Secretarial Duties

TENTH EDITION

Secretarial Duties

John Harrison MinstAM, FSBT, Dip RSA

 LONGMAN

Addison Wesley Longman Limited
Edinburgh Gate, Harlow
Essex CM20 2JE, England
and Associated Companies throughout the world

First published in 1960 by Pitman Publishing
Tenth edition 1996 published by Addison Wesley
Longman Limited

British Library Cataloguing in Publication Data
A catalogue entry for this title is available
from the British Library

ISBN 0-582-27844-9

Library of Congress Cataloging-in-Publication data
A catalog entry for this title is available
from the Library of Congress.

Set by 4 in $11\frac{1}{2}$/13 Melior

Produced by Longman Singapore Publishers (Pte) Ltd.
Printed in Singapore

Contents

Preface

Secretarial Duties is a comprehensive, combined textbook and workbook for secretaries and those employed in a similar capacity in administration. The 10th edition takes account of the present-day needs of both UK and overseas students but retains many of the features that have been so successful in previous editions.

The new edition recognises the increasing role played by computer technology in business administration — with rapid advances in data storage and retrieval, the Internet, speech recognition, automatic call distribution systems, video phones and desktop publishing to mention just a few of the developments that are explained in this book.

In the UK, the recently revised criteria and guidance for National Vocational Qualifications (NVQs) now places greater emphasis on the acquisition of knowledge and understanding. In order to meet the needs of students taking NVQs, the chapters of this book have been re-grouped and new chapters added. These provide the necessary knowledge and understanding to support the achievement of competences as specified in the NVQ Level 3 Administration scheme.

The assessment chart on page xi shows how chapters relate to the different NVQ elements of competence, as well as to the London Chamber of Commerce Private Secretary's Certificate (LCCI PSC) and the Pitman Examinations Institute Office Procedures Level 2 examination (PEI OP2).

In order to assist in establishing competent standards of performance, I have included a wide range of in-tray exercises at the end of each chapter. In working through these realistic simulated business activities, the student is required not only to apply theoretical knowledge to practical, business-related situations, but is also encouraged to develop the necessary NVQ and GNVQ standards of competence. Recently-set past examination questions are also given at the end of each chapter for class, homework and examination purposes.

A new feature of special importance to overseas students is the inclusion, in the Sources of Information Unit, of a cross section of overseas chambers of commerce with their postal addresses and telephone numbers. As chambers of commerce have their own libraries specialising in business information for their local business needs, they are very useful points of contact for secretarial and business studies students.

I hope that this 10th edition will play its part in assisting you to achieve your examination and career objectives, whether you are taking one of the examinations specified in the book or an examination set within your own country.

JH

Acknowledgements

I am grateful for the advice and assistance given freely by many people and organisations, including permission to reproduce photographs and other illustrations. These include:

Acco-Rexel Ltd
The Administration Lead Body
Ms Stephanie Anderson of the Royal Mail Customer Service Centre, Southampton
Bank of Scotland
British Airways
British Telecom
C W Cave & Tab Ltd
Mr J Chew of Longman, Singapore
Ms Julie Ely of American Express Travel Service, Southampton
Ericsson Ltd
GBC (UK) Ltd
The Controller of Her Majesty's Stationery Office
Hewlett-Packard Ltd
IBM United Kingdom Ltd
Mr Peter Joyce of PEI, Zimbabwe
Kardex Systems (UK) Ltd
Kodak Ltd
Larkins Security Ltd
Mr M T McGrave, Hampshire County Reference and Information Librarian
Ms Carolyn Maclay, co-author of The Executive Secretary in Europe
Midland Bank plc
Neopost Ltd
Parcelforce National Enquiry Centre
Philips Electronics UK Ltd
Pitney Bowes plc
The Post Office
Rank Xerox (UK) Ltd
Red Star Parcel Service
Ricoh UK Ltd
Miss Lim Kim See of PEI, Malaysia
Toshiba Information Systems (UK) Ltd
Mrs J Wyeth of Eastleigh College

I am also grateful to the Examinations Boards of the London Chamber of Commerce and Industry and Pitman Qualifications (formerly PEI) for permission to reproduce a selection of questions set in their recent examinations.

JH

Assessment chart

Secretarial Duties Unit		NVQ Level 3 Administration Element (Titles on p xiii)	LCCI PSC Office Organisation & Secretarial Procedures Section	PEI Office Procedures Level 2 Section
1.1	Career development	1.1/1.2	7	1
2.1	Sources of information	5.1/13.1	1	5
2.2	Presentation of information	5.2/13.2	5	5
2.3	Mailing procedures and equipment	5.2	3	1/3
2.4	Mail services	5.2	3	1
2.5	Filing	5.1/5.2	2	5
2.6	Telecommunications	5.2/13.2	3	3
3.1	Business correspondence	6.3/7.1/7.2/13.2	1	2
3.2	Business documents	6.3/7.1/13.2	5	4
3.3	Pay and contracts of employment	6.3/7.1	5	—
3.4	Reprography and paper handling	6.3	2	1/3
3.5	Information technology	6.1/6.2/6.3	4	3
4.1	Health and safety in the office	2.1/2.2	2	1
4.2	Security and confidentiality	2.1/2.2	2	1
5.1	Planning and monitoring procedures	3.1/3.2/8.1/8.2	—	—
5.2	Managing appointments	3.3	1	—
6.1	Working relationships, qualities and responsibilities	4.1	1	2
6.2	Receiving visitors	4.2	1	2
7.1	Office supplies, furniture and equipment	9.1/9.2	2	3/4

Secretarial Duties Unit	NVQ Level 3 Administration Element (Titles on p xiii)	LCCI PSC Office Organisation & Secretarial Procedures Section	PEI Office Procedures Level 2 Section
8.1 Control of cash	12.1/12.2	5	4
8.2 Methods of payment	12.2	5	4
9.1 Servicing and recording meetings	10.1/10.2/10.3	6	6
10.1 Arranging travel and accommodation	11.1/11.2	1	6

NVQ Administration Level 3 Units and Elements

Unit Element   *Competence*
Optional Units

	10.2	Attend, support and record meetings
	10.3	Produce and progress records of meetings
11		Arrange and monitor travel and accommodation
	11.1	Organise travel and accommodation arrangements
	11.2	Monitor and verify travel and accommodation arrangements
12		Contribute to the acquisition and control of financial provision
	12.1	Contribute to the acquisition of financial provision
	12.2	Contribute to the control of financial provision
13		Prepare, produce and present documents using a variety of sources of information
	13.1	Research and prepare information
	13.2	Produce and present documents using a keyboard
14		Prepare, produce and present documents from own notes
	14.1	Take notes and prepare information
	14.2	Produce and present documents using a keyboard
15		Prepare, produce and present documents from recorded speech
	15.1	Prepare information from variable quality recorded speech
	15.2	Produce and present documents using a keyboard

(The above NVQ Units and Elements are reproduced by kind permission of the Administration Lead Body.)

CASE STUDY 1

New Tech Office Services

NEW TECH
Office Services Bureau

Regent House
Regent Street
Leamington Spa
CV15 2AR

Telephone: 01926-342 6189
Fax: 01926-712 3816

Martin is employed as secretary to Mrs Kate Robinson and Mr Gerald Wood, partners of the New Tech Office Services Bureau, a flourishing business which they started five years ago to provide office services for the many small- to medium-sized companies in the Warwick and Leamington Spa area. The bureau offers a wide variety of office services including typing, audio-typing, word processing, copying and an accounting service involving the preparation of accounting records, wages and VAT. The partners also undertake consultancy work for those setting up business for the first time or expanding their operations.

The bureau employs an office manager who looks after the accounts, buying and wages, and is responsible for three text processing operators, a reprographics operator, a computer operator, a receptionist and, of course, Martin, who is a private secretary. In addition, the bureau employs several part-time office workers according to the work demand. Louise Parker will be joining the company on 1 September as a trainee and she is to be given the opportunity to gain experience of different branches of the work.

A telephone-answering machine is operated during the evenings and at weekends to allow clients to leave messages when the office is closed.

Plans are in hand to open a branch at Redditch to cater for the many small companies moving into the new town development there.

The Bureau's suppliers include:

No	Supplier	Products/services
101	Office Products Ltd	Office stationery and equipment
102	Post Office Counters Ltd	PO services
103	EDS (Europe) Ltd (Express Delivery Services)	Delivery and collection services
104	1st Choice Publicity Agency	Advertising
105	Cordon Bleu Cuisine	Catering
106	Waitrose Contract Services Ltd	Cleaning
107	McDowall, Moore & Co	Accounting
108	Dobson Enterprises (Brian Dobson)	Hotels
109	St John Press	Printing
110	Data Services plc (formerly known as Computer Engineering Ltd)	Computer services
111	Mackintosh, Williamson & Randall	Legal services
112	BTC (Europe) Ltd (Business Travel Centre)	Travel

Diaries

		Mrs K Robinson	Mr G Wood
Monday 1 March	1100	Return to office from Belfast	
	1430	Staff meeting	Staff meeting
	1530	Appointment with Mr G Potter of Skyline Advertising Agency re brochures for new branch	
Tuesday 2 March	1400		Office Equipment Exhibition at NEC, Birmingham
Wednesday 3 March	1000	Appointment with Mr R Bird and Mrs T Reynolds, Delta Products Ltd, at 142 Regent Street	
	1300	Lunch with Mr Bird and Mrs Reynolds at Manor House Hotel	
	1930		Chamber of Commerce meeting at Phoenix House
Thursday 4 March	1430	Interviewing for new branch manager	Interviewing for new branch manager
Friday 5 March		Day's holiday	
Saturday 6 March			
Sunday 7 March			

CASE STUDY 2

Office Products Ltd

Office Products Ltd

Parkston Industrial Estate
Derby Road
Liverpool
LL19 2SP

Telephone: 0151-203 4116

Fax: 0151-321 9426

Registered Company No.
109091 England

**OFFICE
PRODUCTS LTD**

**Specialists in Office Equipment
and Stationery Supplies**

Office Products Ltd is a medium-sized company specialising in the manufacture of a wide range of archival storage and filing products, as well as warehousing and marketing other office equipment and stationery supplies for many of the leading manufacturers. Their manufactured products consist of folders, binders, wallets, storage boxes, dividers, record cards, index cabinets, filing trolleys, and a range of personal and office organisers.

OPL is a well-established company with a team of sales representatives covering the whole of the United Kingdom and agents in many parts of the world. Approximately 300 people are employed at the factory, warehouse and head office situated in Liverpool. Five years ago the company moved to a new industrial estate on the outskirts of Liverpool from smaller premises in the city centre, to make way for redevelopment there. The company exhibits regularly at the International Business Efficiency Exhibitions held in Birmingham and Frankfurt, which provide good opportunities to open up new markets.

Maxine is secretary to Mrs Pauline Henderson, the personnel manager. She has a junior secretary, Karen Brown, to assist her with her responsibilities which, in addition to the usual private secretarial duties, include the control of incoming and outgoing mail for the Personnel Department and supervision of the reception office and stationery supplies room for the company. Maxine also acts as secretary to the company's Social Club Committee which meets in the Club House once a month.

The company has established first-class communication facilities with its customers and suppliers by means of a modern electronic telephone system and a fax machine. Sales representatives are equipped with cellular phones to provide the company with an efficient means of communication with them when they are out and about.

The following organisation chart shows the departmental structure of the firm.

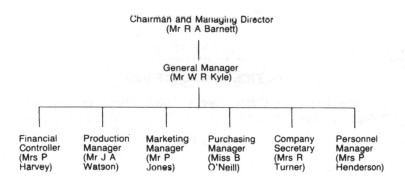

The company's customers include:

No	Name	Trade discount %
01	New Tech Office Services Bureau	10
02	Dobson Enterprises	12.5
03	Manchester City Council	10
04	GST Financial Services Ltd	5
05	British Traders plc	10
06	Chamber of Commerce	7.5
07	McPherson & Platt	12.5
08	Gallagher & Barnet	5
09	3D Visual Arts	5
10	Elmwood Builders Ltd	10
11	Spa Water Garden Centre	7.5
12	Leamington Spa Motors Ltd	12.5

Terms: Net cash within one month after delivery

OFFICE PRODUCTS LTD

Parkston Industrial Estate, Derby Road, Liverpool LL19 2SP
Telephone: 0151-203 4116   Fax: 0151-321 9426

Price List

Catalogue No	Description		Price (including delivery charges)
	OPAL COMPUTER FILES 485 gsm manilla files with 20 mm capacity for unburst sheets:		
	For sheet size 241 × 279 mm		
124680	buff		
124681	blue		
124682	green	packed 25	£33.75
124683	pink		
124684	orange		

Catalogue No	Description		Price (including delivery charges)
	For sheet size 368×279 mm		
124690	buff		
124691	blue		
124692	green	packed 25	£36.25
124693	pink		
124694	orange		
	For sheet size 389×279 mm		
124700	buff		
124701	blue		
124702	green	packed 25	£37.50
124703	pink		
124704	orange		

OPAL PRINTOUT WALLETS
Single pocket wallets for storing burst or unburst computer sheets with 40 mm capacity:

Catalogue No	Description		Price
	For sheet size 297×420 mm		
124800	buff		
124801	blue		
124802	green	packed 25	£17.50
124803	pink		
124804	orange		

OPAL DATA BOXES
Portable filing boxes for computer printout sheets size 76×368×248 mm. Capacity: 70 mm

Catalogue No	Description		Price
124810	charcoal		
124811	blue	packed 10	£16.50
124812	red		

CASE STUDY 3

The Secretairs — professional singers

DOBSON ENTERPRISES

172 Albemarle Street
Mayfair
London W1 2AX

Tel: 0171-306 50112

Jane is private secretary to Brian Dobson, the manager of a group of well-known singers called The Secretairs, consisting of Kenny Martin, Sean Lawrance and Paul O'Connor. She works in Central London at the manager's office and is responsible for all secretarial services to the manager and the singers. Mr Dobson also manages several other less well-known entertainers and owns a small group of hotels in the south of England. Jane began work for Mr Dobson last year after working as a secretary at the BBC for just over five years. Mr Dobson required a mature person with sound secretarial experience as his secretary has to work on her own for long periods when he is away from the office attending performances, meeting artistes and visiting his hotels on the south coast.

The office is small with modern decor but with limited office equipment. An agency has to be used for all printing where large quantities are required. Jane uses an electronic typewriter and as Mr Dobson is away from the office for much of the time he uses a portable recorder to dictate correspondence and leave instructions for work to be done. Mrs Dobson helps out in the office when the need arises.

19 Year Planning Chart – THE SECRETAIRS

	January	February	March	April	May	June
mon						
tue					1	
wed		1			2	
thu		2	1		3	
fri		3	2		4	1
sat		4	3		5	2
sun	1	5	4	1	6	3
mon	2	6	5	2	7	4
tue	3	7	6	3	8	5
wed	4	8	7	4	9	6
thu	5	9	8	5	10	7
fri	6	10	9	6	11	8
sat	7	11	10	7	12	9
sun	8	12	11	8	13	10
mon	9	13	12	9	14	11
tue	10	14	13	10	15	12
wed	11	15	14	11	16	13
thu	12	16	15	12	17	14
fri	13	17	16	13	18	15
sat	14	18	17	14	19	16
sun	15	19	18	15	20	17
mon	16	20	19	16	21	18
tue	17	21	20	17	22	19
wed	18	22	21	18	23	20
thu	19	23	22	19	24	21
fri	20	24	23	20	25	22
sat	21	25	24	21	26	23
sun	22	26	25	22	27	24
mon	23	27	26	23	28	25
tue	24	28	27	24	29	26
wed	25	29	28	25	30	27
thu	26		29	26	31	28
fri	27		30	27		29
sat	28		31	28		30
sun	29			29		
mon	30			30		
tue	31					

Handwritten annotations: HOLIDAY (January, Sun 1 – Sun 8); TOUR (April, Mon 2 – Sat 14); USA (April, around Mon 9 – Sun 15); HOLIDAY (April/May, Tue 24 – Sun 29).

CASE STUDY 4

Scenario — for PEI Office Procedures Level 2 Examination

The tasks are based at the private company of Pinder and Moore, a children's clothing manufacturer, which operates a mail order service as well as supplying various retail outlets throughout the country and a limited number of countries overseas.

The company is owned by two brothers, Arthur and George Pinder.

Arthur Pinder (Managing Director) is in overall control with the following personnel accountable to him:

George Pinder (Company Secretary and Financial Director) and a partner, Geoffrey Moore (Sales and Marketing Director).

There are three senior executives:

Peter Jones (Production)
Anne Martin (Buying)
Lisa Halliwell (Personnel)

The company's address is:

45 The Strand, Bristol
Tel/Telex No   Bristol 37960
Fax No   Bristol 24786

The company's bankers are Central Bank Plc, 110 The Strand, Bristol Account No 4107689

The following organisation chart shows the departmental structure of the firm:

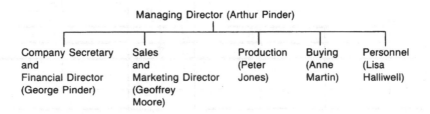

Managing Director (Arthur Pinder)

| Company Secretary and Financial Director (George Pinder) | Sales and Marketing Director (Geoffrey Moore) | Production (Peter Jones) | Buying (Anne Martin) | Personnel (Lisa Halliwell) |

UNIT 1 Introduction

This book is concerned with the work role and responsibilities of secretaries and those employed in administration, as well as the systems, methods and equipment they use in the course of their duties.

1.1 Career development

Staff selection and employment, induction, training and appraisal are considered in this introductory unit as they relate to obtaining jobs and, when appointed, making a success of them.

Recruitment

Employers expect to recruit staff who:

- can develop self to enhance performance (NVQ Element 1.1)
- can contribute to improving the performance of colleagues (NVQ Element 1.2)
- are adaptable with transferable skills, versatile and prepared to accept a changing work situation
- have suitable qualifications and practical training
- are keen and interested in joining the organisation
- are conscientious, loyal and thorough
- enjoy good health and are able to work regularly and punctually
- are acceptable to existing staff and able to work well in a team.

Applying for a vacancy

Very great care should be taken in preparing the letter of application for a post so that the prospective employer will be favourably impressed. The following points are important:

- The letter should be typed neatly, unless the prospective employer has requested a handwritten letter.
- Avoid errors of grammar or punctuation.
- The letter should be worded in a businesslike manner.
- The letter should be planned carefully, covering all the essential points referred to in the advertisement, eg in reply to the advertisement in Fig 1.1 you should refer to

  a your interest in the type of work (publishing)
  b the standard of your secretarial skills (NVQ Level 3)
  c your organising ability
  d your experience of working in a responsible secretarial position
  e your age (must be between 20 and 40), and
  f explain why this job appeals to you.

- The salutation should normally be 'Dear Sir', 'Dear Sirs' or 'Dear Madam' and the complimentary close 'Yours faithfully'.
- If you are asked to state your qualifications and experience, submit a neatly typed curriculum vitae (CV) containing:

  a full name and address
  b telephone number
  c date of birth
  d nationality
  e next of kin
  f education
  g qualifications
  h present employment and previous work experience
  i interests

SECRETARY/PA
£17,500

The Managing Director of this Central London based publishing company requires a top-class secretary.
   Must have excellent secretarial skills (NVQ Level 3) along with good organising ability. Also experience in a responsible secretarial position.
   Age 20–40.

EXCEL RECRUITMENT CONSULTANTS
Tel: 0171-287 2816
or Fax CV on 0171-287 2842

Fig 1.1   Job advertisement

j the names and addresses of persons to whom reference may be made.

- The source of the advertisement should be referred to in the letter of application,eg if the advertisement was read in the *Birmingham Mail*, say, 'In reply to your advertisement in yesterday's Birmingham Mail ...'
- If you receive a letter inviting you to attend for interview, you should reply by return of post confirming that you will attend at the time stated.

On being interviewed

During the course of our lifetime we are faced with all kinds of interviews with headteachers, employers, police, lawyers, clergy and so on, and it is important to approach the interviews in a positive, calm and efficient manner. The following words of advice may prove beneficial:

Before the interview

1 Find out as much as possible about the organisation and the vacancy advertised, ie study the job descrption carefully (see Fig 6.1 on page 252), if one has been supplied.

2 Make a list of likely questions and prepare some good answers to them, eg 'What interests you about the job?' 'What can you offer the firm?' 'What are your career ambitions?' 'Why do you wish to leave your present job?' 'Why have you chosen a secretarial career?' Personal questions about schools attended, best subjects, present employment and salary may also be asked.

3 Prepare some questions to ask the interviewer on such topics as job prospects, the organisation's employment policies and any aspects of the job which are not clear from the job description.

4 Be sure that you know where the interview is taking place and how to get there so that you can arrive in good time.

5 Give careful consideration to your appearance and make sure that you are smart and tidy.

When attending the interview

1 It is advisable to leave outside the interview room any personal belongings, such as a coat, umbrella, etc.

2 Bring with you any documents, writing materials, etc, which were requested in the letter.

3 When answering questions, be perfectly natural, and think before you speak.

4 Be pleasant — a smile always creates a favourable impression.

5 Construct answers logically — make the most of the subjects in which you have gained most experience and knowledge, but remember to keep to the point.

6 Speak clearly and convincingly and do not be afraid to look at the questioner.

7 Be perfectly honest about your capabilities and achievements, drawing attention to any which support your application.

8 Show that you are interested and enthusiastic by your attitude to the questions asked.

9 At the end of the interview, thank the interviewer.

Contract of employment
See page 177.

Induction course
This provides the means of introducing new employees to their company in order to assist them to be effective in their jobs as quickly as possible. The following items might be included in an induction course:

Information about the company
- an outline of the background to the company and its structure, organisation, products and markets. It is useful to issue employees with an organisation chart
- main lines of communication within the company, including arrangements for consultation, grievance procedure and membership of trade unions
- health and safety regulations
- security regulations
- social facilities
- a tour of the premises. The new entrants should have their attention drawn to points of safety, such as the location of fire alarms, fire equipment, fire escapes and first-aid personnel and equipment.

Individual information

- personnel policies relating to conditions of employment including salaries, pensions, hours of work, holidays, etc
- career development: training programmes and opportunities for further education
- training for the job and an introduction to colleagues in the workplace
- training on company equipment, ie telephone, fax, copier and computer.

Training

Training, whether it is at the workplace or off-the-job, has the following benefits:

- improved standards of work performance, resulting in greater accuracy, quality and speed of work
- enhanced morale from improved performance
- higher levels of administrative tasks can be delegated to secretarial staff
- staff motivation as a result of more demanding and satisfying work
- safety standards meet legal requirements
- public relations are improved.

Training programme

The stages involved in organising an internal training programme are as follows:

1 Identify training needs by seeking the views of all concerned — these may be identified as a result of a staff appraisal scheme.

2 Agree methods and objectives of training having regard to existing levels of competence.

3 Plan and organise an appropriate training programme.

4 Follow up the training programme with feedback to the trainees on their performance.

5 Quantify and evaluate the effectiveness of the training programme.

6 Modify plans for future training courses as a result of the evaluation in **5**.

7 Provide opportunities for trainees to apply their newly acquired

skills and knowledge in the workplace as soon as possible after training in order to provide reinforcement of learning.

Staff appraisal

Performance and progress of staff should be reviewed and evaluated regularly. The staff appraisal interview will aim to:

- assess the performance of employees
- help staff achieve their potential
- discuss problems and weaknesses and ways of overcoming them
- identify training needs
- set targets/objectives for staff to achieve
- prepare staff for promotion.

An example of a staff appraisal form for a secretary, or a performance plan as it is sometimes called, is given in Fig. 1.2.

Developing yourself for advancement in your career

'Executive secretaries are in the front line of business communication. They must be able to say what needs to be said assertively, but not aggressively, and to demonstrate their managerial skills. Preparation for advanced secretarial examinations and training in personal development are essential if these needs are to be satisfied. May those words "I am just a secretary" be consigned to the past.' Carolyn Maclay and John Harrison (*The Executive Secretary in Europe*).

Personal development is enhanced when you:

- establish, agree and maintain an action plan for your career
- succeed in achieving the NVQ Level 3 competences on page xiii
- study for and pass advanced-level public examinations, such as the London Chamber of Commerce Private Secretary's Certificate or the Pitman Examinations Institute Level 2 Office Procedures
- use initiative and a logical approach to solving day-to-day problems
- adopt a positive approach to motivation and the motivation of others.
- create and maintain a high standard of professional relationships with colleagues and business contacts
- relate well with people at all levels
- plan, anticipate needs and think ahead unprompted
- are ambitious to succeed in your career.

Objective	Performance criteria	Notes on attainment	Rating
1 COMMUNICATION			
1.1 Ensure a polite and clear telephone manner	No complaints on manner and attitude		
1.2 Where possible ensure messages are clearly understood	No important misunderstandings		
1.3 Use systems to effect internal correspondence	Same-day transfer of notes and messages where possible		
1.4 Ensure a timely and accurate turnaround of typed letters	Same-day completion where possible		
2 PLANNING			
2.1 Maintain up-to-date diaries and plan to minimise last-minute changes	Avoid rearrangements due to overrun and non-attendance		
2.2 Ensure effective preparation for meetings and discussions	Avoid last-minute preparation		
2.3 Administer an effective system of bring-up and follow-up	Timely responses to all requests and required action		
3 ADMINISTRATION			
3.1 Establish budget and monitor expenditure, highlighting potential out-of-line situations	Timely identification of potential problems to allow alternative corrective actions		
3.2 Meet the requirements of the company's safety and security policies	No violations		
3.3 Set up and maintain a secretarial will /back-up file	Up-to-date record		
4 ADDED VALUE			
4.1 Advise on systems usage	Maintain state of the art usage as appropriate		
4.2 Handle correspondence and queries to the limit of knowledge and ability to research	Avoidance of passing on correspondence that could have been previously cleared		
4.3 Ensure that activities such as correspondence and presentations are of the highest quality	No errors and consistency of presentation format		
5 PERSONAL DEVELOPMENT			
5.1 Increase knowledge of external bodies and local and national issues	Demonstrate knowledge through increased added value		
5.2 Learn PC applications to develop efficient system usage	Maintain state of the art knowledge		

Fig 1.2   Performance plan/staff appraisal form

Questions

1 Because of the increased volume of work in your office, it is proposed to appoint a junior secretary to work under you. Draft the advertisement to appear in the press, and give your employer a short note on what you consider to be the necessary qualifications and personal attributes of the person to be appointed, together with some questions which he can put to candidates at an interview.

2 Owing to the introduction of new equipment and methods in office work, the duties of office staff are changing. Apart from text processing, what jobs might a junior secretary be asked to do?

3 Michael Delaney, Administration Manager, has been promoted and will become Director of Administration when Simon Richards retires. His former post as Administration Manager is now to be advertised.

   Briefly describe the actions the Human Resources Department have to take prior to the interview. (*LCCI PSC*)

4 You have seen a job advertisement and are interested in applying. On enquiry you are told that an application form will not be supplied; applicants are asked to write in giving full details.

   a) Why does a firm require a written application?
   b) What type of documents would you submit as your application?
   c) List the sort of information that you would supply. (*PEI OP2*)

5 a) A company is arranging to interview a number of candidates for some vacancies in its office. Before the interviews take place, what information should be prepared for (i) the candidates and (ii) the people in the company who are responsible for the recruitment of staff?
   b) What are the purposes of interviewing candidates?

6 How would you prepare yourself for advancement in your career? (*LCCI PSC*)

7 You have been asked for your views on staff appraisal. Give advantages and disadvantages when using such a system. (*LCCI PSC*)

8 a) Why is induction training important to new personnel?
   b) What would you expect to be included in an induction programme? (*LCCI PSC*)

In-tray exercises

9 You are employed by Mr Dobson, Manager of 'The Secretairs' (Case Study 3). Mr Dobson has recorded the following message for you on his tape:

   I am very conscious that we do not at present organise any systematic induction for the new staff we take on at our hotels. I think it would be a good idea if, say, 2 or 3 times a year we held a day's induction course at one of the hotels for all newly-appointed employees from the hotel group.

Would you give some thought to it and let me see a checklist of the steps we would have to take to set up the course together with a proposed programme for the day indicating the topics to be covered.

Now take the necessary action.

10 You work for the Personnel and Training Department of Madison Confectionery Ltd of Holland Place, Reigate, Surrey, RH42 1PQ.

You have just been promoted from the post of Receptionist/Telephonist to Administrative Assistant (a new post) and are responsible to the Personnel and Training Officer in whose name all letters and memos are prepared.

Staff include:

John Green	Personnel and Training Officer
Mary Mason	Office Manager
Carol Baker	Training Assistant

There is a management post vacant and the following applicants have been invited for interview on the first day of next month:

Sonia Brown, Hugh Black, Carmen White and John Smith.

Your offices are close to The Royal Hotel, Hookwood Road, Reigate, Surrey, RH43 2PQ.

The four applicants invited for interview will need accommodation on the night before the interview and breakfast the following morning. A provisional booking for rooms with bath or shower has been made at the Royal Hotel by telephone.

a) Write a letter of confirmation; ask for details of the cost and that the Hotel Manager sends the bill to the Personnel Officer.

b) Prepare a programme for the day which should include the time of interview for each candidate.

All candidates should arrive by 10 am for a preliminary discussion, lasting about 45 minutes, with John Green. They will then be shown round the offices and factory. Lunch has been booked in the staff restaurant for 12.15. Formal interviews begin at 2 pm and each interview is expected to last about 45 minutes. Candidates will be seen in reverse alphabetical order and will be free to leave after the interview as they will be contacted by telephone the following day with the result.

c) Suggest sources of reference that the applicants might refer to in preparation for the day. (*PEI OP2*)

Note: This task is repeated in Unit 5.2 to encompass the management of appointments dealt with in that unit.

UNIT
2
Researching, preparing and supplying information

2.1 Sources of information

The efficient secretary knows where to locate information when it is required and how to abstract it, and can be relied upon to check the details for accuracy and relevance. This involves a knowledge of the different sources of information and how and when they can be used. Any doubtful points should be checked to prevent them slipping into correspondence without verification.

Sources of information may include:

- files, ie manual, microfiche and computer — as in Unit 2.5
- reference books and directories
- newspapers and journals
- contact with organisations
- statistical returns, graphs and charts — as in Unit 2.2
- timetables and schedules
- manuals, ie parts manuals, operating manuals, etc
- videotex information services – as on page 29.

Examples of the sources of reference in common use are given below:

Information	Publication/organisation
1 **British Standards Specifications**	These may be referred to at reference libraries and purchased from: BSI Standards 389 Chiswick High Road London W4 4AL

Information The following are examples of those relevant to Business Administration:	Publication/organisation
Dictation equipment	BSI 3738: 1980/1985/1993
Duplicators and document copying	BSI 5479: 1977/1981/1985/1993
Envelopes	BSI 4264: 1987/1994
Filing cabinets	BSI 4438: 1969/1981
Mail processing machines	BSI 6191:
Addressing machines	1982/1986
Document inserting machines	1985/1993
Letter folding machines	1981/1986
Letter opening machines	1981/1986
Postal franking machines	1984/1993
Micrographics	BSI 6660: 1985/1991
Office buildings (fire precautions, etc)	BSI 5588: 1983/1985/1990/1991
Office furniture (desks, chairs, workstations, etc)	BSI 5940: 1980
Visual display terminals	BSI 7179: 1990

European standards

Ergonomic requirements for office work with visual display terminals	BSEN 29241 1993
Safety of information technology equipment	BSEN 60950 1992

International standards

Information technology Text and office systems Document filing and retrieval	BS ISO/IEC 10166 1991

2 Business organisations

Business community: home market and overseas trade	Chamber of Commerce Department of Trade and Industry 1–19 Victoria Street London SW1H 0ET

Information	Publication/organisation
Company data: industry and commerce	Dun & Bradstreet's *Who owns Whom*: 1 *Products and services* 2 *Company information* 3 *Financial data*
	Company Annual Reports – from individual companies or Registrar of Companies
Companies: financial data, directors	*The Macmillan Stock Exchange Official Year Book*
Insurance companies	*Insurance Directory and Year Book*
Manufacturers	*Kelly's Business Directory*
Newspapers, journals	*Benn's Media* (UK, Europe and World editions)
	Willing's Press Guide
Prominent firms in the United Kingdom	*Key British Enterprises*
	Britain's Top 50,000 Companies
	British Business Rankings
	The Times 1,000 leading Companies in Britain and Overseas
Prominent international firms	*Principal International Business Exporters' Encyclopedia – the World Marketing Guide*
Trade and Professional Associations Chambers of Trade and Commerce Trade Unions	*Directory of British Associations*
Traders' names, addresses and telephone numbers	*Yellow Pages*
	Telephone directories
	Business Pages
	See also Electronic Yellow Pages on page 122

3 Chambers of Commerce throughout the world

Country	Address	Telephone
Australia	Commerce House Brisbane Avenue Barton ACT 2600	73 2381
Austria	Ministry of Trade and Industry Landstrasser Hauptstrasse 55-57 1030 Vienna	711 02 0
Bahamas	PO Box N665 Shirley Street Nassau	322 2145
Bahrain	PO Box 248 Manama	233913
Bangladesh	PO Box 279 Dhaka 1000	250566
Barbados	PO Box 189 St Michael Barbados	426 2056
Belgium	Britannia House Rue Joseph II 30 1040 Brussels	2 2190788
Dermuda	Front Street PO Box HM655 Hamilton HM CX	54201
Botswana	PO Box 20344 Garbarone	52677
Cameroon	BP 4011 Doula	42 28 88
Canada	Commerce House 1080 Beaver Hall Hill Montreal H2Z 1T2	866 4334
China	93 Beiheyan Dajie Beijing	554231
Cyprus	PO Box 1455 38 Grivas Dhigenis Avenue (6th Floor) Nicosia	449500

Country	Address	Telephone
Denmark	Birsen 1217 Copenhagen K	33 91 2323
Egypt	Sharia el-Ghorfa Altogariya Alexandria	808993
Finland	PO Box 1000 Fabianinkatu 14 00101 Helsinki	650133
France	27 Avenue de Friedland Cedex 08 75382 Paris	42 89 70 00
The Gambia	PO Box 33 78 Wellington Street Banjul	27765
Germany	Adenauerallee 148 5300 Bonn 1	0288 1040
Ghana	PO Box 2325 Accra	662427
Greece	25 Vas Sofias Avenue 106 74 Athens	721 0361
Guyana	PO Box 10110 156 Waterloo Street Cummingsburg	56451
Hong Kong	1712 Shui On Centre 8 Harbour Road	8242211
Hungary	PO Box 106 Kossuth Lajos ter 6-8 1055 Budapest	153 3333
India	Allahabad Bank Building 17 Parliament Street New Delhi 110 001	310 704
Indonesia	Chandra Building Jalan M H Thamrin 20 Jakarta 10350	324 000
Iran	254 Taleghani Avenue Tehran	836031
Iraq	Mustansir Street Baghdad	888 6111
Ireland	Kildare Street Dublin 2	612888
Israel	PO Box 3540 Tel Aviv	259732

Country	Address	Telephone
Italy	Via Agnello 8 20121 Milan	876981
Jamaica	PO Box 172 Kingston	922 0150
Japan	Tokyo 107	505 1734
Jordan	PO Box 287 Amman	666151
Kenya	Ufanisi House Haile Selassie Avenue POB 47024 Nairobi	334413
Korea (South)	CPO Box 25 Chung-ku Seoul	757 0757
Kuwait	POB 775 13008 Safat Chamber's Building Ali as-Salem Street Kuwait City	243 3864
Lesotho	PO Box 79 Maseru	323482
Malaysia	Office Tower Plaza Berjaya 12 Jalan Imbi 55100 Kuala Lumpur	245 2503
Netherlands	Bezuidenhoutseweg 181 2594 AII The Hague	70 3478881
New Zealand	109 Featherston Street POB 1590 Wellington	4722 725
Nigeria	PO Box 109 Lagos	683 486
Norway	Export Council of Norway Drammensveien 40 0255 Oslo 2	43 77 00
Pakistan	Aiwan-e Tijarat Karachi	226091-5
Philippines	PICC Secretariat Building CCP Complex Roxas Boulevard Makati Metro Manila 2801	832 0309

Country	Address	Telephone
Poland	PO Box 361 00-950 Warszawa Ul Trebacka 4	260221
Portugal	Rua da Estrela 8 1200 Lisbon	661586
Russian Federation	103684 Moscow ul. Ilyinka 6	923 43 23
Saudi Arabia	PO Box 1774 Riyadh 11162	401 2222
Sierra Leone	Guma Building Lamina Sankoh Street POB 502 Freetown	226305
Singapore	6 Raffles Quay #05-00 Denmark House Singapore	224 1255
South Africa	PO Box 91267 Auckland Park 2006	726 5309
Spain	Claudio Coello 19 Piso 1 28001 Madrid	275 3400
Swaziland	PO Box 72 Manzini	44408
Sweden	Box 5512 Grevgatan 34 114 85 Stockholm	665 34 25
Switzerland	Freiestrasse 155 8032 Zurich	55 31 31
Taiwan	390 Fu Hsing South Road 6th Floor Sec 1 Taipei	701 2671
Tanzania	PO Box 41 Dar-es-Salaam	27671
Thailand	150 Rajbopit Road Bangkok 10200	225 0086
Trinidad & Tobago	Room 950-952 Hilton Hotel POB 499 Port of Spain	624 6082

Country	Address	Telephone
Turkey	PO Box 190 Karakoy Istanbul	149 0650
Uganda	PO Box 3809 Jinja Road Kampala	58791
United Arab Emirates	PO Box 1457 Dubai	221181
United Kingdom	ICC UK Centre Point 103 New Oxford Street London WC1A 1QB	0171 637 3062
United States of America	1615 H St NW Washington DC 20062-0001	659 6000
Uruguay	Misiones 1400 Casilla 1000 11000 Montevideo	961277
Venezuela	80 Avda Este 2 Los Caobos Caracas	571 3222
Vietnam	33 Ba Treieu Hanoi	52961
Zambia	PO Box 30844 Lusaka	252369
Zimbabwe	Equity House Rezende Street POB 1934 Harare	753444

Information	Publication/organisation

4 Employment

Careers advice, job vacancies and training opportunities	Careers Office Job Centre Training and Enterprise Council (TEC)
Income tax, PAYE, etc	*Inland Revenue Office Employer's* *Guide*
Legislation	*Croner's Reference Book for Employers*

Information	Publication/organisation
National Insurance	Department of Social Security Employer's Guide
Personnel and training	Personnel and Training Management Year Book and Directory

5 Europe

Business methods and marketing opportunities	CCH Doing Business in Europe
	Doing Business in the European Community (Kogan Page)
	The Single Market − Financial Services (DTI)
	The Single Market − A Guide to Public Purchasing (DTI)
	Guide to Exporting (BOTB)
	How to sell to Europe (Danton de Rauffignac, Pitman)
	Selling in the Single Market − A Guide for Exporters (DTI)
Companies in the EU: names, addresses and fax, telephone and telex nos	Kompass: Contact Europe The European Business Directory
Documents of the EU	Documents of the European Communities (OOPEC)
Employment	UK nationals working abroad − tax and other matters (Coopers and Lybrand Deloitte)
General sources of information about the EU	Vacher's European Companion and Consultants' Register Croner's Europe
	Croner's Europe Business Information Sources
Grants from the EU	Grants from Europe: How to get money and influence policy (A Davidson, Bedford Square Press)
Languages: French, German, Spanish and Italian	Hamlyn pocket dictionaries and phrase books

Information	Publication/organisation
	Harrap's pocket dictionaries and vocabulary books
	The Collins Robert French Dictionary
	Collins Klett English German Dictionary
	The Multilingual Business Handbook — *a guide to international correspondence* (Macmillan)
	Pan's Multilingual Commercial Dictionary
	Pergamon's Bilingual Guide to Business and Professional Correspondence: Italian (Harvard & Milotto) *Spanish* (Harvard & Ariza)
Legislation of the EU	*Butterworth's Guide to the European Communities*
	Croner's Europe (an updating service)
	The Single Market – Company Law Harmonisation (DTI)
Members of the European Parliament, Commissioners and officials	*The Times Guide to the European Parliament*
	Dod's European Companion
Statistics	*Eurostat: Europe in Figures* (OOPEC, Luxembourg)
	Monthly *Digest of Statistics* (HMSO)
	Annual Abstract of Statistics (HMSO)
	European Marketing Data and Statistics (Euromonitor)
Translation services	*Directory of Translators and Translating Agencies in the UK* (P Morris & G Weston, Bowker-Saur)

Information	Publication/organisation
6 Financial	
Banking	Banks
	Leaflets supplied by banks
	Banker's Almanac (volumes for banks and branches)
Building Societies	Building societies
	Leaflets supplied by building societies
	Building Societies' Year Book
Stocks and shares	Stockbroker
	Bank
	Newspapers (financial pages)
Taxation	Customs and Excise for VAT
	CCH British Tax Guide
7 General Information	
Background information and reference sources for everyday use, such as political information, economics, money matters, gazetteer of the world, science, literature, computing terms and the environment.	*Pears Cyclopaedia*
News reference service	*Keesing's Record of World Events* *Facts on file – world news digest* (also available on CD Rom)
Sources of information	Libraries
	Walford's Guide to Reference Material
	Croner's A-Z of Business Information Sources
	Whitaker's British Books in Print (microfiche and CD Rom)
	Lists of HMSO Publications

Information	Publication/organisation
	Catalogue of British Official Publications (not those published by HMSO) (Chadwyck-Healey)
	The Oxford Dictionary of Quotations
World affairs	
British and foreign embassies	
Royal family and the peerage	
Cabinet ministers and members of Parliament	*Whitaker's Almanack*
Bank of England	
Law courts	
European Union	
United Nations, etc.	
Exporting	Export Publications Catalogue (BOTB)

8 Government

Central government	Members of Parliament The House of Commons Information Service
Central government complaints	Parliamentary Commissioner for Administration (the ombudsman) Church House, Great Smith Street, London, SW1P 3BW
Civil servants	*Civil Service Year Book*
Government publications	Local office of Her Majesty's Stationery Office or the HMSO Publications Centre, PO Box 276, London SW8 5DT All government reports are published by HM Stationery Office, which has branches or agencies in most of the large towns and cities in Great Britain. There are daily, monthly and annual lists of HMSO publications. HMSO also

Information	Publication/organisation
	distributes publications for the European Union (EU); the Organisation for Economic Cooperation and Development (OECD); the United Nations (UN); the World Health Organisation (WHO) and other international organisations.
Governments of countries throughout the world and international organisations	*Statesman's Year Book* *The Europa Year Book*
Local government	Councillors County/District Council Offices
Local government authorities and officers	*Municipal Year Book* Local Year Books/Town Guides
Local government complaints	Commission for Local Administration in England 21 Queen Anne's Gate London SW1H 9BU (the local government ombudsman)
Members of Parliament	*The Times Guide to the House of Commons* *Whitaker's Almanack* *Dod's Parliamentary Companion* *Vacher's Parliamentary Companion*
Parliamentary reports	*Hansard* – this is the official report of the proceedings in Parliament, and is useful if you wish to obtain details of a debate in Parliament on a particular topic. It is a verbatim report, ie it is reported word for word. Reports are made of the proceedings both in the House of Commons and in the House of Lords.

9 Legal

Barristers, solicitors, judges and legal officers	*Waterlow's Solicitors' and Barristers' Directory*
Court administration (Magistrates courts)	Clerk to the Justices

Information	Publication/organisation
Legal aid and advice	Legal Advice Centre
	Citizens Advice Bureau
	Local Committee of Law Society
Legislation	Acts of Parliament and Statutory Instruments
	Croner's Reference Book for Employers
	Croner's Reference Book for the Self-Employed and Smaller Business
	Croner's Industrial relations Law
	Croner's Employment Law

10   Local information

Books, newspapers, journals reference information	Libraries
Business names, addresses and telephone numbers classified by trades and professions	Yellow Pages Thomson's Local Directory
Local business, trade matters	Chamber of Commerce/Trade
Local services and events	Town guide
	Information bureau
	Tourist office
	Citizens Advice Bureau
Street names and occupiers of houses, flats, etc.	Voters' Lists (Electoral Registration Officers)
Telephone users' names, addresses and telephone numbers	Phone books Many libraries have phone books for the whole of the UK and Europe

11   People

Officers in the armed forces	Army List, Air Force List and Navy List with sections for retired officers
Biographies of eminent living people	Who's Who
	Debrett's People of Today
	Who Was Who provides a record of

Information	Publication/organisation
	eminent people who have died. There are also several other similar books, such as *International Who's Who, International Year Book* and *Statesmen's Who's Who, Who's Who in Art, Who's Who in the Theatre, Who's Who in Finance* and *Authors' and Writers' Who's Who*
Biographies of people of international importance	*International Year Book and Statesmen's Who's Who*
Clergymen of the Church of England	*Crockford's Clerical Directory* (similar clerical directories are published for the other religious denominations)
Dentists	Dentists' Register
Directors and their joint stock companies	*Directory of Directors*
Forms of address	*Black's Titles and Forms of Address*
	Debrett's Correct Form
Medical practitioners	*Medical Directory*
Nurses	Royal College of Nursing
Peers, barons and knights	*Debrett's Peerage and Baronetage*
	Burke's Peerage, Baronetage and Knightage
Qualifications and names and addresses of professional bodies	*British Qualifications*

12 Public services

Broadcast receiving licences	National Television Records Office, Bristol BS98 12L (or Post Office)
Driving licences	Driver and Vehicle Licensing Centre, Swansea SA99 1AN
Motor vehicle taxation	Local Vehicle Licensing Office (or Post Office)
Royal Mail	Post Office and Royal Mail leaflets

Information	Publication/organisation
	Royal Mail Customer Service Centres
	Mailguide
Parcelforce	Parcelforce National Enquiry Centre

13 Safety

First Aid	*The First Aid Manual* (Order of St John)
Office Safety	Health and Safety Executive
	Health and Safety at Work Act 1974
	Health and Safety (Display Screen Equipment) Regulations 1992
	Advice to Employees (Health and Safety Commission)
	Croner's Office Health and Safety
	CCH Health and Safety: are you at risk? *Is my Office Safe? A handbook for Supervisors* (HMSO)
	Various publications from The British Safety Council, National Safety Centre, Chancellor's Road, London, W6 9RS, and the Fire Protection Association, Aldermary House, Queen Street, London, EC4N 1TJ

14 Secretarial services

Office guide for secretaries	*Secretary's Desk Book* (Pitman) or *Longman Pitman Office Dictionary*
	Chambers' Office Oracle
	Croner's Office Companion
Abbreviations and initials	*Acronyms, Initialisms and Abbreviations Dictionary*
Addressing overseas business letters	*A Secretary's Handbook: addressing overseas business letters* (Allen, Foulsham)

Information	Publication/organisation
Forms of address	*Black's Titles and Forms of Address* *Debrett's Correct Form*
Printing terms and procedures	*Authors' and Printers' Dictionary*
Synonyms and antonyms	*Roget's Thesaurus of English Words and Phrases*
Information technology	*Croner's IT*

15 Telecommunications

Telephone numbers	*The phone book* (local area)
	Yellow Pages
Telex numbers	*British Telecom Telex Directory*
Answerback codes	*Telex Answerback Directory*
Fax numbers	*British Telecom Fax Directory*

16 Travel

Advice to business executives travelling abroad	*Hints to Exporters* (Department of Trade and Industry) from DTI Export Publications, PO Box 55, Stratford-on-Avon, CV37 9GE
	Royal Mail International Business Travel Guide
	ABC Guide to International Travel
Air services	*ABC World Airways Guide*
	Airline timetables
Hotels and restaurants	*Automobile Association Members' Handbook*
	ABC UK Holiday Guide
	ABC Worldwide Hotel Guide
	Hotels and Restaurants in Great Britain
	Financial Times World Hotel Directory
	Good Food Guide
	Michelin Guides
	RAC Hotel Guide

Information	Publication/organisation
Location of places, names of towns, etc.	Ordnance Survey Gazetteer of Great Britain
	Chambers World Gazetteer
	The Times Atlas of the World
Motoring information: road maps, hotels, garages, distances between towns	Automobile Association Members' Handbook
	Royal Automobile Club Guide and Handbook
	AA and RAC Guides for motoring in Europe
	AA Big Road Atlas for Britain
Passports	Regional Passport Offices
	Post Offices (for application forms)
Shipping services	ABC Passenger Shipping Guide
	Lloyd's International List
Travel information	ABC Rail Guide
	Great Britain Passenger Railway Timetable
	Travel agencies
	British Rail
	Airports
	AA/RAC offices
	Travel Trade Directory
	ABC Guide to International Travel
Visas	Consulate of country to be visited

Library resources

If a reference book is not available at your workplace, try your local library, where many of the books listed in the preceding pages will be in the quick reference section. The simplest way to obtain them is to ask a librarian to help you.

The normal procedure for locating a book is:

1 First check the library's catalogue to find out whether the book you require is stocked and, if so, where it is kept. The catalogue may be on cards, computer printout, microfiche, or accessed via a computer terminal. If you look in the title A-Z catalogue you will find the classification number of all books held by the library. The Dewey decimal system is used in most public libraries, but other libraries may use different systems. The Dewey decimal classification numbers, which are made up of three digits, may be followed by a decimal point and further digits to represent particular subject areas, eg a general reference book such as *Whitaker's Almanack* has a classification number of 030; a book on office services will be placed at 651.189. Books in the reference section of the library may have the letter 'R' placed before the classification number, eg R301.31.

2 If the book you require is not in stock, ask the librarian whether there are alternative books which may provide the same information.

3 When you have found the book, check the date of publication (usually on the reverse of the title page) to see if the book is a recent edition; otherwise the information it provides may be out of date.

4 Look first at the contents page at the front and the index at the back to find the page number where the information can be located.

5 When you have located the correct page, write down the relevant information and its source, ie the reference book title and its page: it is unwise to rely on remembering important facts. It may be possible, subject to copyright law, to take a photocopy of a particular page if you require detailed information.

6 If you cannot find a reference book on the subject you require, there may be some information about it in one of the major specialist encyclopaedias (classification No 030).

7 Even current editions of reference books cannot provide details of recent developments and changes and, if you require the most up-to-date information, you will need to refer to newspapers and journals available at most libraries or on-line databases at larger libraries. See also the information services provided by videotex.

Videotex information services

Quick access to a wide range of information through the medium of a television receiver or communicating data/word processing equipment is available using the television companies' teletext services or British Telecom's viewdata service. These services may be used for supplying information on a wide range of topics including stock market prices, exchange rates, world markets, tourist rates, weather conditions, travel guide, advertisements, etc.

Teletext

Ceefax (BBC) and Oracle (ITV) are computer-based information retrieval systems transmitting pages of data to television sets specially adapted for the purpose. The page of data required is selected by a remote controlled push button handset to provide a one-way source of information.

Viewdata

The British Telecom Prestel Service, as illustrated in Fig 2.1, uses the telephone network to connect the user's television receiver with the computer supplying pages of data. This is an interactive two-way service in which users can receive and send data from their homes or offices, eg placing orders for goods, making payments through a bank, reserving hotel accommodation, etc. The *Prestel Users' Guide and Directory* gives full details of the providers of information, their numbers and the services available.

Some of the information providers connect their own computers to the main Prestel computer in order to allow subscribers to gain access to their data through a gateway link. For example, British Airways provides up-to-the minute information about aircraft arrival and departure times on its computer which is linked to the Prestel computer.

Messages may be sent and received by the Prestel Mailbox Service. Subscribers have their own 'mailbox' which is used for receiving and transmitting their messages. Telex messages may also be sent and received via a Prestel mailbox.

A special financial information service, called Citiservice, is provided by British Telecom for investors, traders, financial advisers and business executives who require a knowledge of immediate market conditions. It provides instantaneous updating of prices in real time as well as on-line investment services, such as

Fig 2.1   Prestel viewdata

automatic portfolio valuations and electronic share ordering. Dedicated data lines connect the Citiservice Computer Centre direct to exchanges, banks and brokers around the world, providing a continuous flow of financial data 24 hours a day.

Private viewdata systems are used by organisations requiring specialised or restricted information. They are operated within a closed circuit for such needs as police, investment and travel. Access may be via Prestel or directly through the public telephone network.

Questions

1   From where can the following information be obtained? Indicate any further data you would require before applying to the various sources of reference.

   a) the value of 1000 pesetas
   b) the price of a motor-car licence
   c) how to dispatch a camera to Kenya
   d) how to engage an interpreter
   e) the name of a good hotel in the Western Highlands
   f) the value of 100 shares in a well-known public company (*LCCI PESD*)

2   Where would you go to get, or to deal with, the following for your employer:

   a) a new passport
   b) a driving licence
   c) a television licence
   d) a query relating to VAT
   e) a government publication
   f) a complaint about a local government service
   g) information about the foreign country where the employer will be spending
       his holiday?

3   Various forms of on-line databases are now often used in preference to sources
     of reference such as books, reports and newspapers. Give six examples of
     business information which can be obtained 'on-line' and outline the various
     advantages and disadvantages of these databases over the more traditional
     sources of reference. (*LCCI PSC*)

4   Where would you look for information about:

   a) a qualified medical practitioner
   b) a solicitor
   c) a clergyman of the Church of England
   d) the population of a town
   e) a company
   f) the road mileage between two towns?

5   For his forthcoming visit to the United States Mr Watson, your employer, has
     asked you to obtain as much information as possible about the country, the
     companies and opportunities for developing trade with the States in the field
     of safety goods. List the sources you will use for this purpose and the information
     you are likely to obtain.

6   Find out the following information relating to the European Union and state the
     reference books or other sources you used:

   a) The name and address of your MEP
   b) The number of British MEPs serving in the European Parliament
   c) The names of the EU Commissioners appointed by Britain
   d) The percentage of Britain's total trade with the EU for last year
   e) The title of a reference book listing the names, addresses and telephone
      numbers of manufacturers in another member country of the EU
   f) The current currency exchange rates for £ sterling in each of the EU member
       states
   g) The name and address of a UK government department providing advice to
      businesses trading within Europe

7 Suggest a reference book that would be of particular relevance to each of the businesses in Case Studies 1—4 and explain in what ways they would be helpful to the organisations.

In-tray exercise

8   You are employed at Office Products Ltd (Case Study 2). Your company is considering opening a factory and offices in Belgium, where they already do a great deal of business. A conference is to be held next week to discuss some basic considerations. The Marketing Manager's Secretary is off sick and you are asked to assist Mr Jones in undertaking the following tasks:

a) Will you please prepare a memo containing the following information which may be required at the conference:

1 The current rate of exchange of Belgian francs against £ sterling.

2 The total population of Belgium.

3 The population, position and industries of the town of Charleroi in Belgium.

4 How much does it cost to telephone, fax and telex to the company's agents in Belgium?

5 The address and telephone number of the Belgian Embassy in London.

6 The name of the government department which is able to assist in this project and any government publications which may be helpful .

7 The name and address of our local Member of the European Parliament whom we may wish to consult on the proposed project.

8 The local sources we can contact in order to engage an interpreter.

b) Our two Belgian agents will be arriving next Tuesday for the conference on Wednesday and they will return to Belgium after lunch on Thursday. Select a good local hotel (at least three stars) and reserve suitable accommodation for them. Arrange to book a table for dinner at the hotel at 2000 hrs so that I can join them for a pre-conference discussion. Please let me have two copies of your letter of confirmation to the hotel for the agents' use.

P Jones

2.2 Presentation of information

Statistical information is much more clearly grasped when illustrated on a graph, chart or planboard than when it is given in typed or printed form. Visual control systems enable progress and situations to be observed and controlled systematically and efficiently, and they are even capable of indicating current trends and future requirements. The information is clearly displayed so that the observer can digest facts and figures at a quick glance.

Line graphs

Line graphs can be used to show almost any kind of statistical information concerning, for instance, sales, purchases, gross profits, net profits, imports and exports, average prices, mark-up, margin figures, working capital and wage fluctuations. The graph should be drawn on as large a scale as the paper will allow, and the divisions should usually represent units of multiples of five.

Fig 2.2 is an example of a line graph chart which answers the following question:

A chart is required to show the weekly home and export sales over a period of three months. Plot the data on pages 34 and 35 on line graphs, using scales of 10 mm = £1000.

The following points should be noted in connection with the question and answer given:

1 The weeks are set out on the bottom horizontal line (or axis), each week occupying 10 mm.

2 The scale of money is given on the side vertical line.

3 Two or three colours may be used, eg red to represent home sales, and blue to represent export sales. If colour work is not permissible, contrasting lines, such as a continuous line and a dotted line, may be used, as in this example.

4 '0' takes the bottom line position and the largest sum takes the top line. In the example, each group of 10 mm represents £1000.

5 Care should be taken in joining up the lines, and the first few transactions of the example are described, as follows. Home sales start at £8500. A dot should be placed at the point of this figure immediately above 5 October. On 12 October home sales dropped to £7000, and a dot should be placed in line with the £7000 point

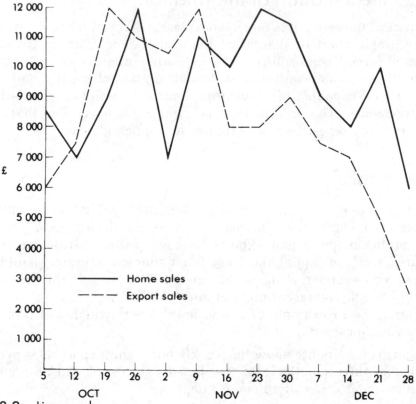

Fig 2.2 Line graph

and above 12 October. The two dots should now be joined together with a continuous line. On 19 October the sales rose to £9000 and at this position another dot should be placed over the correct date. The line ending on 12 October should now be joined up with the dot for 19 October, and so on.

6 Clear keys or footnotes must be displayed on the chart, giving the colour scheme or line formation adopted

Week ended		Home sales	Export sales
		£	£
Oct	5	8 500	6 000
	12	7 000	7 500
	19	9 000	12 000
	26	12 000	11 000
Nov	2	7 000	10 500
	9	11 000	12 000

Week ended	Home sales	Export sales
Nov 16	10 000	8 000
23	12 000	8 000
30	11 500	9 000
Dec 7	9 000	7 500
14	8 000	7 000
21	10 000	5 000
28	6 000	2 500

Bar graphs

Bar graphs are also an effective means of displaying information and are similar in many respects to line graphs, except that individual bars instead of continuous lines are used for each week or month. Bar graphs are more suitable for illustrating and contrasting figures for short periods; for example, in monthly statistics for a six-month period. Fig 2.3 is an example of a bar graph which answers the following question:

A chart is required to show the monthly sales of computers, filing cabinets and copiers over a period of six months. Display the following data on bar graphs, using scales of 10 mm = £10 000.

19-	Computers	Filing cabinets	Copiers
	£	£	£
January	40 000	34 000	41 000
February	29 000	20 000	50 000
March	31 000	31 000	50 000
April	39 000	22 000	49 000
May	12 000	29 000	48 000
June	20 000	35 000	45 000

The following points should be noted concerning this example:

1 The left-hand vertical line shows the sums of money ranging from £0 to £50 000.

2 The bottom horizontal line gives the months; each bar occupies 5 mm.

3 Coloured bars are most effective, but contrasting black designs can be used.

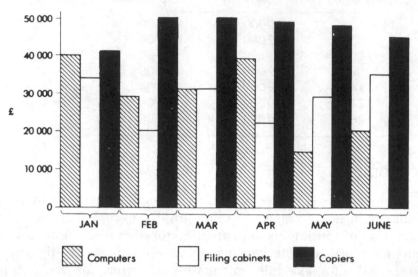

Fig 2.3   Bar graph

4 As with line graphs, the keys or footnotes must be clearly displayed.

Pie charts

A pie chart formed by means of a circle is another method sometimes used to display information, often in reports, journals and newspapers. The full circle represents the total amount involved and the sections making up the full amount are ruled off in proportion. The pie chart illustrated in Fig 2.4 analyses the sales to different parts of the UK during a week.

Computer graphics

Computers with graphics application software packages can be used to display graphics on VDUs and to supply printouts of columnar tables, line graphs, bar charts, pie charts, etc. A light pen may be used as a drafting aid for plotting images on the screen. An example of a computer displaying graphics is given in Fig 2.5.

Spreadsheets

Spreadsheets with graph facilities can be used to calculate and re-

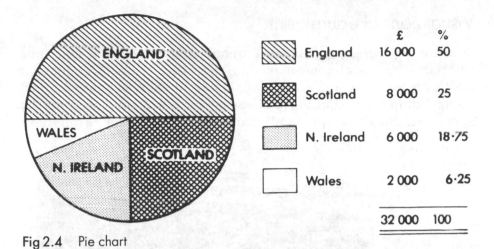

		£	%
	England	16 000	50
	Scotland	8 000	25
	N. Ireland	6 000	18·75
	Wales	2 000	6·25
		32 000	100

Fig 2.4   Pie chart

Fig 2.5   Computer graphics

calculate data and print it out in the form of line, bar or pie charts. Spreadsheets are dealt with in more detail in Unit 3.5. By using a spreadsheet data can be updated quickly and easily and the results reproduced in printed form.

Visual control equipment

Situations, progress and current trends can be watched and thus controlled by visual control boards and other types of equipment which are versatile and readily adaptable to show changes as they occur. Equipment requiring adjustment once a month need not be elaborate, and the graphs and charts described earlier in this unit

Fig 2.6   Visual control system

may be all that is required; but if the data requires altering from hour to hour a much quicker and more highly mechanised arrangement would be needed. As with graphs and charts, different colours are used in most visual control systems to distinguish and contrast the situations.

Visual control systems as in Fig. 2.6 are not only employed in controlling production, sales, progress, stores, parts available for assembly, stock control, shop loading, dispatch work and statistics but they can also be used to indicate trends in expenditure, the allocation of personnel, and many other purposes. Several kinds of visual control systems are manufactured using channel type planboards; perforated panels and pegboards; magnetic boards and plastic sheets.

Questions

1 The diagram below shows in £m the value of imports and exports for a period of three and a half years, each year being divided into its four quarters. Answer the following questions:

   a) What kind of graph is this?
   b) What are the names given to the lines along which the £m and the years are shown?

c) At what period did imports exceed exports by the greatest amount?
d) In what periods did exports exceed imports?
e) How large was the greatest gap between imports and exports?
f) What was the difference between the gap at the beginning of 1992 and the gap at the end of the second quarter of 1995?

2 Describe the various methods which can be used to display facts and figures in the office.

3 a) What are the advantages of recording statistical data in graphic form?
  b) Explain the difference between a line chart and a bar chart and give an example to show when each might be used. (*LCCI PSC*)

4 What is the purpose of using graphs? Suggest an occasion when a graph might be of value in:

  a) your college or school
  b) an office

5 a) Twenty management trainees are employed by your company and during their training they spend three months in each department. Design a visual control board or display chart, to be kept in the Personnel Manager's office, to show clearly the location of trainees during the current three-monthly period.
  b) Describe briefly other visual aids which can be used in the office to display facts and figures.

6 From the chart given below state:

  a) in which years home sales exceeded £10 000

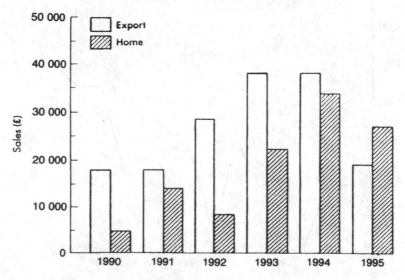

b) in which years home sales exceeded 50 per cent of total sales

c) in which years total sales exceeded £35000

7 Construct a line graph from the following information to show the comparative sales of a London branch and a provincial branch of a trading concern.

	London £	Provincial £
1988	5 000	20 000
1989	10 000	17 000
1990	12 000	15 000
1991	15 000	10 000
1992	17 000	8 000
1993	12 000	12 000
1994	10 000	20 000
1995	4 000	23 000

8 Draw a pie chart showing the information given below.

The turnover of a garage consists of:
Sales of cars — 50 per cent
Sales of accessories — 25 per cent
Sales of petrol and oil — 25 per cent.

9 Sales figures of selected toys are faxed in from the different sales regions. Figures faxed in today are for three toy ranges: 'Masters of Space', 'Cinderella' and 'Football Fanatics' and cover sales for May. More often than not these figures remain on Mr Hadfield's desk for a long time before he is able to study them. Today he has passed the latest figures (see below) back to you with the attached note. Using graph paper, show how you will prepare these figures in an appropriate way for Mr Hadfield.

SALES ('000 units)					
	North	Midlands	South	East	Wales
M of S	450	900	880	400	440
Cinderella	20	50	200	150	10
FF	600	45	350	100	200

Liz – can I burden you with yet another job? Please give some thought to how these figures can best be presented in a visual form each month to give us 'at a glance' information. Perhaps you can use these figures as a basis and prepare a sample graph. I shall need to be able to compare sales of each range in areas. Can I leave it with you?

M H

In-tray exercise

10 This task is based at Pinder and Moore (see Case Study 4).

The Sales Director is making a two-day visit to the North during which he will present the figures for the last three years for the sales of children's clothes both home and overseas. He has drawn up the figures in the form of a line graph but has decided that his presentation will be more effective as a bar chart.

Using the line graph you have been given convert it to a bar chart showing the start of the year figures for both overseas and home.

Children's clothes sales figures

(PEI OP2)

2.3 Mailing procedures and equipment

Incoming mail

The handling of incoming mail in an office needs to be carried out systematically and efficiently in order to have the correspondence quickly available for distribution. The staff responsible for opening the mail will usually arrive at the office earlier than the normal starting time so that the incoming correspondence is sorted and distributed without delay. The steps normally taken to organise this work include:

1 Sorting the mail into the following categories:
   a registered mail (signed for on receipt)
   b private, personal and confidential letters
   c mail marked 'urgent'
   d mail not addressed to the firm (reposted unopened)
   e all other mail addressed to the firm

2 Opening the urgent mail c first and giving it top priority delivery.

3 Opening the mail in a and e, using a paper knife or letter opener.

4 Unfolding the contents of the envelopes, checking that any enclosures are there and that they are pinned to the letters which they accompany. Any missing or incorrect items should be reported promptly using an enclosure slip (a note drawing attention to the omission).

5 Stamping the date on every document received, taking care not to obliterate typewritten or printed matter.

6 Entering all remittances, whether registered or not, in a remittances book. Check the remittances with the amounts indicated on the letters or accounts to which they are attached, and inform the supervisor of any discrepancies. The amount, method of payment (eg cheque, PO or cash) and your initials should be written on the corner of the document. The remittances are then detached from the correspondence and passed to the cashier, who signs for them in the remittances book.

7 Scanning each item of mail in order to allocate it to the appropriate departmental tray.

8 Delivering the mail to departments, including the private, personal and confidential mail b which is delivered unopened to the persons concerned.

9 Rechecking all envelopes to make sure that nothing has been left in them.

If an incoming letter contains a number of matters which require the attention of several departments, a special arrangement may be made so that each department concerned deals promptly with its particular matter. There are several ways in which this can be done. Three are given here:

1 A circulation slip which lists the various departments could be attached to the letter and, as it is sent round the offices, the representative of each department crosses their name off the slip after taking the necessary action.

2 The department dealing with the major part of the letter could be given the original and be responsible for passing on the minor matters to the other departments concerned.

3 The mailroom clerk could have several copies made of the entire letter and send one copy to each of the departments concerned.

The third method is normally the most satisfactory provided that the replies are co-ordinated.

Suspicious postal packets

When sorting incoming mail you should take care to look out for any suspicious items which might contain letter bombs; for example, such packages might be identified by:

- an unusual shape or size
- wires attached
- oil or grease marks on the cover
- weighing heavier than the size suggests
- having a smell of almonds
- a pin hole in the wrapping.

If you discover a suspicious package which complies with any of the above descriptions, you are advised:

1 Not to open it or allow anyone else to deal with it

2 To handle the package gently, placing it on a flat surface above floor level and away from a corner of the office

3 To leave the office as soon as possible, lock the door and hold on to the key for use by the police or security officer when they arrive

4 To inform your security/safety officer, who will assume responsibility for the incident and, if necessary, inform the police

5 To keep the entrance to the office clear of people.

Automatic time and date stamping machine

This machine may be used for automatically stamping the time and date of receipt on incoming correspondence. It is an electrically operated machine which prints the year, month, date and time, in the form given below:

```
19--JAN 10  AM 9: 13
```

Printing is performed automatically once the document is inserted in the machine. Additional information such as a company name, department, trademark, etc may be incorporated on the printing plate. It is similar to a clocking-in machine and may be used for any documents which require precise timing.

Outgoing mail

The procedure for outgoing mail will depend on the volume of post handled and the equipment available, but after letters have been typed they will generally receive the following treatment:

1 Letters are delivered to the executives for signature.

2 If there are any enclosures, these are checked and attached to the appropriate letters.

3 The letters and enclosures are collected from the departments and delivered to a central mailing office. To ensure that the mail is prepared for the post on time, a deadline will be set after which letters will not be accepted by the mailing office for dispatch that day.

4 The addresses on the envelopes are checked with the addresses on the letters. Window envelopes, which have an opening (or window) in the front, may be used to save typing the name and address twice.

5 The letters are folded and inserted into their envelopes.

6 The flaps of the envelopes are sealed.

7 The packages are weighed and stamped or franked by machine.

8 Details of the mail may be recorded in a postage account.

9 Special items of mail, such as registered, recorded delivery, air mail, etc which require labels or forms or have to be handed over the counter of the post office, will be kept apart from the remainder of the post.

10 The envelopes are tied in bundles with all the addresses facing in one direction.

11 The mailroom clerk arranges for the mail to be delivered to the post office, completes any necessary forms and collects the receipts for the items referred to in 9.

This procedure is explained in more detail in the following paragraphs.

Post Office automation

To facilitate the sorting of mail by using electronic machines, Royal Mail requests its customers to post their mail in envelopes within a preferred range of sizes. Envelopes should be at least 90 mm x 140 mm and not larger than 165 mm x 240 mm.

Royal Mail advises its customers that high-speed postal deliveries depend on correct addressing and, in order to comply with good practice, postal addresses should normally comprise:

- name of addressee
- house number (or name) and street
- locality name, where necessary
- post town (in block capitals)
- county name where required
- postcode

Example:
Mr J A Knight
142 East Street
HARLOW
Essex
CM12 8RP

Modern sorting methods increasingly depend on the postcode — a shortened form of the address which can be read by machine — allowing mail to be processed automatically at all stages. Every UK address has a postcode. The full list is published by Royal Mail in a set of postcode directories and can be consulted at public libraries or most main post offices. The code should be written in block capitals on a line by itself, with a space between the two parts. At the outgoing sorting office, the code is translated into two rows of phosphor dots. The lower row, representing the first half of the code, conveys enough information for the letter to be computer-sorted to the right sorting office for its destination post town. By a similar process on arrival there, the upper row of dots allows automatic sorting right down to an individual postman's delivery round. Without the postcode, a letter may at some stage be diverted for sorting by hand which is much slower than machine. The postcode is not a substitute for any of the other parts of the address. Certain items must be sorted by hand and the code does not identify single addresses except for major postal users, for whom a full address is still needed. Most codes are shared by several addresses and the full address is essential for delivery to the individual address.

Addressing envelopes

Computers, word processors and copiers can be used to print out names and addresses and other repetitive data on sheets, with adhesive backing if required, thus providing a rapid and efficient means of supplying address labels for envelopes and other mailing applications. An automatic document printer with an ink roller may be used for overprinting data on coupons, vouchers, tickets, labels and forms, as well as cheque signing.

Enclosures

All outgoing mail has to be checked to ensure that the correct enclosures are attached to the letters. They are usually indicated by 'enc' typed at the bottom of the letter.

Folding

Letters and enclosures for posting should be folded carefully and neatly. Care should be taken not to fold a document more than is necessary to fit it into its envelope.

Where large quantities of circulars, invoices, statements, price lists, etc have to be folded for the post, a folding machine may be used.

Folding machines will automatically feed, fold and stack papers. The positions of the folds are changed simply by adjusting a knob on a setting scale to provide for single and double folds. The papers are ejected on to a moving conveyor system which stacks them in strict sequence. Machines are also capable of making perforations in the paper where a tear-off portion is required and a slitting wheel may be brought into use to cut away any unwanted paper.

Inserting and sealing

Machines can also be used to carry out the combined processes of folding papers, inserting them into envelopes and sealing the flaps. This equipment, as illustrated in Fig 2.7, uses the latest microcontroller technology, and enables large quantities of mail to be assembled at speed ready for franking.

Stamping of mail

It is important that the letters all have stamps to the correct value; if they are insufficiently stamped, the deficiency plus a surcharge becomes payable on delivery. A good reliable pair of scales is indispensable in the mailing room for weighing the post to calculate the correct charges.

Franking machines

If a franking machine is used, postage stamps are dispensed with and printed impressions are made instead on the envelopes. A certain amount of credit is secured at the post office or by arranging for a Royal Mail representative to visit the premises, and, every time the machine prints an impression, the amount of postage used is recorded

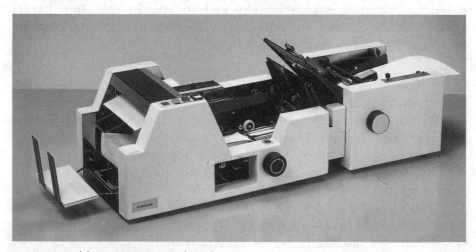

Fig 2.7 Folding, inserting and sealing system

on the machine's meter. The amount of credit in hand and the total postage used can be seen in the visual display at the touch of a button. All types of mail can be franked, including ordinary inland letter post, postcards, registered letters, parcels and foreign letters.

Franking machines are purchased, leased or rented from certain office equipment manufacturers, and a licence must be obtained from Royal Mail.

To operate the machine, the required postal value is keyed in, and when the envelopes are passed through the machine an imprint is made, showing the date, postal district and value. An advertising slogan, or the user's name and address can also be printed on the package at the same time.

If a package is too thick to pass through the machine, a label device is used to dispense a self-adhesive label. The amount of postage which can be printed at one impression depends on the size of the machine, but the most comprehensive models print denominations up to a maximum of £99.99.

The mailroom clerk is responsible for changing the date on the machine and ensuring that the supply of red ink is adequate. Modern machines use disposable cartridges for the ink. A lock is fitted to prevent unauthorised use and the machine should be locked at the end of the day's work and whenever it is not required. A refund can be obtained from Royal Mail for any envelopes franked in error. Such envelopes must be retained and submitted periodically to Royal Mail, who will supply a refund for the value of the impressions less 5 per cent.

The following procedure should be used for dispatching franked mail:

1 Separate the mail into first-class and second-class packages.

2 Tie the packages in bundles, arranged with the names and addresses facing in the same direction.

3 Place the bundles of first-class letters in a red pouch and the second-class letters in a green pouch.

4 Keep franked mail separate from other post.

5 Call for a collection or deliver the packages to the specified post office or, by arrangement with the Royal Mail Customer Centre, post the packages in any posting box if the franked mail is enclosed in the special envelopes provided for the purpose.

The electronic franking machine, when interfaced with electronic

Fig 2.8   A franking machine with interfaced electronic scales

scales, automatically combines the weighing, postage calculation and franking operations. This equipment is illustrated in Fig 2.8.

When electronic scales are used, there is no need to refer to postal rates as these are programmed into its memory. To obtain the correct amount of postage for a packet, you place it on the scales and press the appropriate key for the service required, eg first class, and the rate appears instantly in a digital display panel. It also reveals the exact weight, which is useful for recording on customs declaration forms.

A remote meter-resetting system using a special telephone data pad may be used for purchasing additional units and for resetting your franking machine by telephone instead of having to deliver the machine to the specified post office.

An alternative system for resetting the franking machine is the use of a credipac module, which is sent with a cheque to the post office or Royal Mail in a special reply-paid pouch. The module registers the units used and the amount of credit in hand and, after resetting by the post office, it is returned to the user within 72 hours. The franking machine remains with the user during resetting and continues to be used without a break.

Modern franking machines can include such features as:

- a date-change control which flashes 'set date' immediately after switching on the machine to alert the operator to set the new date

- a warning light when the credit begins to run low
- a safeguard in printing high values, as a signal flashes when amounts in excess of £1 are set
- a credit management control system which provides a printout of usage by individual departments
- a built-in diagnostic system can keep the operator informed at all times with messages at every stage of the mailing process.

Advantages

1 A saving in time compared with choosing, tearing off, moistening and fixing stamps.

2 Greater security by eliminating the use of stamps which may be lost or stolen. Franking impressions do not exist until the machine is operated and then they are non-negotiable.

3 Ease of planning future requirements as there is no need, which there is with stamps, to forecast the varying quantities of different denominations required.

4 Better control of expenditure as the meters show at a glance the amount used and the amount of credit.

5 A saving in printing costs as an advertisement or return address can be printed simultaneously with the franking impression.

6 Assists in speeding up the dispatch of mail from the post office as the envelopes are not held up for franking by Post Office officials.

7 A postage book may be dispensed with when a franking machine is used since the machine meter indicates the amount of postage paid.

8 Eliminates the drudgery of moistening and sticking stamps on to envelopes.

Disadvantages

1 The savings must be set against the cost of the machine and the fact that operators may waste postage by franking wrong amounts or not producing legible impressions.

2 A franking machine is unlikely to be an economic proposition for small companies with fewer than 20-30 letters daily.

3 Because of security, a franking machine cannot be made available to a large number of people, which necessitates the use of loose

postage stamps for mail which has to be dispatched after the franking machine has been locked away.

4 Although a franking machine indicates the amount of postage used, it does not provide a record of letters posted.

5 Franked envelopes cannot be posted as easily as those which are stamped as they must be taken to the post office or posted in a specially prepared envelope.

Postage book

After the letters have been stamped, particulars of the letters posted may be entered in a postage book which serves as:

a a check on the number of stamps used, and

b a record of all letters posted.

The mailroom clerk brings down the balance in the postage book

Stamps bought			Stamps used		Total	
£		Number	Denomination		£	
			1st October 19_			
25	00		Balance b/f			
		33	20p		6	60
		36	25p		9	00
		12	30p		3	60
		2	35p		0	70
					19	90
			Balance c/f		5	10
25	00				25	00
			2nd October 19_			
5	10		Balance b/f			

Fig 2.9   Daily stamp record

every morning showing the difference between the amount of stamps purchased and the amount used; the value of any remaining stamps must agree with the balance shown in the book.

Postage books are not kept in many offices today mainly because of the time taken to record them and the popular use of franking machines which automatically register the amount of postage used. Where postage stamps are still in use and details of correspondents are not required, the mailroom clerk may simply keep a record of the total number of stamps used each day, as illustrated in Fig 2.9.

Collection of mail by the post office

Instead of the mailroom clerk having to deliver large quantities of mail to the post office, arrangements can be made for a postman to collect it from the company.

A free collection of letters is available on request if you are posting at least 1000 letters or letters and packets to the value of £190. Charges for collecting parcels vary depending on collection patterns and on the number of parcels involved.

A parcel contract can be arranged with Parcelforce for regular large postings of parcels (over 750 per annum) and this includes free delivery of parcels to the post office.

Automatic mailroom system

The equipment, as illustrated in Fig 2.10, performs laborious paperhandling functions automatically. It is capable of collating enclosures; folding and inserting them into envelopes; sealing the envelopes; and counting them in one non-stop operation.

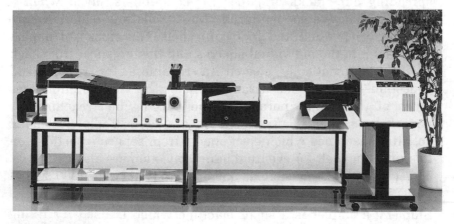

Fig 2.10   Multi-component system for feeding, collating, folding and inserting mail

Electronic mail

Electronic mail or teletex, as it is sometimes called, does not have to be placed in an envelope, stamped and posted in the normal way, as it is transmitted electronically over telephone lines from one word processor to another, which may be situated in another town or country.

Mailroom equipment

In addition to the various items of equipment already referred to in this unit, the following may be used in the mailroom to assist in the efficient handling of the post:

- Jogger: a machine which vibrates papers into alignment ready for stapling or binding.
- Document destroying machine: for shredding confidential and secret documents or providing packing material for parcels.
- Package tying machine: for tying tape round parcels.
- Tucking and folding machine: for preparing notices which are to be mailed without envelopes.
- Rolling and wrapping machine: for preparing newspapers, magazines and journals for mailing.
- Trolleys or baskets: for the collection and distribution of mail.
- Rubber stamps: for various purposes, such as marking the firm's name and address or the name of the postal service on packages, or for stamping a facsimile signature on a document.
- Collators: the considerable table space normally used for spreading out stacks of paper for collation is saved when a collating machine is employed. Most collating machines are electrically operated and foot controlled. The stacks of papers are fitted into the individual shelves and the top sheet from each shelf is automatically ejected in readiness for rapid hand collection. The compact arrangement of the shelves eliminates much of the fatigue normally experienced when reaching for papers from stacks spread out over a table. Fully automatic collating machines which eject sheets from separate sections on to a revolving belt for eventual hand collection are also available. This type of machine enables one operator to collate 2000 sets of papers in an hour.
- Staplers: a stapler is a small machine which is used for fixing wire staples into the pages of a document. The wire staples,

which are issued in blocks of 50 to 100, are clamped into the machine by means of a spring clip. The document to be stitched is inserted into the stapler and the knob is pressed down with a sharp instant action. If this sharp action is applied, the jamming together of several staples in the machine is avoided. An electric stapler is faster as the staple is automatically fixed when the papers are inserted into the machine. A long-arm stapler is used for stapling the centre of folded documents such as magazines, manuals, etc.

- Guillotine: a razor-sharp cutting device used for slicing quantities of paper and cardboard to the required size and for straightening tattered or uneven edges of paper.

Questions

1   Draft a report to your employer, suggesting steps which could be taken to deal with a greatly increased volume of incoming and outgoing mail. This is at present handled by one clerk, who keeps the postage book and stamps.

2   Mr Paul Wood, Operations Director of Comlon International plc, has agreed that you help the Personnel Department by showing a newly appointed secretary around as part of her induction. She previously worked for a small company, has no experience of franking machines and wants to know the advantages. What would you tell her? (*LCCI PSC*)

3   There is some concern in your company because letters appear to be going astray. You are asked to devise a system for handling the incoming mail ensuring the maximum of security, especially for remittances. Set out in detail your plan.

4   Give the following information about each of three machines of your choice which you would expect to find in a mailroom:

- its purpose
- its advantages
- very briefly, how it is operated.

5   a) Machines for franking the post can be purchased or hired from certain office equipment firms, but the user must comply with various Royal Mail conditions. List any such conditions which you know.

b) It may not be economical to use a franking machine if the number of items posted each day is not very large, and there are also disadvantages in its use, even to a large company. What are these disadvantages and why do many companies consider that franking machines should nevertheless be used?

6   Some incoming mail needs to be seen by more than one person or department in a firm. Suggest what can be done to make sure that three people see the contents of a letter:

   a) when there is no urgency
   b) when the matter is urgent.

7   If you were responsible for operating a franking machine, state what action you should take for the following:

   a) faint impressions of printed information
   b) an envelope franked in error
   c) preparing franked mail for dispatch
   d) closing the franking machine at the end of each day.

8   Describe a variety of methods and equipment which might be used to reduce to a minimum the time spent addressing envelopes. (*LCCI PSC*)

In-tray exercise

9   You are employed at the New Tech Office Services Bureau (Case Study 1). As you will shortly be going on holiday, Mrs Robinson has asked you to help your replacement by listing the points he/she should cover when handling:

   a) incoming mail, which arrives unopened on your desk each morning
   b) outgoing mail, which you organise for the bureau. The mail is delivered daily to the post office by the firm's delivery van
   c) addressing the envelopes and mailing a circular letter to 300 customers.

2.4 Mail services

Anyone who is concerned with the dispatch of mail should know about the many services offered by Royal Mail, Parcelforce, and the other delivery agencies. The following is a summary of the essential details. Current charges can be obtained from the Royal Mail leaflets for UK and international letters, from Parcelforce and from price lists supplied by the independent delivery agencies.

Letters and cards

United Kingdom

Letters and cards may be sent by two classes of service, known respectively as first class and second class. Royal Mail endeavours to deliver first-class mail the next working day after collection and second-class mail within three working days after collection. The class of a letter is determined by the amount of postage paid. No written indication of service is necessary, except where this is separately specified for certain categories of mail. There is a limit of 750 g weight for second-class letters, but there is no weight limit for first-class letters.

Special Delivery
If a letter is urgent, it can be sent by the Special Delivery service for a special fee, which is in addition to first-class postage. The letter receives priority and is guaranteed next-day delivery (Monday to Friday) by 1230 hrs to most UK destinations. Items posted on Friday or Saturday are guaranteed delivery on Monday.

The despatch procedure is as follows:

- Complete the sender's and addressee's names and addresses on a special delivery form.

- Peel off and attach the top portion of the form 'Guaranteed Delivery' to the top left-hand corner of the front of the envelope.

- Peel off and attach the middle portion of the label which includes barcodes and sender's details to the reverse of the envelope.

- Stick stamps to the envelope to the value of first-class postage and the special delivery fee.

- Hand in the certificate of posting with the package at a post office counter.

- The certificate is date-stamped and initialled as the sender's receipt. This should be kept safely for reference in the event of a claim or enquiry.

To confirm delivery of a special delivery, registered or recorded delivery package it is necessary to make a local telephone call to 0645 272100 and quote the 13-digit number on the receipt. A copy of the delivery signature can be requested on payment of an additional charge.

Mailsort

A contract can be arranged with Royal Mail to allow discounts on letters posted in bulk, ie a minimum of 4000 items, which have been presorted by postcodes. Exceptionally, a minimum of 2000 letters will be accepted for a discount, provided they are all for delivery within one postcode area and are all posted within the same postcode area. To qualify for a discount the items must normally be of the same size, shape and weight and at least 90 per cent of the addresses must have postcodes.

This service may be used for the following categories of mail:

Mailsort 1 for first-class mail:
target delivery the next working day
Mailsort 2 for second-class mail:
target delivery within three working days
Mailsort 3 for non-urgent second-class mail:
target delivery within seven working days

Door-to-door delivery service

This service provides for the delivery of unaddressed material (usually promotional leaflets) on a door-to-door basis with the normal mail. No stamps are required, and the mail can be delivered enveloped or unenveloped. It is cheaper than the normal postal services and less costly in preparation.

Europe

Business letters, packets (up to 2 kg in weight) and cards are sent by airmail and are usually delivered within two to four days in cities. Letters and postcards to the EU up to 20 g are charged at the same rate as inland first-class letters.

Airmail items should have the blue airmail labels stuck on them or the words PAR AVION – BY AIRMAIL written boldly on the package.

A special high-speed overseas letter post, called Swiftair, delivers airmail letters at least one day earlier than those sent by ordinary airmail. In this case a red Swiftair label should be stuck on the envelope in the top left-hand corner and, when posting, it should be kept separate from other mail to ensure prompt delivery.

Items of mail requiring more urgent delivery should be sent by the Datapost service (see page 62).

International - outside Europe

Airmail services may be used for letters and cards for delivery within two to seven days in cities, depending on the country of destination. Airmail labels, as explained above, should be used and delivery can be speeded up with the Swiftair and Datapost services, as for Europe.

Aerograms (airletters) may be sent to any address in the world for a cheaper rate of postage, provided they are written on either the stamped printed forms which are obtainable from post offices or on privately manufactured forms with the necessary postage included. They must not contain enclosures.

Large business users sending at least 2 kg of airmail per day may take advantage of the Airstream contract service, in which Royal Mail arranges to collect mail, complete the documentation, and stamp the packages.

Surface mail is the cheapest way of sending letters and cards abroad but delivery to some countries can take up to 12 weeks.

Faxmail

This is a fax/courier service which uses the Electronic Mail Centre for transmitting urgent documents up to A4 size to most towns and cities in the UK and to over 40 countries worldwide (see page 126).

Printflow

Printed papers up to 5 kg in weight may be sent abroad by airmail or surface mail at reduced rates of postage by the Printflow service. Printed papers include newspapers, magazines, directories, calendars, photographs, books and non-personalised mailshots.

There are three different types of Printflow service, allowing the sender to select the best combination of speed and cost for their particular needs:

Printflow Air   used when speed of delivery is a major consideration.

| **Printflow Airsaver** | for a less expensive but moderately fast delivery service outside Europe. |
| **Printflow Surfacesaver** | used for optimum economy when speed of delivery is not essential. |

Overseas small packets

This service provides for the transmission of goods, whether dutiable or not, in the same mails as Printflow which, as a rule, travel more quickly than parcels. The sender must write their name and address on the outside of the packet and must write the words *Small packet* in the top left-hand corner on the address side of the packet. Small packets may be sent by air mail or surface mail. The packets may be sealed and contain personal correspondence if it relates to the contents being sent.

Airpacks

Prepaid, specially manufactured airpacks for European and world-wide destinations may be used for sending goods weighing up to 500 g by airmail. Additional postage has to be paid for heavier weights. A customs (C1) label is incorporated on the front of the packaging and must be completed by the sender.

Customs declarations

All packets posted for abroad at the letter rate of postage and containing goods, whether or not dutiable in the country of destination, must be declared to customs. If the value of the goods does not exceed £270, a green label (form C1) is sufficient, but for goods in excess of £270 a form C2/CP3 plus a green C1 label should be completed.

Parcel services

United Kingdom

The following Parcelforce services are available for the delivery of parcels up to 30 kg at the different delivery times given below:

Service	*Delivery time*	*Inclusive cover for loss or damage (per parcel)*
Datapost	Guaranteed next morning with money back guarantee in the event of late delivery	Up to £500

Parcelforce 24	Guaranteed next working day with money back guarantee in the event of late delivery	Up to £500
Parcelforce 48	Guaranteed within two working days with money back guarantee in the event late delivery	Up to £500
Parcelforce Standard	Normally within three working days	Up to £20*

* It is necessary to obtain a certificate of posting (available free of charge) as evidence of despatch should the need arise to make a claim

Confirmation of delivery by telephone or in writing can be arranged with all services.

The compensation fee parcel facility provides a higher level of compensation for the Parcelforce Standard service. By paying this fee, a parcel can be insured against loss or damage during transit up to a maximum value of £500. The sender must complete a certificate of posting with the addressee's name and address, and the amount of compensation required, and hand this certificate to the post office counter clerk together with the parcel, fee and postage. The clerk then initials and date stamps the top portion of the certificate of posting and returns it to the sender. Posting lists may be used, instead of separate certificates of posting, when posting a large number of parcels.

Under the Parcelforce Datapost service, consequential loss from £100 to £5000 per consignment is included. A consequential loss is a loss to the sender arising out of some failure in the Parcelforce service and is over and above the actual value of the articles lost, damaged or delayed, eg in the case of manufactured or sample goods delayed or damaged in the post, this could result in the consequential loss of sales and profits.

Addressing and packaging

When addressing a parcel, the address should be written on the parcel itself and not merely on a label, which may become detached. In case the wrapping becomes damaged, or the parcel cannot be delivered, the sender's address should appear both inside the parcel and on the cover. On the cover it should be kept distinct from the address to which the parcel is sent, and should preferably be to the left and at right angles to the addressee's name and address. Pack the contents securely to avoid any movement within the package. It is advisable to use 38 mm or 50 mm plastic or re-inforced carton sealing tape rather than adhesive tape. String should not be used around boxes but can be used around other wrapping materials.

Contracts
Large business users of Parcelforce services may enter into contracts which provide for flat-rate charging, account facilities, free collection, weekly data reports itemising all consignments sent and access to printed postal impressions instead of using meter machines.

International

Parcelforce services
The following international parcel services are offered by Parcelforce:

International Datapost	For urgent parcels of documents or goods. Guaranteed express deliveries can be made to some 200 countries and territories worldwide with money-back guarantees in the event of late delivery. An inclusive charge covers compensation, consequential loss and collection from the sender's premises.
International Standard Service	For less urgent deliveries to Europe from three working days and the rest of the world from five working days. The charge includes compensation.
International Economy Service	Use for optimum economy. Delivery to Europe from ten working days and the rest of the world 20 working days.

The Parcelforce charges, guaranteed delivery times, weight and size allowances, prohibitions and import licence requirements for each country are listed in the *Parcelforce International User Guide* This guide can also be used to look up time zones, working days, dialling codes and contacts, eg Overseas Chambers of Commerce, for most countries abroad. All merchandise must be accompanied by three signed copies of commercial invoices to verify the value of the contents. Advice on customs documentation requirements for international parcels can be obtained from the Simpler Trade Procedures Board (SITPRO) Tel: 0171-287-1814.

Checklist for sending international parcels

1 Select the parcel service according to the price and speed you need, referring to the *Parcelforce International User Guide* (PIUG).

2 Check that the contents of the parcel are acceptable for despatch to the country of destination as listed in PIUG.

3 Pack the parcel securely and address it clearly (see page 61 and PIUG). If the parcel is going by Standard Service, you will need to fix a service label (available at post office counters) to the parcel.

4 Check the weight and size limits imposed by the country of destination, using PIUG.

5 Weigh the parcel, calculate the postage required and frank a label (or attach stamps).

6 Complete the necessary docket set (for Datapost) and despatch pack (for Standard and Economy Services). The pack combines the customs declaration, despatch note and customer receipt in one document and, after completion, it should be attached to the front of the parcel. Check with SITPRO for advice on customs documentation requirements.

7 Complete any other documentation required, such as:

- VAT label 444 for items valued at over £100
- commercial invoice or bill of sale to verify the value of goods
- export licence or certificate of origin as required for customs purposes.

Place these documents in the despatch pack on the outside of the parcel.

8 Deliver the parcel to a post office or arrange for the post office to collect it from your premises.

9 Collect and retain a certificate of posting as evidence of despatch.

Registered post and recorded delivery services

A comparison

	Recorded Delivery	Registered	Registered Plus
Uses	For the correspondent who requires not only proof of posting but, if necessary, proof of delivery and is not so concerned in receiving compensation for loss. It is especially suitable for despatching documents of little or no monetary value for which proof of delivery may be required in a court of law. It should not be used for sending money or jewellery.	For next-day delivery by 1230 hrs of money, jewellery, documents and any other items up to £500 in value with entitlement to compensation for loss or damage.	For next-day delivery by 1730 hrs of the items in the previous column but up to £2,200 in value with entitlement to compensation for loss or damage.
Maximum compensation payable	£25	£500	£2200
Confirmation of delivery	Telephone 01645-272100 and quote the 13-digit number on the receipt. Call the day after delivery is due. A signed receipt of delivery may be requested for an additional fee.	As for Recorded Delivery except that the sender can call at 1400 on the day after posting.	As for Recorded Delivery.
Cost	First- or second-class postage plus the recorded delivery fee.	First-class postage plus the registered/ compensation fee.	First-class postage plus the registered plus fee.

Preparation	(1) Detach and stick the top portion of the label to the top left-hand corner of the envelope. (2) Enter the sender's name and address on the middle portion of the label which contains the bar coding. Detach and affix it to the reverse of the envelope. (3) Fill in the name and address of the recipient on the remaining portion of the label. (4) Affix postage stamps to the envelope for the total cost of the service (as above). (5) Hand in the label and envelope at a post office or give it to the Royal Mail driver who collects the mail. The label will be date stamped and initialled for the sender to keep as a receipt.	As indicated in points (1) to (5) of Recorded Delivery. Ensure that the envelope or wrapping material is strong enough to hold the contents. Seal the package with gum or other adhesive substance. String alone is not enough. Make sure that the contents cannot be removed without breaking a seal, tearing the wrapper or forcing two adhesive surfaces apart. If adhesive tape is used it must be marked with a stamp or a signature. If several Registered, Registered Plus or Recorded Delivery packets are to be sent, they should be accompanied by a list, in duplicate, of the names and addresses; one list is retained at the post office and the other, when completed and signed, is returned to the sender. These are usually kept in book form and are obtainable from the Royal Mail Customer Service Centre	As for Registered.

Response services

Business reply service

This service enables a firm to receive cards or letters from their customers without prepayment of postage. The postage at the first- or second-class rate, with a fee on each item, is paid by the addressee. A licence to use the service must be obtained from Royal Mail. A priority service may be used on payment of a small increased fee to target delivery by the first scheduled post on the following day.

Freepost

A person who wishes to obtain a reply from a client or a member of the public without putting them to the expense of paying postage may use a special address which includes the word 'FREEPOST' in the communication or advertisement. The reply bearing this address can then be posted in the ordinary way but without a stamp and the addressee will pay postage on all the replies that are received.

Freepost can be used with both first- and second-class post when a pre-printed envelope, card or form is the response device, but only second-class post is permitted when customers respond by writing the freepost address on their own stationery. This service can be used to attract a response not only through the press, but through television and direct mail. The postage, plus a small fee on each item, is paid by the addressee. A priority service is also offered, similar to the one applied to the business reply service explained above.

Postage forward parcel service

The postage forward parcel service enables a company to receive parcels from customers without prepayment of postage; the postage, with a small fee on each parcel, is paid by the addressee. A licence to use this service must be obtained from Parcelforce. This service is designed primarily to meet the needs of companies who wish to obtain a parcel from a customer without putting the customer to the expense or trouble of paying postage.

Reply coupons overseas

International reply coupons, obtainable from post offices in the UK, enable anyone sending a letter to a place abroad to prepay a reply, ie instead of enclosing a stamped addressed envelope, the sender encloses a reply coupon which is exchangeable for postage stamps at post offices abroad.

Other services
Other services and devices which traders can use to encourage prospective customers to communicate with them include:

Freefone telephone service (page 121)
Telephone-answering machine (page 113)
Telex service (page 123)
Fax service (page 125)
Electronic mail (page 54)
Videotex (page 29)

Other outgoing mail services

Newspapers and magazines
A special application of Mailsort (page 58) called **Presstream** is available to publishers who have large quantities of magazines and periodicals to dispatch. In this service they pay lower prices in return for postcode sorting before posting using a Mailsort Database.

Cash on delivery
A service in which the recipient of a parcel, registered letter or datapost package pays for the cost of the item on delivery. Up to a maximum sum of £500 can be collected and credited to the sender's bank account. Sums in excess of £100 (£250 for businesses) must be collected at a post office or special arrangements made for delivery.

Late posting facility
Registered letters, first-class letters and recorded delivery packets are accepted in travelling post offices at railway stations up to five minutes before the departure times of the trains on payment of a fee in addition to the postage. The stamps for the postal fees must be stuck on the package before it is presented at the station.

Printed postage impressions
An alternative to franking and stamping mail for organisations which send average daily mailings of over 250 items or average annual postage expenditure of £12 000 is to send letters or packets with

printed postage impressions (PPIs). They can be used for large quantities of identical inland or international letters or packets at first- or second-class postage.

Envelopes, labels or wrappers are pre-printed and may be used for regular or occasional postings. Royal Mail invoices the user for the cost of the postage after the items have been despatched.

Incoming mail services

Selectapost

This service is provided by Royal Mail for mail to be sorted into specified categories, such as departments, before it is delivered.

Private boxes

Instead of the mail being delivered in the ordinary way, a private box may be rented at a post office for the reception of postal packets 'to be called for' by the renter or their agent. The box must be taken for a definite address in the postal district in which the service is required and letters and parcels addressed to the renter must include the private box number, eg:

John Payne Enterprises plc
PO Box 149
BLANKTOWN
BN8 3AP

The renter can also arrange for normally addressed mail to be transferred to their private box.

By means of this service the renter can obtain mail before the normal delivery time. Correspondence is handed over only on production of a check card.

Poste restante

Poste restante means post waiting. To assist travellers with no fixed address, correspondence and parcels may be addressed to them at any post office except town sub-offices. The words 'Poste restante' or 'To be called for' must be included in the address. At the expiry of two weeks (one month for a packet originating abroad) postal packets are treated as undelivered. To ensure delivery to the right person, addressees must produce evidence of their identity when calling for mail.

Redirection of postal packets

Letters, registered packets, postcards and newspapers are

retransmitted by post without additional charge, provided the packet is unopened and reposted not later than the day after delivery, Sundays and public holidays not being counted. If an adhesive label is used to indicate the new address, the name of the original addressee must not be obscured; otherwise the packet will be liable to surcharge as unpaid.

Registered and recorded delivery packets must not be dropped into a letter box but must be handed over the counter of a post office.

Redirection of mail by Royal Mail

If a person or business moves from one address to another, redirection of letters, parcels and other postal packets is undertaken by Royal Mail and Parcelforce at various rates depending on the period of redirection required. Forms should be completed and sent to the Royal Mail Redirection Centre and Parcelforce Customer Care Unit serving the old address.

Red Star parcel delivery services

The following parcel delivery services are offered by British Rail.

United Kingdom

1 Station to station

A railway delivery service which connects British Rail's network of 200 parcel points. Packages must be handed in to a railway station at least 30 minutes before the chosen train leaves and they are then available to be collected at the destination station 30 minutes after the train's arrival.

2 Door to door

A courier service with collection from the sender's premises and delivery to the consignee's address for same day or overnight dispatch.

The documentation required for these UK services is a Red Star consignment note.

Insurance cover is offered at no extra charge for most items, with up to £15 000 compensation per package. If a consignment is not delivered to the door by an agreed time, or is not available for the recipient to pick up within one hour of the scheduled arrival of the train, a full refund of fees will be made.

International TCX Service

This service combines the use of road, rail and air transport for delivering parcels to addresses in countries around the world.

The Red Star consignment note must be completed and commercial goods must be accompanied by four signed copies of a commercial or pro-forma invoice. The pro-forma invoice should contain:

- the document's title: Pro-forma invoice or commercial invoice
- invoice date
- consignee's full name, address and telephone number
- the sender's and consignee's VAT numbers
- an accurate description of the goods, including the customs' tariff number if known
- country of origin – if from the UK and destined for an EU country, state 'goods in free circulation within the EU'
- total number of packages and total weight of consignment
- commercial value of the goods
- a statement explaining whether the goods are new or if the consignment is being sent abroad for processing, repair, examination, temporary use or exhibition and for future reimportation.

There are also many private delivery firms offering courier services for express delivery of packages.

Sources of reference on mail services

Publication	Contents
Mailguide	A comprehensive guide to Royal Mail services
UK Letter Rates Comprehensive Guide	UK letter services and rates of postage
Address Magazine	Latest developments in Royal Mail services
Royal Mail International Services Guide	Services provided by Royal Mail International
Parcelforce UK User Guide	UK parcel services and prices
Parcelforce International User Guide	International parcel services and prices
Postcode Address File	Database of every UK address and postcode

The Postcode Guide	Lists of postcodes linked to postcode maps
The Post Town Gazetteer	An index of post towns in postcode order
Red Star Services	British Rail Red Star delivery services
Red Star Price Guide	British Rail Red Star prices
Yellow Pages	Other delivery, collection and courier services

Questions

1 a) What are the main points to follow when packing and labelling a parcel?
   b) What steps have to be taken when sending a parcel overseas?
   c) What steps should you take before signing for a parcel in the office?

2 a) Explain the Royal Mail regulations regarding the redirection, by the public, of letters and parcels. Are redirected parcels subject to additional postage charges?
   b) If your company is moving to new premises, what arrangements can be made with Royal Mail for the redirection of letters and parcels? Is any charge made for this service?

3 What is the difference between recorded delivery, registered and registered plus?

4 Describe the Royal Mail services which can be used to ensure that written or verbal communications are received:

   a) speedily
   b) safely

5 What happens if:

   a) a letter weighing under 60 g bears a 15p stamp
   b) a letter bears no stamp
   c) there is no reply when a postman brings a registered letter?

6 One of your colleagues is moving to a new branch office in another town. In her work at your office she has relied on you to tell her the correct postal service to use for the various items sent by mail and you are asked to supply her with some notes of guidance. Under subheadings First-Class, Second-Class, Datapost, Special Delivery, Registration and Recorded Delivery, give an example of an appropriate item which you would recommend for dispatch by each method. Explain why you have chosen that particular service for each item.

7 The day's mail consists of the following items: *Weight*

   a) Legal documents to be dispatched urgently. They are valuable
     (not in terms of money) and you may wish to have proof of delivery. 80 g
   b) A silver vase, value £200. 50 g
   c) A letter containing enclosures (not valuable). Not urgent. 100 g
   d) Three books (not valuable) to be sent to an addressee in the same
     town. Not urgent. 4 kg
   e) An urgent letter about a meeting to be held the following day. 40 g

Select the appropriate Royal Mail services and, by reference to a current edition of the UK Letter Rates Guide, calculate the amount of postage to be used for each item.

8 Praxitoys, a toy manufacturing company based in Chester, frequently has sales promotion tours which may last two/three weeks. It is quite usual that extra sales literature, documents and copies of correspondence have to be sent urgently to the sales venue. Ordinary Royal Mail services have proved to be too slow in the past.

   The matter came to a head last week when some documents failed to arrive in York in time for an important meeting. In the discussions which ensued many similar situations were focused on:

- parcels of advertising literature needed urgently
- contract forms which need proof of posting/delivery
- demonstration toys of some value, both small and large

In an attempt to rectify the situation, you decide to prepare an information sheet for general use outlining the appropriate Royal Mail services and those offered by other agencies, under two headings: 'Speed' and 'Security'.

9 Mr Tony Witt, Cruise Director of Comlon International plc, wants urgent information to be sent to all the main offices — New York, Ontario, Genoa and Athens. These offices must reply to Mr Witt on certain aspects to be discussed at a meeting in four days' time.

   a) Explain which method you would choose to send this information, giving your reasons for the choice.
   b) If your chosen fast and effective method is not available to you, it may be necessary for you to use one of the Royal Mail delivery services. Which of the range of services would be most suitable for your purposes? (*LCCI PESD*)

In-tray exercise

10 You are employed at the New Tech Office Services Bureau (Case Study 1). Mrs

Robinson has asked you to draft a reply to the following message received last night on the telephone answering machine:

Roger Mitchell here from Royston Products Ltd, 148 Lillington Road, Leamington Spa.

.We have used your bureau on a number of occasions for producing mail shots and I thought you would be the best people to advise us how to go about some of our mailing tasks.

We shall be moving shortly to a new factory at Kenilworth. How can we make sure that our mail is forwarded to the new address?

We would like to mail all householders in Kenilworth letting them know of our arrival in their town. Which Royal Mail service could we use for this?

Is there any way that we can encourage the Kenilworth householders to place orders with us by paying for their replies?

Occasionally we have to dispatch urgent parcels to various parts of the country requiring delivery the same day. How do you suggest we should arrange for their dispatch?

I shall be pleased to receive your advice on these various matters.

2.5 Filing

An important function of the office is the filing and finding of information, which may be held on paper, disk or film, and to ensure quick and reliable access to it. Developments in electronic data storage have revolutionised the speed of retrieval and allowed greater and easier access to vast quantities of records without the need to store papers in bulky filing cabinets. While recognising the potential of these electronic filing methods, you should also appreciate that most offices continue to generate, receive and dispatch paper documents that need to be stored and controlled in cabinets, using traditional methods of filing.

Records, whether they are in their original paper form or processed electronically, must be filed accurately so that they can be retrieved instantly. A document filed incorrectly can be the cause of a delay in a business transaction, resulting in frustration and irritation to the staff concerned, and it may even contribute to the cancellation of an important contract. Only when the filing system is efficient can the office function properly. A failure to retrieve information when it is required will have serious repercussions for all sections of a business.

Filing systems for paper records

Filing systems can be arranged in a variety of ways but several considerations must be taken into account in choosing a filing system. It must be:

- quick and simple to operate
- easily accessible, ie the cabinets must be conveniently situated, and the files within the cabinets easy to locate
- suitable for the particular type of correspondence dealt with; the size, volume and nature of the correspondence must be considered
- capable of expansion, if required
- appropriate in size, ie not using unnecessary space
- used to hold current papers only
- capable of safeguarding documents and in particular confidential information

In a large organisation, filing may be organised centrally or departmentally. The points in favour of each of these methods are given.

Central filing

1 All files are kept and controlled together in one room.

2 A clerk or number of clerks is able to specialise in filing and to administer the system efficiently.

3 Accommodation and equipment are economically used in the central arrangement of filing cabinets.

4 A standardised system of filing can be established throughout the organisation.

5 More effective supervision is possible.

6 Files are more complete as all aspects of a subject are filed together and fewer copies of correspondence are required for departments.

7 Effective and efficient follow-up and absent file systems can be organised.

8 Terminals can be used to capture computerised records held centrally.

Departmental filing

1 The departmental files are kept in the department and are, therefore, more readily available.

2 The type of filing system may be employed which is most suitable for the correspondence with which the department deals, eg an export department would generally use a geographical system, whereas an advertising department would find subject filing more useful.

3 Departmental staff will have a better knowledge of the work of the department and should be more expert in filing departmental papers.

4 It is more suitable for confidential files.

5 The filing system is not so large and therefore is easier to handle.

6 Departmental code letters may be employed in correspondence and on file titles for easy recognition, eg 'S' for sales department, 'A' for accounts department, or colour coding may be used for this purpose.

Methods of classification

General alphabetical filing

In the alphabetical method each folder contains the name of a correspondent and is arranged in strict alphabetical order. Guide cards, 'miscellaneous' suspension files, or individual letter bars, may be used to divide the letters. The first letter of the surname (not first name) is the preliminary guide to the position of the file in the drawer. To determine the exact position of a file, the letters subsequent to the first letter of the surname are the determining factor, eg Collins, Thomas should be filed before Cryton, Philip.

Miscellaneous files are generally allocated to most letters of the alphabet for the purpose of holding small amounts of correspondence where individual files are not needed. An index of the correspondence contained in each miscellaneous file should be given on the front cover. An example of the general alphabetical method of filing is given in Fig 2.11.

Subject filing

Instead of being filed under the name of the correspondents, letters are filed under subject headings. The subjects are filed in alphabetical order. The primary guides in subject filing give the main headings of the subjects which are relevant to the business, eg advertising, shipping, sole agents, progress, purchasing, management, etc.

Most offices have a certain amount of correspondence which can be filed to advantage by subject. These subjects usually concern the general management of the business and its relation to branches, agencies, trade connections, etc. The advantage of filing by subject is that all relevant data and correspondence are grouped together for quick and easy reference (see Fig 2.12).

Geographical filing

In the geographical method, correspondence is classified according to the county, town, country, etc. The principle is identical with that of the general alphabetical and subject methods, except that papers are filed by alphabetically arranged names of counties or towns instead of correspondents or subjects. This enables all correspondence relating to a county or town to be grouped together and individual files to be allocated to the agents or representatives. Obvious uses for geographical filing are in transport and export offices, planning departments and sales departments, where it is frequently necessary to group papers in district or territorial order. An illustration of this system is given in Fig 2.13.

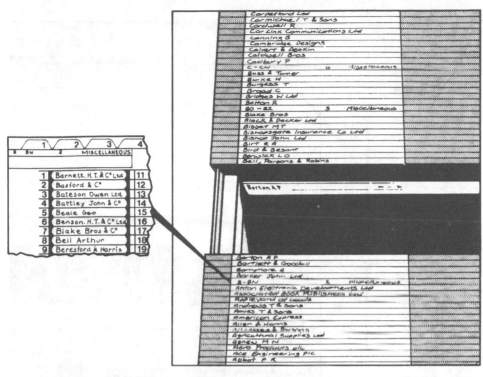

Fig 2.11   General alphabetical method

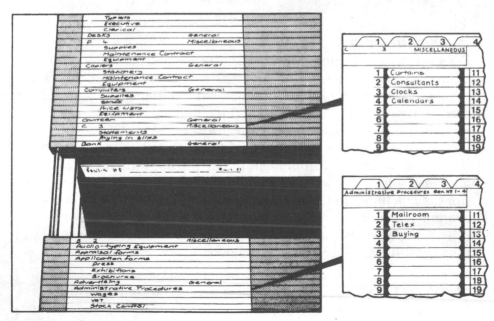

Fig 2.12   Subject method

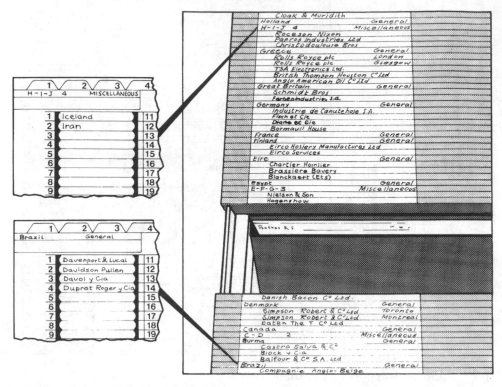

Fig 2.13   Geographical method

Numerical filing

Files are arranged numerically, each correspondent being allotted a number. Index cards or index strips are required to connect the numbers with the names. Each index card contains the name of the correspondent and their allotted file number, and is arranged in alphabetical order in an index-card drawer.

When a certain file is required, the name of the correspondent is located in the index-card drawer, under the appropriate letter of the alphabet, and the number of the file ascertained. The numbered file can then be found in the appropriate filing cabinet. Fig 2.14 shows an example of the numerical method.

The advantages and disadvantages of the alphabetical and numerical filing methods are as follows:

Method	Advantages	Disadvantages
Alphabetical	1 A convenient method of grouping papers by company, subject or location.	1 Difficulty may be experienced in locating common names.

Method	Advantages	Disadvantages
	2 A direct and quicker method of filing without the meed for a separate index.	2 Uncertainty of file location when subjects are used.
	3 Less cost in materials.	3 Difficult to assess space requirements for expansion.
Numerical	1 Numbered files are more easily found than alphabetical files and are less likely to be misplaced when they are returned.	1 Reference to an index causes a delay in locating a file.
	2 The file number may be used on letters for reference.	2 More costly in materials and time taken to maintain the system.
	3 Capable of indefinite expansion as new files are placed at the back of existing files.	3 Transposition of figures can be serious in misplacing papers and files.
	4 The index card or strip may be employsed for other purposes.	

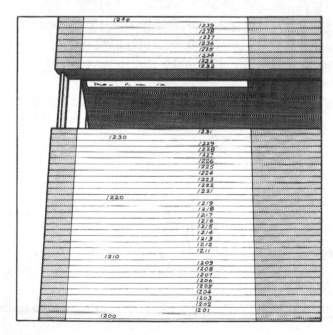

Fig 2.14   Numerical method

Guidelines for placing names in alphabetical order

- The surname is placed before first names, and if the surnames are the same, the first name determines the position, eg Jackson, John would be placed before Jackson, Thomas.

- If the first name and surname are embodied in the name of the company, the surname is written first, followed by the first name and finally the remainder of the name; for example, Leonard White and Co should be filed under 'White, Leonard, and Co.'

- If a company has several names, the first name is taken as the surname for filing purposes, eg Messrs May, Jones and Jenkins should be filed under 'May'.

- When 'The' is the first word of the name, it is either omitted, or placed at the end, for indexing purposes, as follows — High Pressure Tools Limited, The.

- In hyphenated names, the first name is used, eg in Smith-Ryland use Smith.

- Titles are placed after the surname and before the first names, eg Champion, Sir G H.

- Names beginning with Mac, Mc, or M' are treated as if they were spelt 'Mac'.

- Names beginning with 'St' are treated as if they were spelt 'Saint'.

- In names such as De La Rue, De La Mare, etc the prefix is regarded as part of the surname and indexed as if they were one word, eg Delarue.

- Nothing comes before something, ie a name without an initial precedes a name with an initial, as in the following names:

  Roberts
  Roberts, A
  Roberts, A A

- Names which consist of initials are placed before full names, eg BRS (Parcels) Ltd precedes Brown Bros.

- For impersonal names such as government departments, use the name that distinguishes it from the others, eg Education and Employment, Department.

- Names which begin with a number should either be listed before the alphabetical names in numerical order or converted to words and placed in the appropriate alphabetical position, depending on the rules of the organisation, eg 3 Stars Trading Company treated as 'Three ...'.

Chronological filing

This is where the documents are filed according to their dates in numerical order. Chronological filing is not often used as a basic system, but it is the normal method of filing papers within files.

Systems of filing

Vertical filing

In this system, the papers or documents are placed into files, which are arranged vertically (upright). The files are effectively displayed with title strips or labels on the top edges. Papers can be placed in or taken out of the folders without the folders having to be removed from the filing cabinet. The files can be stored in cabinets, drawers, racks and shelves.

Folders or pockets may be suspended vertically from metal runners fitted inside cabinet drawers (see Fig 2.15). These metal runners and chassis rails suspend the pockets in such a manner that they are held clear of the bottom of the drawer. The files are thus protected from wear and tear and, no matter how heavily they are loaded, retain their neat, tidy appearance.

The actual correspondence is filed, not directly into the suspended pockets, but in inner folders. The pockets may be connected together to form a 'concertina' arrangement. This prevents loose papers from being mislaid underneath the pockets. The 'concertina' can be broken at any point for an additional pocket to maintain an alphabetical method.

The titles, which must be clearly given on both the pocket and the inner folder, may be displayed in a number of ways. Upright tabs or flat strips are in common use. The cards for the tabs or strips are supplied in perforated lengths. The cards are completely covered and their titles kept clean and legible with shields of cellulose acetate or similar material which melts under extreme heat but does not burst into flame. Celluloid is rarely used because of the risk of fire. The cards are supplied in a variety of colours for classification purposes.

System

Fig 2.15 Vertical filing

Advantages
1 The files are more compact and there is less chance of losing documents, particularly if files are suspended.
2 Papers can be inserted and replaced without removing the file.
3 Titles can be read clearly.
4 Cabinets have greater protection from fire and dust.

Disadvantages
1 Extra space is required for opening drawers.
2 More expensive equipment.
3 Only one person at a time can have access to a filing cabinet.

System

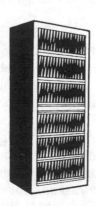

Fig 2.16 Lateral filing

Advantages
1 Saving space as there is no need to allow for opening drawers.
2 Can be built up higher than vertical cabinets.
3 Can be accommodated in alcoves which would not be suitable for vertical cabinets.
4 Larger range of files can be viewed at one time.

Disadvantages
1 Difficulty in reading file titles in a vertical position.
2 Files may become dusty because of the large opening.
3 Location of files from a height can be a hazard.

Lateral filing

Lateral filing is a system of storing files side by side, rather like books on a shelf. The files are generally suspended from rails placed laterally in cupboards, racks or on open shelving. They are fitted with title holders which can normally be adjusted for the required angle of vision. Where accommodation is limited, lateral installations are ideal, as space does not have to be allowed for the opening of drawers and they can be built up as high as the ceiling will allow (see Fig 2.16).

Shelf filing has the same advantages as the lateral system but the files, instead of being suspended from rails, are arranged securely along open shelves.

The advantages and disadvantages of the lateral and vertical systems of filing are given on page 82).

Plan filing

Plans and drawings may be stored horizontally in flat drawers or vertically in storage cabinets where the drawings are arranged in an upright position. Vertical cabinets contain compartments with wave-like dividers enabling large drawings to stand erect without buckling. A vertical plan cabinet occupies less than a third of the floor space of a horizontal cabinet of equal capacity. Each compartment has its own indexing strip so that the drawings can be easily identified.

Rotary suspended filing unit

This system accommodates files, suspended and linked on rotating platforms, so that the filing clerk has easy and quick access to a larger number of files.

Electronic filing system

This is a computerised document management system which allows files to be retrieved at the touch of a button. When a file is required, the operator keys in its index code on a push-button panel (as illustrated in Fig 2.17) at the front of the filing unit and presses a retrieve button. This activates the system to locate the required file container and deliver it automatically to the operator. Once the file has been retrieved or the desired information extracted, the 'restore' button is pressed and the file container is returned to its storage location. This system can also be used for locating records kept on microfilm or computer disks.

The index and location of every file in the system is entered into the computer using a pc keyboard, or automatically with a swipe of a barcode scanner if identifying barcodes are present on the files.

Each time a file is stored or retrieved, the date, file number and user's name are keyed into the pc, providing a useful record of the whereabouts of the file.

Fig 2.17   Computerised document management system

Documents for filing systems

File absent cards/'out' guides

One of the most frequent sources of delay and annoyance in filing is to find that a folder has been removed from its place in the cabinet, and a lengthy, irritating search all over the building is necessary to trace it. This can be avoided by monitoring the movement of files on absent cards (see Fig 2.18).

Another system is the suspended absent wallet. In this particular system the wallet is suspended with the pocket from which a folder is removed. A completed docket showing the number or name of the folder, the name of the person to whom it has been issued, the department concerned and the date is placed in the wallet and retained until the folder is returned. This absent wallet, while providing a check on the whereabouts of the folder, has the further advantages of:

1 Providing a container for the receipt of papers while the folder is out.

2 Determining at a glance which folders are out and, if required, enabling their recovery to be made without delay.

FILE ABSENT CARD

File no/Name:

Borrowed by	Department	Date borrowed	Date returned

Fig 2.18   File absent card

Cross reference slips

These are used whenever a file may be known by more than one title. A cross reference slip, as in Fig 2.19, is placed in the section of the cabinet for the secondary title, stating the name or position in the cabinet where the file can be found, eg GST Financial Services Ltd (formerly known as Peter Robinson & Sons) is filed under 'G' and a cross reference slip filed under 'R' to indicate that the file can be found in the position for GST Financial Services Ltd.

CROSS REFERENCE SLIP

For information on
refer to file   *Peter Robinson & Sons*
                             G S T Financial Services Ltd

Signed   *M Clarke*   Date   *12 - 3 - 9 -*

Fig 2.19   Cross reference slip

Bar code tracking system

This system provides a means of controlling the movement of files within an organisation. It uses bar codes to identify files and their location. A hand-held 'datawand' scanner, as in Fig 2.20, records from a bar code the name and place of every file each time it moves. The

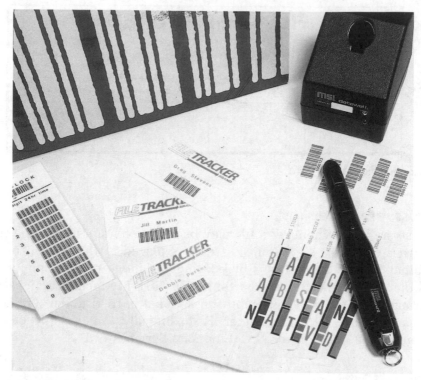

Fig 2.20   A datawand scanner

stored information flows from the datawand through a 'datawell' terminal into a personal computer, which can then be accessed to discover the whereabouts of a particular file.

Follow-up system

There are several systems which can be used satisfactorily for following up correspondence, and one very effective system is given here. A follow-up system is used to ensure that a matter is not overlooked. If, for example, an executive writes a letter on the 11th of the month, the executive may wish to send a further letter on the 21st if a reply has not been received. When signing the letter on the 11th of the month, the executive completes a memo form, attaches it to the copy of the letter in question, enters on it the date when the letter is next wanted, and places it in the filing tray. The filing clerk fills in the name of the correspondent and, if necessary, the subject matter, and then detaches the form, which is filed in the appropriate monthly pocket of the 'follow-up' filing cabinet. The letter itself is then filed away in its proper file with other correspondence, where it can be found at any time it is wanted.

The 'follow-up' filing cabinet drawer contains twelve pockets, titled January to December; the pocket for the current month contains a file which is sub-divided by thirty-one daily insert sheets. The memos are placed in the appropriate monthly pocket and are sub-divided on a daily basis when the month becomes current. The system can have a separate pocket for each day of the current month if the quantity of papers requires it.

Each day the filing clerk extracts any memo forms from the current daily insert, finds the papers or letters to which they refer, couples the forms and letters and passes them to the individual whose initials appear on the form. After appropriate action, the executive places the form and the papers back in the filing tray with, if necessary, a further date marked in for follow-up, and the whole process is repeated. Appointments for future dates and many other items can be dealt with by this system, which is almost automatic in operation.

Fig 2.21 Follow-up system

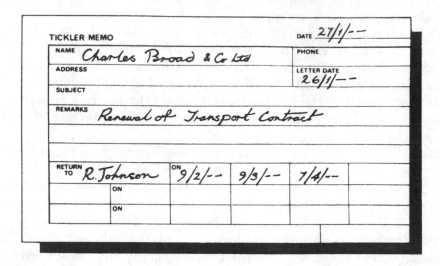

Fig 2.22   Follow-up system memo

Note the information recorded on the memo form and the arrangement of the pockets in the follow-up system given in Figs 2.21 and 2.22.

See also the computerised desk diary planner (page 242) which can be used for following up correspondence.

Document sorting

Correspondence should be sorted and classified before filing, and a document-sorting cabinet is a valuable aid to arranging the names or subjects into alphabetical order; a suspended folder is provided for each letter of the alphabet, and the documents are placed in or behind the appropriate folder.

Flap sorters are commonly used for sorting documents for filing. The flaps are hinged to a steel base and arranged in such a manner that they overlap each other with the titles of each being clearly visible. The titles will generally contain the letters of the alphabet, but numbers, subjects or other classifications may be used. Papers, as they are sorted, are placed under the appropriate flaps and are held securely in position. The filing clerk can sort a large number of documents while remaining seated and the compact arrangement of the sorting device avoids unnecessary reaching or other tiring movements.

File retention policy

If correspondence is retained unnecessarily, files become bulky, occupy valuable space in cabinets and make the retrieval of documents more difficult. For this reason it is necessary for a file retention policy to be agreed by the organisation and to take account of:

- any legal requirements for the documents to be retained
- the need to retain documents for auditing purposes
- the possible need for documents to be produced in their original form as evidence in a court of law
- records which may be duplicated elsewhere in the organisation — both copies need not be kept
- whether the organisation would be at a disadvantage if the records could not be produced on a future date.

Filing code of practice

- Ensure that all papers are passed (or authorised) for filing.
- File neatly and methodically by:
  - **a** sorting and grouping all correspondence before filing (sorting equipment is referred to on page 88) and
  - **b** placing the papers on to the files squarely, so that all the edges are perfectly straight.

- Ensure that the correspondence is placed in the correct file.
- Place the correspondence in the files in the correct sequence of dates so that the most recent document is on top.
- Avoid large bulky files by thinning them out regularly as directed in a file retention policy (see above).
- Do not remove individual papers from a file. If an individual paper *must* be removed, a note stating the date, name of correspondent, and name of the person holding the paper should be placed in the file.
- Provide cross-references for files known by more than one name (see page 85).
- If a file is temporarily removed, complete an absence marker or card (see page 84).
- Seek guidance when in doubt concerning the filing of nonclassified papers and any which are unclear.

- Always close filing cabinet drawers after use for reasons of safety and security.
- Seek to maintain the efficiency of the system and recommend modifications or improvements to it as appropriate.
- Lock filing cabinets before leaving the office at night or for any length of time.
- File daily so that the filing system is always up to date.

Microfilming

Microfilming is a process for making film records of documents so that bulky originals need not be stored. They are used for recording business documents, legal documents, drawings, parts manuals, newspapers, journals and reports by reducing them in size for storage and quick retrieval.

Microfilm can be viewed from a viewer or from a VDU on-line to a computer.

A VDU microfilm retrieval device has the ability to communicate directly with a computer or with any other element of the electronic office, in addition to its microfilm viewing capacity. The computer records exactly where the appropriate source document is filed on microfilm and can access it very quickly, and if additional data is required from the computer this can be accessed at the same time.

The following different types of film may be used:

Roll film: commonly used and suited particularly to sequentially filed documents, such as archival records where no insertions are required.

Cartridge: this holds roll film but it is easier to handle because there is no lacing of the film, no rewinding and the film is completely protected.

Microfiche: a sheet of microfilm with rows of images, which is appropriate for quick reference to a large number of related documents which do not require updating, eg approximately 400 A4 pages on one piece of 6" x 4" microfiche.

Acetate jacket: a 'loose-leaf' system with horizontal grooves to hold strips of film, ideal for applications which require periodic updating, eg quarterly or annual reports.

Computer output on microfilm: directly transferring the data from a computer on to microfilm at speeds of up to 120 000 characters per second.

The microfilming process has the following advantages:

1 It saves space and weight as bulky correspondence files are reduced to film. For example, the contents of a four-drawer vertical filing cabinet can be condensed into four rolls of microfilm and you can store up to 120 000 A4 pages on microfilm in a single binder.

2 Documents can be sent abroad at reduced postal rates.

3 There is little risk of misplacing information or losing records.

4 Film is more durable than paper and provides a much more permanent record.

5 The film can be enlarged on to paper, thus providing quick and accurate duplicate copies of the original documents.

6 Reference to documents is quicker, as it is easier to find a section of a film than it is to search through files.

7 The film is tamper-proof, but for legal purposes certificates of authenticity must be filmed with the documents.

These benefits should, however, be judged against the cost of installing the necessary equipment, the time taken to film the documents and index them, and the inconvenience of having to use a viewer or terminal every time reference is made to a document.

Microfilm equipment

1 Filming/microimaging
This equipment produces microfilm images from the source documents. Kodak's Imagelink Microimager, as illustrated in Fig 2.23, is an example of advanced equipment used for creating microfilm images. Controls have been minimised to reduce the need for operator intervention and the possibility of error. The 37-key keyboard includes eight predefined keys and two programmable keys that make the most frequently-used functions easier, such as paper printer on/off. An 80-character display communicates information about the job and the machine's status in plain language messages. A smart cassette has its own microprocessor memory. It stores information such as job number and film status and downloads it automatically to the microimager, eliminating the need for operator programming.

2 Readerprinter
A machine called a readerprinter, using cartridges, microfiche or microfilms, simplifies searching for documents, displaying them on a

Fig 2.23   Microfilm imagemaker

screen and, if required, printing copies on paper. Fig 2.24 (onpage 93) illustrates Kodak's 'Starmate' readerprinter with its enhanced retrieval keyboard attachment. This facility enables the operator to retrieve document images at the touch of a button for viewing and/or printing.

3   Digital workstations
The Kodak Imagelink Digital Workstation scans and digitises 16 mm microfilmed images and transmits them electronically to printers and fax locations. The operator keys in an image address, inserts the relevant microfilm roll and the digital workstation automatically retrieves the image and positions it correctly. All the operator has to do is verify the image and choose whether to print, fax or transmit the document. When faxing complex requests, the system can merge images from separate reels of film. It can do several things at once, such as transmitting information while an operator continues retrieving images. It can be programmed to advance film, scan a series of images and, if required, deliver the images to different fax locations during non-working hours for cheaper transmission.

Fig 2.24   Microfilm readerprinter

Computer data storage and retrieval

Whilst paper continues to be used as the principal means of transmitting information, traditional methods of filing using cabinets will remain. Alternative computerised filing systems, which are quicker and occupy considerably less space, are, however, gradually reducing the need for paper files and replacing them by disks, tapes, cartridges, etc.

Data may be stored in the following ways:

Floppy disks

Sometimes called flexible disks or diskettes, these are used with personal computers and range from those which store about 40 A4 pages of typed data to those which accommodate about 1000 A4 pages.

Magnetic tape

This may be reel-to-reel, cassette or cartridge. Updating is similar to the process used for an ordinary tape recorder, in which the updated material on one tape is transferred to record over the existing data tape.

Hard disks

Sometimes called Winchester disks, capable of holding vast quantities of data on one disk, eg 100 megabytes or 100 million bytes/characters.

Optical disks

Digital optical recorders use laser beam technology to scan documents and provide permanent facsimile records. Most optical disks used for this purpose are of the 'write once, read many' WORM type using 13.5 cm or 30.5 cm disks which are capable of recording between 600 megabytes (mb) and 4 gigabytes (gb) (1 gb = 1000 mb) from a computer or scanner by a laser assembly. The data is unalterable and can be accessed quickly from any terminal on a network system. Document image processing of this kind is generally used to store information that is no longer active but may need to be located quickly, such as business reports, financial statements and correspondence.

The optical disk system (see Fig 2.25) includes a personal computer, optical disk storage and a high-resolution scanner and printer. Documents are scanned into the system and stored on an optical disk. During this process the operator can verify the quality and accuracy of the scanned image and make any necessary adjustments from the keyboard of the personal computer. Each document is indexed by the operator.

Using the keyboard the operator can:

a retrieve a document and display it on the screen

b refer to multiple documents simultaneously and make comparisons

Fig 2.25   Optical disk system

c print a 'hard' copy from the printer

d transmit a document by fax to a distant location.

If the system is networked, data can be accessed and printed at multiple terminals using personal computers or image terminals. The system can also be linked to an existing computer for interacting with mainframe data.

Printout of computer data

Commonly referred to as 'hard copy'.

Computerised filing

Advantages
- Speed of retrieval
- Saving office space
- Reduced paperwork
- Interaction with other data, eg mainframe computer, and other services such as fax
- Ease of access to centralised records through a network system

Disadvantages
- Cost of acquiring equipment
- Cost and time taken to print out copies when it is necessary to work away from the terminal
- Time taken to input data and verify it using a keyboard, for systems which do not use optical character recognition

Advantages
- Greater security by using passwords
- Files are not removed when access is made to them

Disadvantages
(OCR). OCR converts text and graphics into images for computer storage and eliminates the need for keying in data
- The danger of an operator accidentally erasing data from the memory of a computer
- The need for back-up copies
- The problems incurred when there is a power cut or a system breakdown

Visible records

The cards or forms are arranged to overlap in such a manner that their edges are exposed to view. The exposed portions carry, in addition to the title, various control features which summarise essential details contained in entries on the records.

Visible card records

The cards are housed in flat trays, in such a manner that while they overlap each other, the title of each is clearly visible. The trays are kept in cabinets which are normally made of steel, with locking devices to safeguard confidential information. Colour markers or indicators may be affixed to the cards to focus attention on vital facts. Sixty to seventy cards can be accommodated in each tray, and as many as twenty-one trays fitted into a single cabinet. Transparent plastic shields are generally fitted over the exposed portions of the cards, to protect them from dirt and to provide a suitable carrier for the coloured markers (see Fig 2.26).

Strip indexing equipment

In most offices there is a need to find certain items of information, such as names and addresses, telephone numbers in current use, current commodity prices, etc, frequently and quickly, and the line reference equipment strip-indexing method is the most efficient and practical. The information in the container is visible to the clerk without having to search through sheaves of papers, books or loose cards. Individual references, each on its own strip, can be pinpointed instantly.

Fig 2.26 Visible card records

Each item of information is recorded on a separate strip, and these are built up one above the other in suitable carrying devices, so that all the information contained in them is visible. The strips are generally supplied in sheets which can be printed. Additions, amendments and deletions can be made without affecting the continuity of the records.

Strips are available in a number of different shades, which facilitates colour classification. In addition, various forms of signalling devices can be employed. The strips may be housed in

Document	Recommended equipment							Recommended classification				
	Vertical	Lateral	Plan	Microfilm	Visible cards	Loose-leaf binders	Strip indexing	Alphabetical	Geographical	Subject	Numerical	Chronological
Accounting records						X		X			X	
Application forms (jobs)	X			X				X				
Artwork, blueprints, photographs	X	X	X	X						X		
Bank paying-in slips						X						X
Catalogues and price lists	X	X						X		X		
Computer printout						X				X		X
Current prices				X			X			X		
Export documents	X	X							X			
Insurance policies	X	X	X								X	
Invoices	X	X				X					X	X
Mailing lists							X	X				
Maps	X	X	X						X			
Minutes of meetings						X						X
Orders	X	X				X					X	X
Petty cash vouchers						X					X	
Receipts						X					X	
Share transfers and records of shareholders						X		X				

panels, wall fitments, books, stands, revolving units or cabinets.
   The advantages of the visible record cards are:

a The records can be seen at a glance; it is not necessary to fumble
   through many cards.

b The visible portion of the card lends itself to various effective
   control features.

c The cards are less likely to become dirty as transparent plastic
   shields are fitted over the exposed portions.

d Arrangement and rearrangement of records is simple and speedy.

Filing methods

The chart on page 98 shows the most suitable methods of filing
various business documents. It should be noted, however, that it is
necessary for each filing requirement to be studied individually in its
true environment, taking into account quantities, contents, sizes, etc,
and that the subjects are dealt with in general terms only.
Computerised filing methods may also be used in all cases.

Questions

1 a) Place the following names of individuals, professional bodies and trading
     organisations in the order and form in which you would index them:

L M Macintyre	St John Courtney Salon
British Plastics plc	E A Sanford & Co Ltd
1990 Express Services	Dennis O'Donovan
Borough of Bexley	Stephen Watts–Owen
A M McBridie	Henry Levene plc

   b) Draw up a typical 'Out' guide and discuss its importance.

2 a) Explain the uses and advantages of visible card records.
  b) Design a visible record card for use in a personnel department. Your
     illustration should also indicate:
     i the information conveyed on the visible edge and
     ii the use of signalling devices.

3 The head of your department has asked you to examine some new systems of
  filing and recording information with the object of saving office space and at
  the same time having the records available for quick and easy reference. In a
  memo to your head of department explain the features of:

  a) microfilming

b) lateral filing and

c) one other method which you consider should be introduced.

4 How would you indicate in your filing system:

a) that you had removed a file from the filing cabinet

b) that a letter filed in file 77 also referred to the subject matter dealt with in file 88?

5 Mr Webb, Purchasing Manager, has asked you to redesign his unwieldy system of approximately 400 files and suggests that you use a numerical classification.

a) Outline the advantages and disadvantages of using a numerical classification for Mr Webb's work. How would you attempt to overcome any perceived disadvantages?

b) Outline the procedure which you would adopt for successfully converting the old system to the new. (*LCCI PSC*)

6 It has been considered that investment may be required in a central resource area where all Managers can have access to information. It is expected that this would be under the Office Manager's jurisdiction. Mr Nicholls, the Office Manager, has asked you to collate ideas and carry out a feasibility study.

Describe how you would go about this. (*LCCI PSC*)

7 Mr Davies, Sales and Marketing Director, has told you that when you get a little time he would like you to suggest ways of improving the present alphabetically-arranged departmental filing system. The files in the department go back to 1980 and there is now a considerable problem in filing new customer records, especially within the more commonly used alphabetic letters. He has complained that he never knows quite where to find a borrowed file and consequently wastes a large amount of time tracking down missing files. He also finds it frustrating when a company ends up changing its name in a takeover bid and the previous documentation filed under the old name gets forgotten or lost.

Suggest to Mr Davies, in a brief report, how the above problems could be resolved.

8 The Directors and Management Consultants have a habit of taking files out with them on visits without notifying you. You have expressed concern to Mr Hamilton, Marketing Director. He has suggested you write him a memo outlining how these problems could be overcome.

9 Gerald & Peters plc has a suggestion box scheme whereby all staff are given the opportunity to put forward practical ideas. At the end of each month the most suitable idea is chosen and earns a £50 bonus for the contributor.

With the rapid expansion of the Company, you recognise the need for rationalising storage of different types of information — letters, memos, reports, personnel records, etc. At present a numerical system of filing is in operation but your idea is that an electronic filing system would be far more appropriate to the Company.

Suggest why a computerised system of filing should be introduced and mention the possible benefits of such a system.

10 What effect is computerisation having on filing procedures? Select any one procedure to illustrate your answer.

11 Referring to the organisation chart in Case Study 4, suggest suitable filing equipment and classification systems for four of the five departments. Provide reasons to support your suggestions.

The Managing Director should not be included as his secretary deals with all his paperwork. You are expected to use suitable different classification systems. (PEI OP2)

12 Some documents cannot be found in the filing system. Draft a report to the Office Manager in which you:

a) Identify four likely reasons for this failure.
b) Describe ways in which these problems can be avoided.
c) Recommend appropriate action. (PEI OP2)

13 Your employer is considering installing microfilming for the storage of documents and has asked you to find the answers to the following questions. Let her know in a memorandum:

a) Four advantages of microfilming.
b) Four disadvantages of microfilming.
c) Three forms of storing microfilm, giving a brief description of each. (PEI OP2)

In-tray exercises

14 You are employed at Office Products Ltd (Case Study 2) and are asked to deal with the following message left on the dictating machine by Mrs Henderson:

'As you know, we will be exhibiting at the International Business Efficiency Exhibition next month and the Marketing Department expects to receive many enquiries from potential customers. Jeremy Bates, the Exhibition Co-ordinator, would like Karen Brown to join the team of staff manning the stand. I hope it will be possible for you to spare her as the experience will do her good. In view of your substantial knowledge of filing systems, Jeremy would like you to suggest the content and layout of a record card for keeping details of potential customers, bearing in mind that we may need to follow up these enquiries. Please let me see your proposal before it is sent to Jeremy.'

15 You are employed at the New Tech Office Services Bureau (Case Study 1).
    Using the list of suppliers on page xvi:

   a) complete cross-reference slips for any of the suppliers where you consider
      they may be needed;
   b) prepare an alphabetical list of suppliers' names, including the names given
      in the cross-reference slips in (a);
   c) prepare a second list of suppliers arranged alphabetically by subject, ie
      products/services;
   d) complete file absent cards for files 103 and 109 borrowed today by Mr
      Wood;
   e) complete a tickler memo to arrange for a letter written today to Office
      Products Ltd by Mrs Robinson to be followed up in 10 days' time.

2.6 Telecommunications

Using the telephone

Most of the information which passes in and out of an organisation is handled initially by the telephone system operator. The operator has a key role in influencing first impressions, which are frequently lasting, that customers gain about the organisation. If the telephone inquirer does not receive a clear and courteous greeting, a poor opinion of the firm as a whole is immediately formed. What the telephonist says and the tone and manner in which it is said can also influence the response received from the caller. Time is money in business, especially when it is spent on the telephone, and it is important to guard against conducting unnecessarily long conversations.

When speaking on the telephone, the operator should always try to sound friendly and helpful. It is important to listen to, and show an interest in, what the caller has to say, and to speak clearly and unhurriedly. Words with the same vowel sound, eg 'five' and 'nine', can sound alike on the telephone and special care is therefore necessary when quoting amounts, names and unfamiliar words. The telephone alphabet (see page 104) can be used to spell out words which the caller may have difficulty in recognising. Avoid the use of slang expressions such as 'hang on', 'OK', etc, which do not give a good impression in business.

Matters overheard on the telephone must be treated in the same strict confidence as the contents of correspondence. Above all, the telephonist must have a good speaking voice and should learn to recognise all who use the telephone in the organisation by sight, name and voice. Familiarity with the organisation's work is desirable and also a knowledge of the part played in the organisation by each executive, section and department. The telephonist is then able to handle calls efficiently and connect callers quickly to the right personnel.

The private secretary responsible for handling telephone calls for an executive must also have the qualities of a good telephonist. It is necessary to shield executives from receiving unnecessary calls which will waste their time. The secretary has to recognise those callers to whom the executive will wish to speak and to know how to handle the others tactfully.

Telephone alphabet

When it is necessary to emphasise or identify any letter or word it can be done by using an alphabetical code, such as:

A	for Alfred	J	for Jack	S	for Samuel
B	for Benjamin	K	for King	T	for Tommy
C	for Charlie	L	for Lucy	U	for Uncle
D	for David	M	for Mary	V	for Victor
E	for Edward	N	for Nellie	W	for William
F	for Frederick	O	for Oliver	X	for X-ray
G	for George	P	for Peter	Y	for Yellow
H	for Harry	Q	for Queen	Z	for Zebra
I	for Isaac	R	for Robert		

A guide for telephone users

When answering the telephone

- Always answer promptly when it rings and announce your identity. If the caller is received via your telephone operator, give your name and department (if necessary). If you are receiving an incoming call direct, state the name of the establishment, for example, 'Brown and Company'. A greeting such as 'Good morning, Brown and Company', has a pleasing effect. If an internal call is being received, state your own name and position, if necessary; for example, 'Jane Brown, Production Manager's Secretary' .

- Avoid saying 'Hello' as this wastes time and does not help the caller.

- Try not to keep a caller waiting. If there is likely to be a long delay in connecting the caller, it may be better to ring them back and save their time on the telephone. This is particularly important if the call is made from a pay telephone where the caller may not be in possession of additional coins.

- Have a message pad and pencil to hand so that you can write down a message. Pick up the receiver with your left hand so that your right hand is free for writing (vice versa, of course, if you are left-handed).

- You may have to leave the telephone for a while in order to make an inquiry or collect some information. If so, let the caller know how long you expect to be and ask if they would prefer you to call them back. In these circumstances, arrange for your calls to be answered in your absence.

- When an incoming call has to be transferred from one extension to another, convey the caller's name and request to the new extension so that they do not have to repeat their message.
- If a delay occurs before a caller can be connected, keep them informed of the action you are taking.
- If an incoming call is disconnected, replace the telephone receiver so the person making the call can re-establish the connection as soon as possible.
- If you receive a call which is a wrong number, remember that the intrusion is not intentional and that it is probably just as irritating to the caller as it is to you. No apology is required of you, but one made by the caller should be accepted politely.
- Always try to make a conscious effort to greet people cheerfully, even at the end of the day, and if you know a caller's name, do not hesitate to use it when addressing them. The telephonist is responsible for seeing that each caller is connected to someone who can deal with their business. A caller who wishes to speak to an executive absent from the office should not be kept waiting but asked whether they would like to:

  a speak to someone else
  b be rung back by the executive
  c ring again later, or
  d leave a message.

Whatever the answer, the caller's name, business address and telephone number should be noted.

Taking messages

Calls and messages should never be entrusted solely to memory, which may well prove unreliable, and the important facts should be written down while they are being received.

The following important points should be noted:

- Date and time of the call.
- The name of the person for whom the telephone call was made.
- Caller's name, address and telephone number.
- Precise details of the message received.

The message should be repeated back to the caller to make sure it has been taken down correctly.

Fig 2.27 is an example of a typical message sheet. As soon as the

```
┌─────────────────────────────────────────────────────┐
│                                                       │
│              MESSAGE FOR                              │
│                                                       │
│   M r...........G.H.Ellis...........                 │
│              WHILE YOU WERE OUT                       │
│   M r..............P.Spike...........                │
│                                                       │
│   OF ...Melvin Manufacturing Co. Ltd.                │
│                                                       │
│   TELEPHONE NO. 0161-416 392                         │
│                                                       │
│   ┌──────────────────┬───┬──────────────────┬───┐  │
│   │ TELEPHONED       │ X │ PLEASE RING      │ X │  │
│   ├──────────────────┼───┼──────────────────┼───┤  │
│   │ CALLED TO SEE YOU│   │ WILL CALL AGAIN  │   │  │
│   ├──────────────────┼───┼──────────────────┼───┤  │
│   │ WANTS TO SEE YOU │   │ URGENT           │ X │  │
│   └──────────────────┴───┴──────────────────┴───┘  │
│                                                       │
│   MESSAGE   Mr Spike expects to be in                │
│   the Leadington area next week, when                 │
│   he would like to call on you to                     │
│   discuss the matter referred to in                   │
│   your letter dated 3 January. Will                   │
│   you please ring him back                            │
│   to-day?                                             │
│                                                       │
│                                                       │
│   DATE  5 January 19--  TIME 0930 hrs                │
│   RECEIVED BY ...Lorna Phipps...                     │
│                                                       │
└─────────────────────────────────────────────────────┘
```

Fig 2.27   Message sheet

message has been recorded, it should be placed on the executive's desk so that it can be seen by them immediately on their return.

When making a telephone call

- Check the correct code and number before dialling. If you are in doubt, look it up in the telephone directory and make a note of it.

- Dial your number carefully and allow sufficient time for the call to connect.
- If you make a mistake while dialling, replace the receiver for a short while and then start dialling again from the beginning of the number.
- When the person you have called answers, say who you are and to whom you wish to speak.
- If you are connected to a wrong number, remember to offer an apology. It may be your fault, or it may be an equipment fault, but it is certainly never the fault of the person called.
- Familiarise yourself with the telephone tones (see page 108).
- When the call is answered, say to whom you wish to speak and then give your name. Also state the extension number of the person you require, if you know it. If you do not know it, ascertain this and make a note of it for future use.
- If a number cannot be dialled, dial 100 and ask the operator to obtain it for you, stating the number required and your own telephone number.
- A telephone call should be planned in exactly the same way as a business letter and before even dialling the number you should be prepared with any necessary papers at hand. It is also advisable to prepare beforehand a short list of points to be discussed.

Private external calls
The use of the business line for private calls is inadmissible, except in special cases of urgency. The rules governing this matter should be known to all members of the staff and should be strictly kept.

When making a telephone call abroad
- Check the correct codes and number and write them down. If you do not know these numbers you can look them up in the international codes section of The phone book or obtain them from the appropriate international operator by dialling the number given in the international dialling section of your telephone directory.
- With International Direct Dialling (IDD) you can dial the call yourself. Dial the four groups of digits in the following order:

a international code (00)

b country code

c area code

d subscriber's number.

If you are not able to dial direct, the call must be placed with the international operator (dial 155).

- Be prepared to wait up to a minute before you are connected because of the long distance involved.
- Bear in mind the time differences for each country. Note that between March and October, British Summer Time is one hour later than GMT (Greenwich Mean Time).

Telephone tones

Dialling tone

A low-pitched burr indicates that the equipment is ready for you to start dialling.

Ringing tone

A repeated double beat tells you that the number is being rung. Allow two minutes for the number to answer; if there is still no reply, replace the telephone, wait a little while and try again.

Engaged tone

A single high-pitched note repeated at regular intervals usually means the number being called is in use, but it can also mean that the equipment is engaged. In either case, you should replace the telephone and try again in about five minutes.

Number unobtainable tone

A continuous high-pitched note indicates that the number is either out of service or spare. If you hear this tone, check that you have the correct number (and dialling code) and then dial again. If you hear the tone again, dial 100 and tell the operator what has happened.

'Lines engaged' announcement

On some calls you may hear a pre-recorded voice saying: 'Lines from ... are engaged, please try later.' This means that there is overload on the lines from the district mentioned and you should replace the handset and wait a few minutes before dialling again.

Foreign tones
It should be noted that the above descriptions apply only to UK inland telephone calls. Some of the tones you may hear if you dial your own calls to other countries are different.

Telephone charges

British Telecom's charges (excluding VAT) for dialled inland calls are as follows:

Type of call	Local (within 15 miles) per minute	Regional (15–35 miles) per minute	National (more than 35 miles) per minute
Day-time rate Monday to Friday 0800–1800	3.4p	7.0p	8.4p
Cheap rate Monday to Friday 1800–0800	1.4p	3.4p	5.0p
Weekend rate Midnight Friday to Midnight Sunday	0.9p	2.8p	2.8p

Notes: A minumum charge of 4.2p is made for all calls.
Charges are correct at time of publication.

It is essential for staff to use the telephone sparingly, not to waste time with unnecessary conversation and to avoid making calls at peak rate times whenever possible. When answering an incoming call the telephonist must be ready to deal with it promptly, since charging starts as soon as the call is received.

British Telecom charge cards

A telephone charge card enables you to make telephone calls from any telephone and to charge the costs to your business or personal telephone account. Every charge is itemised on a quarterly statement of account so that you are able to keep a check on expenditure incurred on telephone calls made from the charge card. There is no charge for the card, which can be used for both dialled and operator-connected calls. Each cardholder has a PIN (personal identification number) to use when dialling calls direct from payphones and some other telephones in the UK.

Many companies find it useful for their outside representatives to be supplied with telephone charge cards as they can then use customers' telephones without incurring any expense to them. From the company's point of view, it is also a useful control on the telephone calls made, as a separate statement of account is issued for each representative holding a charge card.

Phonecards

Cardphones, which use a plastic card instead of coins, provide the public with a coinless telephone service. The cards are purchased from post offices and certain shops.

To make a telephone call, the user inserts the card into the cardphone and enters the telephone number on a keypad. A visual display shows the number of units stored on the card at the beginning of the call and, as the call progresses, the units are reduced accordingly for the amount of time used. At the end of the call, the card is returned for future use.

Telephone numbers

A complete and up-to-date list of frequently-called telephone numbers should be maintained, including the names of contacts and their dialling codes, telephone numbers and extension numbers. An example of a page of a telephone number index is given in Fig 2.28. The index should be placed where the operator can refer to it while seated at the telephone. A strip indexing system may be used for this purpose, as explained on page 96.

Telephone equipment

Switchboards

Incoming calls will usually be received at a switchboard and routed through an operator to the various extensions. External calls may also be made from the switchboard, although it is normal for such calls to be made from the extensions. Modern private telephone exchange switchboards, call-connect systems or call distribution systems as they are sometimes called, incorporate microprocessor technology and are operated electronically to provide fast and

H

Name and address of company	Name of contact and position	Telephone numbers			
		Country code	Area code	Customer Tel No	Extn No
Heckel Sportwaren Artikel Gmbh Hauptstrasse 18 6200 Wiesbaden Germany	F Schmidt Sales Director	49	6121	31425	42
Huffman Inc Schwanenplatz Lucerne Switzerland	T Bleuler Sales Manager	41	41	241886	5
Hutton International Traders Ltd 146 Mason's Hill Feltham Middlesex TW13 40P	R Hutton Director		0181 751	130329	1

Fig 2.28   Telephone number index

efficient communication links both within the organisation and externally. The facilities may include:

- Internal and external calling from all terminals — internal and external calls are distinguished by different ringing signals and calls can be made with press-button speed.
- A memory stores the last number called and will reconnect the caller at the press of a button — tedious redialling of engaged numbers is eliminated.
- Repertory dialling — automatic dialling from a directory of stored 'frequently used' numbers.
- Ring back when free — an engaged extension rings the caller back when the current call is finished.
- A call can be held 'on line' while you make an inquiry by ringing another number or transferring the call to another extension.
- Group hunting — a call can be diverted to another extension or a group of extensions in order to leave you undisturbed.
- Call forwarding — incoming calls may be transferred to another venue.
- Telephone conferences can be held with several extension users.
- Selected terminals can be allowed to interrupt calls to convey urgent messages.
- Appointment reminders — an extension is called at a specified time.
- Incoming calls are automatically placed in a queuing system so that the operator can answer them in order.
- When connected to recording equipment, all calls can be logged, providing a printed record of numbers dialled and the extensions making the calls.
- Music on hold — music is played to callers while they wait to be connected to their extension.
- A liquid crystal display on the system gives the time, date, number/extension number called or a message received from an extension.

Automatic call distribution systems (ACD)

ACD, as illustrated in Fig. 2.29, uses computer technology to provide a fast and efficient means of answering and handling incoming calls quickly and in sequence. As soon as an incoming call is accepted the system automatically identifies and distributes it to a person in the

Fig 2.29 Automatic call distribution system

organisation who is available to deal with it. If all the staff are busy, the call is queued, to wait its turn for the next available person who can deal with it. A visual display unit assists by providing the staff with relevant information about the incoming call.

A voice response unit can also be used to handle a variety of routine functions which will supply information and advice to callers. It can answer the call, ask for the caller's identification or order number and then route the call and relevant information to the member of staff who is available to deal with the call.

ACD is designed to provide a flexible communications system which will satisfy the needs of callers and reduce their waiting time to an absolute minimum.

Telephone-answering machines

Telephone-answering machines may be employed when the office staff are not available to receive telephone calls. When the office staff leave at night or at lunch time, the machine can be fitted to the telephone to provide a continuous telephone answering and recording service. Callers hear a prerecorded announcement inviting them to record a message. The message should give the name of the organisation, a greeting, the reason for the recording, how to record a message, action to be taken with it, and an acknowledgement. The calls received are then transcribed from the recording machine and message sheets are prepared for the staff concerned. These machines are suitable for businesses in which urgent messages are delivered at all hours of the day and night, such as with television servicing, motor vehicle repairs and servicing, import and export, as well as covering telephone calls at lunch times and weekends.

If an interrogator is used, a business executive can extract information from a recording machine by remote control. The interrogator is fitted to a telephone and, when callers ring in, a prerecorded announcement is given and messages are recorded. By using a special code number, executives can telephone in to their office and listen to the messages received on the machine. They can also record a message themselves and program the machine to erase the messages and reset itself to continue recording more messages. Alternatively, they can leave the messages intact for future reference and the interrogator will continue recording.

The interrogator is a useful device for people who travel a great deal and who are required to keep in touch with information at their base of operations.

Voicebank

This is a development of the telephone-answering machine using a computerised 'mail box' for recording spoken messages when staff are not available to receive calls in person. It is linked to an existing telephone system and a caller's message can be played back by dialling the voicebank number and keying in a PIN number. A pager may be used to alert the user to a message in the mailbox. Each extension user is allocated a box number which is usually the same as their extension number. Messages can be reviewed, deleted and, if necessary, re-recorded before being transmitted. You can be informed when a message has been cleared by the recipient. Urgent messages can receive top priority treatment by automatically being placed at the front of all other messages in the mailbox. If a message is exceptionally important, the system can be requested to ring the telephone of the recipient at repeated intervals. If a person is away from the office, any messages received can be diverted to another box number. Voicebank ensures that messages are delivered quickly and accurately without the harassment of making repeated telephone calls when people are not available to receive them.

Mobile telephones

Another means of speedy communication with colleagues and clients when they are on the move is provided by cellular phones. Two-way battery-operated radio telephones can be used to keep in touch with other people operating within a closed circuit, but the advent of cellular phones has extended the area of coverage, with the setting up of 'cells' each with their own transmitter in different parts of the country.

A cellular telephone enables you to call an ordinary telephone number or another cellular phone user. You can also receive calls from either source, providing that you are in an area served by your operating network, Cellnet or Vodaphone.

There are three different types of cellular phone:

- mobile — one which is permanently installed in a motor vehicle
- portable — one which can be used in any situation and is powered by battery
- transportable — one which can be used in or out of a motor vehicle and is powered by a rechargeable battery, as illustrated in Fig 2.30.

Mobile telephones can incorporate a number memory device which stores frequently used numbers for automatic dialling at the touch of only one or two buttons. Other features may include automatic redialling and illuminated display panels.

The use of a car telephone must never be allowed to distract your attention from driving. *The Highway Code* states:

1 Do not use a hand-held microphone or telephone handset while your vehicle is moving, except in an emergency.

2 You should only speak into a fixed, neckslung or clipped-on microphone when it would not distract your attention from the road.

3 Do not stop on the hard shoulder of a motorway to answer or make a call, however urgent.

Pagers

Light-weight, pocket-sized pagers may also be used to locate staff when they are away from their offices, either moving around the firm's premises or outside as they go about their normal business. Some pagers operate bleeps to provide the user with a signal that

Fig 2.30   Mobile telephone

there is a message for them on the firm's telephone number, while others display messages on the pager's screen. Multiple tone pagers employ different tones so that the user can distinguish the source of the sender by the sound of the tone.

People wishing to contact a pager are required to dial the special number allocated to it. The UK is divided into 40 paging zones, ie geographical areas within which paging messages can be sent and received. British Telecom Mobile Communications, for example, operates a nationwide area paging network which covers 97 per cent of the UK population, but you select and pay for the size of area you need. Some pagers have mailboxes, as in Voicebank, to allow messages to be stored and dealt with at the user's convenience.

A paging system, as illustrated in Fig 2.31, can be integrated with the office telephone system and allows each of the telephones to act as paging terminals. In this system a paging bleep alerts users that their phone is ringing even when they are away from their offices and

Fig 2.31   Pager with alpha-numeric display receiver

calls can be picked up from the nearest phone. Internal calls display the extension number or name of the person trying to contact the user.

Paging in Europe
The BT Euromessage Pager operates in major cities, towns and industrial areas in France, Germany and Italy. This pager, which can be hired for the duration of single visits, can receive and store up to 40 written messages, each up to 15 words long.

Videophone
A videophone, as illustrated in Fig. 2.32, combines the benefits of videoconferencing with those of telephoning. It enables people to 'meet' by telephone, face to face for meetings without the expense of travel and time costs.

Tannoy loudspeakers
Another means of contacting staff internally when they are moving around the premises is by tannoy loudspeakers operated by the telephonist from the switchboard. This is commonly used in retail stores but less frequently in offices because of the distraction caused by frequent announcements.

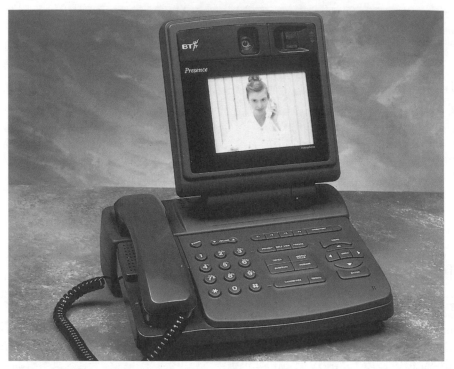

Fig 2.32   A videophone

Cordless telephones

British Telecom's Freelance cordless telephone allows the user to operate the telephone anywhere within 100 metres from the base unit. It can also be used to provide a two-way intercom service between the base system and the handset. Special features of the Freelance cordless telephone include:

- a memory device capable of storing nine 'frequently used' numbers
- a last number re-dial button which saves time re-dialling numbers which are engaged
- a volume control on the handset which enables you to increase the volume when using the telephone in a noisy environment
- a secrecy button so that the conversation cannot be heard on another telephone extension
- the use of security codes to prevent unauthorised access
- a 'call diversion' service which provides for calls to be diverted from an extension to the cordless telephone

- a 'call waiting' service in which the cordless telephone is bleeped when a person is trying to get through to you while you are on the phone.

Loudspeaking telephone

A loudspeaking telephone, which is supplied by British Telecom on a rental basis, can be connected to exchange lines and most types of extensions. The microphone and loudspeaker are built into the equipment so that the user does not have to hold a handset and both hands are free for taking notes, searching through files, etc. It is also useful for small conferences as the people sitting round the desk on which the loudspeaking telephone is placed can all hear what is said by the incoming caller and anyone at the meeting can reply.

Telephone services

Emergency calls

The procedure for making an emergency telephone call should be clearly understood as, in times of trouble, an emergency call efficiently conducted could be a vital factor in saving a life.

For the Fire Brigade, Police, Ambulance, Coastguard, Cave or Mountain Rescue Services, dial 999 unless the dial label on your telephone tells you otherwise. It is important to remember that you are first connected, not to the emergency service you require, but to an operator who will put you through to the required emergency service.

When the operator answers give:

- details of the emergency service required
- your telephone number.

When the emergency service answers give:

- the address where help is needed
- all other information for which you are asked.

Emergency calls are free of charge.

Temporary transfer of calls

Arrangements may be made with British Telecom for calls to be automatically transferred from one number to another, for example a doctor on his holiday or weekend off duty may have calls automatically transferred to another doctor's telephone number.

This is arranged on modern equipment by entering a simple code into the system followed by the number where you wish the calls to be transferred.

Charge advice service

A charge advice service, formerly known as ADC (advice of duration and charge), is arranged by dialling 150, and the local exchange then reports back to you as soon as possible after the call with the cost incurred.

Collect calls

The charges for a telephone call can be reversed from any telephone number in the United Kingdom to any other number by calling the operator and asking for a collect call. When abroad, collect calls can be made to the UK by going through to the international operator in over 140 countries.

UK Direct

By dialling the special UK Direct telephone number when abroad in certain countries, you reach a British Telecom operator who is then able to place a collect (reverse charge) call for you, so avoiding any language problems or procedural difficulties.

Reminder calls

This is an 'alarm clock' service in which the exchange rings you at a requested time. Customers served by a modernised exchange can arrange reminder calls by keying in a simple code to their local exchange. A small charge is made for this service.

Accurist Timeline

This is the 'speaking clock' service which may be used to supply the correct time. Refer to your local telephone directory for the number to dial for this service.

Directory enquiries

This service is used to provide telephone numbers not available in the directory. For UK inland numbers dial 192 (142 within London for London numbers) and tell the operator the place and name you require, and for international numbers dial 153 and tell the operator which country you require.

Caller display

This equipment is used with the telephone to register the telephone numbers, time and date of your most recent incoming calls. It enables you to see the phone number of a person calling you before answering the call.

Call return

A free service offered by British Telecom which tells you the telephone number of the last person who has called you. The code 1471 is dialled and a message system in the network tells you the number of your last caller, whether it was answered or not. If you call someone who is out, when they return, they can dial 1471 and, if your call was the last received, it will be recorded in their system.

Call waiting

This service lets you know, with a gentle beep, if someone is ringing your number while you are on the phone. You can then arrange for the first call to be on hold while you speak to the second caller.

Marketing services

1 Freefone 0800
This is a telephone service which enables customers, clients, agents or employees in the UK to telephone an organisation without cost to themselves. It encourages customers to place orders by telephone and it can also be used by representatives and employees to save them time and trouble of using coins and claiming refunds for calls made to their company. The calls are made by using a special freefone 0800 number. The company is required to pay the normal telephone call charge and the caller pays nothing.

2 International Freefone 0800
This service allows customers in many overseas countries to dial firms direct in the UK free or for no more than the price of a local call. It can also be used with a fax machine number to allow customers to fax their enquiries and orders free of charge. The international 0800 service is available for use in major European markets, USA, Australia, Japan, Hong Kong and Canada.

3 Lo-call 0345
This service enables customers, potential customers and staff to phone or fax your organisation over any distance within the UK for

the price of a local call. The balance of the call charge is paid by the organisation. It enables companies to maintain a customer service presence in a locality without having to provide the local resources.

4 BT Direct Connect
A service which automatically connects callers to a pre-programmed number when they pick up a remote handset. It provides customers and potential customers with a fast and simple means to make contact with a company without having to dial a number and at no cost to themselves.

Sources of information on telephone services

The phone book
This lists, in alphabetical order, all the names of telephone subscribers in a locality with their addresses and telephone numbers. It also contains local, national and international codes, and general information about British Telecom services. There are 99 telephone directories covering the whole country.

The phone book companion
A British Telecom publication which helps you to identify where in the country a particular telephone number is located.

Yellow Pages
These directories list the names of businesses and other organisations with their telephone numbers and addresses under their respective trade classification or profession, eg office equipment dealers, solicitors, hotels. They also contain local town maps with a street index.

Yellow Pages directories are also offered as an on-line computerised database (known as Electronic Yellow Pages) with details of some 1.8 million businesses and services throughout the UK which can be accessed for the cost of a local call.

Tele Directory
This is a dial-up or dedicated Global Network Services (GNS) link access to BT's database of over 17 million telephone numbers on an annual subscription basis plus a standard charge per enquiry.

Alternatively, a quarterly subscription can be paid for a Phone Disc which is a BT single compact disc for tracing telephone numbers in any of the UK phone books. An IBM-compatible PC and a CD-ROM reader are required for this service.

British Telecom booklets, newspapers and catalogues
These are obtainable free from British Telecom (telephone: 0800 800 968).

Telemessage service

Telemessages are transmitted by telephone, fax or telex, but not delivered to post office counters. When telephoning a telemessage you are required to dial 190 and ask for the Telemessage Service. A typed message is then delivered by first-class post next morning. Special telemessages printed on attractively designed greetings cards may be used for special occasions.

International telegrams

International telegrams may be sent to most parts of the world. They are accepted by telephone, fax or telex, but not from post office counters. When telephoning an international telegram you are required to dial 190 and ask for the International Telegram Service.

Telex

The main teleprinter communication service in Britain is known as telex and is maintained by British Telecom. It provides a quick means of communication in printed form among subscribers, combining the speed of the telephone with the authority of the printed word. The printed copy of the message is produced on teleprinters at both the sending and receiving subscribers' installations. Calls may be made to any telex subscriber in the UK and to subscribers overseas in more than 200 countries. The service is available day and night and messages may be transmitted to a subscriber even though their teleprinter is unattended, provided it is switched on. The message is then available for attention when the operator returns to the machine.

There is a standard rental charge for the provision of the necessary equipment and for hiring the line to the telex exchange. Charges are based on the distance between the calling and called subscribers' telex centres and the duration of the calls.

Electronic teleprinters use microprocessors which have 'memories' so that telex messages can be stored and sent automatically at fast speeds when required. If the number called is engaged, the electronic teleprinter will make further attempts, and the same message can be sent to more than one destination. Other facilities include message editing (similar to a word processor) by which operators can insert,

Fig 2.33 An electronic teleprinter

correct or delete parts of a message and the text can be rearranged.

The teleprinter in Fig 2.33 has a visual display screen. Outgoing messages are typed into the electronic store and presented to the operator on the screen, while the teleprinter continues to receive incoming messages or transmit other outgoing messages. Copies of the messages transmitted are produced on the teleprinter's printer.

With the use of a 'mailbox' facility, telex messages can be operated directly from a computer, giving many more people access to telex communications. The messages received can be read on a VDU screen or printed.

The uses of telex:

- It provides an instant written communication which is ideal for many business purposes.

- It is a reliable and clear means of communication for messages of a technical, legal or quantitative nature.

- Foreign languages can be translated more easily in the written form provided by telex.

- It can be used to receive messages when the office is closed, particularly useful for communications from overseas.
- It prepares and electronically 'posts' messages.

Fax machines

Fax (facsimile) machines use the telephone network to transmit, within a few seconds, any form of printed, typed or handwritten matter, drawings, diagrams or photographs from one location to another.

Replicas of documents can be sent any distance with complete accuracy by combining the speed of the telephone with the reproduction facility of the office copier. Equipment of the same type has to be in use at both the sending and receiving ends.

Operation of the equipment is simple and in the more sophisticated models loading is automatic; the originals to be transmitted are stacked in a loading tray and, after making telephone contact with the recipient, the operator presses the start button and the copies are reproduced automatically at the recipient's machine. Copies can also be transmitted automatically without using the services of an operator. An important advantage over telex is that the input material does not have to be typed and checked, and complicated, detailed orders and other business documents can be sent with complete accuracy. Other applications for this equipment include the distribution of technical drawings to branches; gaining access to records stored centrally at a head office; and transmitting advertisement copy to printers.

By combining the use of the Freefone 0800 and Lo-call 0345 services with fax, your customers can call you free or for the cost of a local call and leave their written order or message without any delay in the postal service.

Fax numbers are listed in the British Telecom *Fax Directory*.

The fax machine illustrated in Fig 2.34 serves as a plain paper, high-quality laser copier as well as a fax machine. It has a memory which can store up to 20 A4 pages of text, and can be used to send documents to several locations and to store received transmissions. There is a 100-number memory for storing regularly dialled numbers and a 30-page input tray for automatic document transmission at a speed of 10 seconds per copy.

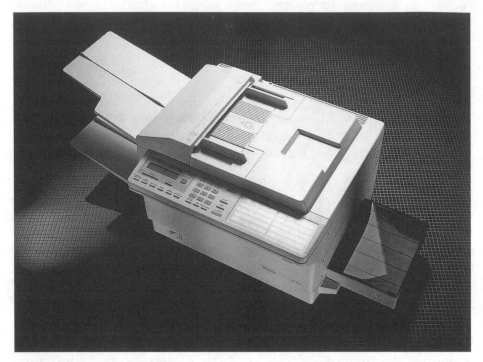

Fig 2.34 Fax machine

Faxmail

This is the Royal Mail's fax service for the transmission of documents between more than 112 Faxmail Centres in the UK and over 40 countries abroad. Documents up to A4 size may be handed into certain post offices for direct transmission to another centre. At the destination the copy is delivered to the recipient, either the same day or next day, depending on the option selected. Greetings cards with a facsimile handwritten message can also be sent by Faxmail for delivery the same day by courier. Private users of fax equipment may receive or send items by this service, provided their machines are compatible with those used by Faxmail.

Integrated Services Digital Network (ISDN)

ISDN is BT's digital dial-up public network offering integrated voice, data, images and videoconferencing communications. The following are some typical applications of ISDN:

- data file transfer

- faxing documents
- voice communication
- videoconferencing and desktop conferencing.

Manufacturers have created a new generation of equipment to capitalise fully on the capabilities of ISDN but special terminal adapters can also be used to make use of existing equipment.

The UK ISDN network is also connected to many overseas countries, including France, Germany, USA, Hong Kong, Australia and Japan.

Costs involve installing a single ISDN line, a quarterly rental charge and usage of the line on a time basis, similar to installing a conventional phone line. It provides so much more than the phone, with its facility to move files from computer to computer, send faxes and print-quality text and photographs, transmit stock control bar codes and maintain remote video surveillance of premises.

Telecommunications services for meetings and conferences

Conference calls

This is a British Telecom service for meetings and conferences held on the telephone. Between three and 60 individuals may be linked up by telephone at locations throughout the UK and worldwide at any time, day or night. If required, the telephone service may be supplemented by video aids, such as slow-scan TV or fax. It is an efficient and economic way to run meetings without the expense of travel and hotel accommodation. Organisations requiring regular teleconferences will normally acquire their own equipment, but for occasional conferences the Conference Call Service may be used to link the participants by their own telephones.

An interpreter can be provided for most languages and a tape recording and play-back service avoids the need for anyone to take minutes while the meeting is in progress.

See also videophone (page 117).

Videoconferencing

The British Telecom closed-circuit television service links groups of people at different locations for meeting and conference purposes. Using videoconferencing can save companies a considerable amount of money and travelling time for their executives and yet still retain the face-to-face interaction and visual presentation. Studios are located in Birmingham, Bristol, Glasgow, Ipswich, Isle of Man, London and Manchester, and links can be established with 150 centres abroad. Each conference room is equipped with cameras and monitor screens. Slides, videos and charts can be displayed, as well as close-ups of documents, drawings or samples, using a video display station.

Business television

This is a private satellite-based network for broadcasting a message or presentation to a specific audience anywhere in the world. It can be prerecorded or live, and can be transmitted to the audience at their places of work at a number of different locations. Live 'feedback' from the audience can be arranged, if required. Business television can be used for training sessions, company announcements, product launches, staff briefings, etc. British Telecom arranges the television link-up and can also offer a complete programme-making service with the necessary operating crew and equipment.

Questions

1 As a secretary you are often called upon to make telephone calls on behalf of your Principal, many of which require particular tact and diplomacy. Briefly explain how you would prepare for and conduct the following telephone calls:

   a) explaining to a prospective author that an idea for a new publication was not of interest to the company;

   b) cancelling a provisional hotel booking for a sales conference involving 50 people;

   c) informing a job applicant that he/she has been unsuccessful in obtaining the post. (*LCCI PSC*)

2 Explain the methods of communication you would expect to use between:

   a) various local offices and Head Office;

   b) the main USA office and Head Office;

   c) Head Office and commissioning editors travelling within the UK and Europe. (*LCCI PSC*)

3 Among the modern office technology is a call-connect system incorporating all the latest features. Describe how the call-connect system enhances communications within Comlon by the use of four of the following features:

a)	abbreviated dialling	d)	call diversion
b)	automatic call-back	e)	conference facility
c)	automatic recall	f)	override facility (*LCCI PSC*)

4

> When I was at a meeting yesterday, a customer complained informally to me that one of our telephone booking clerks had been off-hand with him. I suspect this is not the first complaint about telephone usage and feel we should take steps to make improvements in company telephone technique.

Will you:

a) prepare a list of good telephone techniques; and

b) write down some suggestions on how we can tackle this problem without upsetting anyone.

5 The Office Manager has been instructed to take steps to reduce the expenditure on telephone calls. Investigate the present position regarding the internal and external telephone calls, and prepare a report on your findings together with your recommendations.

6 Assuming your company has up-to-date equipment, suggest ways in which the Managing Director might communicate with:

a) other managers in the building

b) someone whose work takes him to all parts of the factory

c) someone in a provincial branch office.

7 In what circumstances is a telephone answering machine useful? Suggest a suitable pre-recorded message to be received by every caller who is put through to such a machine.

8 What are the main points to bear in mind when dialling an international telephone number? Name two other ways in which a message can be sent overseas using Royal Mail or British Telecom facilities.

9 Yesterday the Headmaster asked you about Faxmail. He has seen it advertised on TV and wishes to have more information. Basically he wishes to know what can be sent, where it can be sent and what the UK services cost. From an information sheet supplied by the Royal Mail, list for him this information.

10 You work for Sarah Patel, Assistant Sales Manager. You are just going to lunch when you receive a telephone call from John Smith of Orpington Social Club. The latest batch of packets of salted cashew nuts are not of the usual quality. The outer boxes appear to have had something spilled on them, and he says that there were similar problems with the last batch. He would like Sarah to ring back as soon as possible (after 1600 hours as he will be out of the office until then). Sarah is in a meeting but will be back shortly. Fill in the message form. (*PEI OP2*)

11 a) Briefly describe the main features of three means of communication (other than the telephone) your office could use to send information abroad which requires action today.
    b) Compose a message to be recorded on the new telephone answering machine to be used when the office is unstaffed. (*PEI OP2*)

In-tray exercise

12 You are employed by Mr Brian Dobson (Case Study 3). Mr Dobson called in to the office early this morning and left you the following note prior to leaving for a two-day visit to Northern Ireland:

> Jane
>
> Last night's concert at Llandudno was cancelled after the Group had set off and unfortunately I had no way of contacting them — very annoying and costly as they wasted a whole day in unnecessary travel. Can you suggest what arrangements we could make in the future to make contact with them whilst they are on the road if we have to change their plans at the last minute?
>
> Also, is there any way that telephone callers enquiring about concerts - even cancellations - could be given details when they ring in the evenings and at weekends when you are not there?
>
> Will you please make some enquiries and let me have a memo with your suggestions — don't forget to supply costs too!
>
> BD

Drafting and preparing documents

3.1 Business correspondence

The secretary is required to initiate and respond to correspondence, both internal and external to the organisation, for self and on behalf of others. This entails drafting and researching letters, memos and reports from notes given, as well as preparing correspondence from shorthand or recorded dictation.

The following specimen NVQ Level 3 performance criteria indicate the standards required for two of the competences in this range of skills:

Unit 14 — Prepare, produce and present documents from own notes

Element 14.1 — Take notes and prepare information

a Accurate notes are taken, at an average speed of 100 words per minute, under workplace conditions.

b Uncertainties, arising in taking notes, are identified and clarified.

c Instructions are interpreted correctly and actioned appropriately.

d Additional information, when required, is located, selected and incorporated into the integrated material.

e Work practices are in accordance with legal and regulatory requirements and organisational procedures.

f Security and confidentiality of information are maintained.

Element 14.2 — Produce and present documents using a keyboard

a Error-free documents, of approximately 1500 words, are produced, under workplace conditions, from selected material, in two and a half hours.

b Selected presentation conveys the information effectively, appropriately and in accordance with house style.

c Spelling, grammar and punctuation are consistent and correct.

d The language, style and tone of the finished document are suited to its purpose.

e Work practices are in accordance with legal and regulatory requirements and organisational procedures.

f Security and confidentiality of information are maintained.

g Work is achieved within agreed deadlines.

h Documents are finished for presentation and appropriate routes determined.

Letters

What is it that a business letter sets out to do? It has two primary functions:

1 to provide a communication between two persons

2 to preserve a permanent record of the communication.

The purpose of the business letter is to convey information and/or to ask questions.

Key pointers in writing a business letter:

- Plan your message carefully so that you have a clear idea of what you want to say or what you want to ask.
- Write clearly and concisely but be careful that courtesy of tone and exactness of meaning are not sacrificed to brevity.
- Write simply and directly and with the right amount of emphasis to enable the reader to grasp the contents instantly. No room should be left for ambiguity.
- Check the letter carefully to ensure that no spelling, grammar and punctuation errors are made. Whenever there is the slightest doubt over the spelling of a word, consult a dictionary.
- Quote the correspondent's reference if one is given in an earlier communication.

- Use a heading if it provides a quick identification to the contents of the letter.

- Select the appropriate salutations and complimentary closes, as given in the forms of address on pages 135 to 137.

- Divide the letter into paragraphs, each dealing with one major point only and arranged as follows:

  a opening paragraph: introducing the subject;
  b the body of the letter (further sub-divided into paragraphs);
  c closing paragraph: with a concluding remark.

  Grade the points so that they follow logically in their correct sequence.

- Display the letter clearly and consistently. The layout given in Fig. 3.1 is the fully-blocked style, but other forms of layout and punctuation are equally acceptable as long as consistency is maintained throughout.

A specimen letter written by a private secretary, embodying many of the above principles, is given in Fig. 3.1.

Receiving dictation

The secretary must possess an adequate shorthand speed to be capable of taking down bursts of dictation at high speeds.

If the author deletes a passage dictated, you must be certain to cross it out completely in your notes. If a corrected passage is to be inserted, it is advisable to put a mark or number in the place where it is to go, and then, in the margin of the corrected passage, repeat the mark or number.

You are justified in interrupting the executive during dictation if you have not fully understood or heard some aspect of the dictation; never guess a word or phrase, nor be afraid to ask questions when in doubt. It is advisable, however, to avoid interrupting immediately a query arises, as this may cause the dictator to lose track of their thoughts; instead, you should wait for a suitable opportunity, eg when there is a brief pause in dictation.

Before leaving the executive's office, try to be quite certain about all the correspondence dictated, eg if you are doubtful about the salutation or complimentary close to use in a particular case, be sure to ask.

Computer Products Ltd
Enterprise House, Elm Road, Buckingham, BM3 4AS

Telephone: 0128-02 3296
Tax: 0128-02 1876

Your ref: RTH/PT
Our ref: GF123/BNS

14 August 199-

Mr R T Hollis
Office Manager
Paramount Financial Services Ltd
14 Wansworth Road
York
YS2 3PT

Dear Mr Hollis

DISPLAY SCREEN EQUIPMENT

Mr Buckingham, who is abroad on business at the present time, has
asked me to thank you for your letter of 12 August, suggesting
that you and he should meet on Thursday 22 August for a
demonstration of our new VDU Glare Filters on your VDUs.

I am pleased to confirm that this date is convenient for Mr
Buckingham. He will also be pleased to explain how this
equipment conforms to the EU Directive on VDU Operator Health and
Safety.

You are probably already aware that VDU users are exposed to
Computer Vision Syndrome and that this can lead to eye strain,
headaches and double vision; symptoms which are known to affect
staff welfare and productivity in the office. A small investment
in VDU Glare Filters, therefore, makes good sense, not only in
complying with legislation but in enhancing staff morale.

I have pleasure in enclosing our catalogue and price list for the
VDU Glare Filters, together with an extract from the Safety
(Display Screen Equipment) Regulations 1992 which I hope you will
find useful.

Mr Buckingham will look forward to meeting you at your premises
on 22 August at 1100 hrs.

Yours sincerely

Beryl Stowe

Beryl N Stowe
Private Secretary to Mr Hugh Buckingham,
Marketing Manager

encs

Registered No 1375400 England

Fig 3.1   A displayed business letter

FORMS OF ADDRESS FOR LETTERS TO EUROPE

Country	Form of address	Salutation	Complimentary close
United Kingdom			
Men	Mr —	Dear Sir or Dear Mr —	
Married women	Mrs — or Ms —	Dear Madam — Dear Mrs — Dear Ms —	Yours faithfully or Yours sincerely
Unmarried women	Miss — or Ms —	Dear Madam — Dear Miss — Dear Ms —	
Belgium			
Use French (as for France) or Dutch (as for The Netherlands)			
Denmark			
Men	Hr —	Hr —	
Married women	Frue —	Fru —	Med venlig Hilsen
Unmarried women	Frøken —	Frøken —	
Finland			
Men	Herra —	Arvoisa vastaanottaja	Parhain terveisin
Married women	Rouva —	or	or
Unmarried women	Neiti —	Hyvä —	Ystävällisin terveisin

Country	Form of address	Salutation	Complimentary close
France			
Men	M —	Monsieur	Veuillez agréer (name) l'expression de mes sentiments distingués
Married women	Mme —	Madame	or
Unmarried women	Mlle —	Mademoiselle	Avec mes meilleurs sentiments
Germany			
Men	Herr —	Sehr geehrter Herr —	Mit freundlichen Grüssen
Women	Frau —	Sehr geehrte Frau —	

Note: When writing formally to a company, address the letter to Sehr geehrte Damen und Herren

Greece			
Men	Kyrios	Agapete Kyrie	Eilikrina dikos sas
Women	Kyria	Agapete Kyria	Eilikrina dikos sas (if the letter is signed by a man)
			or
			dike sas (if the letter is signed by a woman)

Note: The majority of unmarried women wish to be called 'Mrs'. There are, of course, some exceptions who wish to keep the title Despoinis, so say Despoinis X but write to Despoinida X.

Italy			
Men	Egr Signore	Egregio signor —	Cordiali saluti
Married women	Gent ma Signora	Gentile signora —	or
Unmarried women	Gent ma Signorina	Gentile signorina —	Distinti saluti

Note: The titles **Dottor** (Dottoressa) and Professor (**Professoressa**) and **Avvocato** are always used where relevant.

Luxembourg
Use French (as for France) or German (as for Germany)

The Netherlands

Men	De heer —	Geachte heer —	*Formal:* Hoogachtend
Women	Mevrouw —	Geachte mevrouw —	*Informal:* Met vriendelijke groeten

Portugal

Men	Exmo —	Senhor —	Com os melhores cumprimentos
Women	Exma —	Senhora —	

Spain

Men	Señor D	Señor *or* Estimado Sr	le saluda atentamente *or* le saluda cordialmente *or* un atento saludo *or* un cordial saludo
Married women	Señora Da	Señora *or* Estimada Sra	
Unmarried women	Señorita Da	Señorita *or* Estimada Srta	

Note: Married women keep their family name even if they get married. They take the name of their husband for social events or when they are named together, but the married name is never used in commercial transactions.

Switzerland
Use French (as for France), German (as for Germany) or Italian (as for Italy).

137

Recording dictation

A guide for the recording of dictation

At the beginning of the whole dictation:

1 Announce your name and department.

2 Indicate any special reference to be used for your correspondence.

3 Say if you wish any item to be given priority.

At the beginning of each passage:

4 Assemble your facts before you start dictating.

5 Indicate the document required and whether it is for internal or external use.

6 Mark the index or scale to show the starting point of each passage.

7 Say how many copies you require with any instructions concerning distribution.

8 Quote the reference number/file number.

9 Dictate names and addresses of correspondents or refer to their names in correspondence which will accompany the recording.

10 Say if you require a variation from the normal layout of correspondence.

11 Dictate the salutation.

During the course of dictation:

12 Indicate paragraphing and capital letters *before* the text to which the instruction refers.

13 It is advisable to dictate the full stops, question marks, colons, semi-colons, dashes, exclamation marks, brackets and quotation marks. You are not expected to dictate every comma, but you can assist the typist by the inflections of your voice. It is also helpful if you can give special instructions, ie 'open brackets ... close brackets', in a slightly different tone from your normal voice, so that they can be recognised as instructions and not typed by mistake.

14 Spell out foreign and unusual words, using the phonetic alphabet (if necessary) and pronounce difficult words slowly and clearly.

15 Keep the volume of your voice as low as practicable.

16 Hold the microphone fairly close to the mouth and speak directly into it.

17 Do not speak too quickly or in jerks, but speak into the microphone

at a normal conversational speed.

18 Avoid clipping words using the 'on-off' switch.

At the conclusion of each passage:

19 Dictate the complimentary close.

20 If there are enclosures, state the size of envelope required.

21 If a correction has to be made, refer to it on the index slip.

22 Mark the index or slip to show the end of the passage.

At the conclusion of the whole dictation:

23 Indicate that you are signing off.

Transcribing recorded dictation

The following points should be observed when transcribing recorded dictation:

1 Pay attention to any special instructions and corrections accompanying the recording.

2 Letters required urgently should be processed, checked and returned to the author first of all.

3 The size of each letter must be assessed before typing, to enable the correct size of paper to be used.

4 Any doubtful points in the dictation should always be checked with the author or another responsible member of staff.

5 Consult a dictionary whenever there is any doubt about the spelling of a word.

6 Insert the proper punctuation marks and allow adequate paragraphs.

7 Every transcription must be accurately typed and the utmost care must be taken in checking letters, etc, before they are printed.

Invitations

Invitations are generally in the form of printed cards, with the guest's name inserted. The secretary will usually be expected to know how to reply to invitations after the employer has said simply 'accept' or 'refuse'.

The style of reply must be based on the invitation text itself, eg an invitation written in the third person is replied to in the same form.

> 'The Meadows'
> Fulham Road
> Wandsbrook
>
> Telephone: 0142–126 8973
>
> Major Terence Field thanks the Chairman
> and Committee of the Boldingham Musical
> Society for their kind invitation to the
> Society's Tenth Annual Dinner to be held
> at the Town Hall, Crockington on Tuesday
> 2 September 19 __ at 1945 hrs, and he has
> much pleasure in accepting.
>
>
> 25 August 19__

Fig 3.2   A formal acceptance of an invitation

No salutation, subscription or signature is required.

Fig 3.2 gives an example of the acceptance of an invitation.

When refusing an invitation, it is more courteous to give a reason. Note the wording for a refusal in Fig 3.3.

Reports

The efficient secretary should be able to prepare a report of a meeting, a discussion, an interview or even a report on a document. It is necessary to present the essential facts so that the executive can deal with the major items of business swiftly without having to delve into a large number of unimportant details.

A report must be accurate, clear, concise and logically arranged. It should be concise to the extent that there is no 'padding' or irrelevant details. The writer should 'telescope' phrases wherever possible and avoid using long, involved sentences.

If the report is an individual one, ie from the secretary to the office manager, it should be a narrative written in the first person, but if the report is of a meeting it should be written wholly in the third person. A report of an event or a meeting should always be in the past tense.

Planning

The preliminary preparation of a brief outline is an essential so that the matters are introduced in their correct sequence and each point will lead naturally to the next. Here is a suggested plan:

```
'The Meadows'
Fulham Road
Wandsbrook
Telephone: 0142–126 8973


Major Terence Field thanks Mr and Mrs

Geoffrey Lloyd for their kind invitation

to a party to be held on Tuesday

9 September 19__ at 2000 hrs.

He regrets very much that owing to a

previous business engagement in Scotland,

he must decline their invitation.




25 August 19__
```

Fig 3.3 A formal refusal of an invitation

1 The heading or title containing the following information:

    a the subject of the report, eg the type of meeting
    b the date of the meeting or interview
    c the place
    d if a meeting, those present — specifying the chairperson and officers
    e file reference numbers for future identification
    f the name of the person to whom the report is sent
    g if the report is confidential or secret, care must be taken in marking it accordingly.

2 The opening paragraph, which should set out clearly the circumstances which called for the report, for example, the office manager's memo, or changing circumstances which called for the discussion of future policy.

3 The body of the report containing the general business discussed: if it is a report of a meeting, adequate sub-headings should be used; if it is an individual report, the facts of the case should be stated clearly and concisely.

4 Recommendations or conclusions.

5 The action necessary to effect the recommendations, including the following:

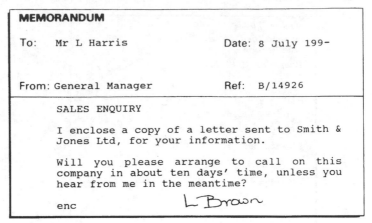

```
MEMORANDUM

To:   Mr L Harris            Date: 8 July 199-


From: General Manager        Ref:  B/14926
```
```
SALES ENQUIRY

I enclose a copy of a letter sent to Smith &
Jones Ltd, for your information.

Will you please arrange to call on this
company in about ten days' time, unless you
hear from me in the meantime?

enc                    L Brown
```

Fig 3.4   A memo

    a the names of the persons who should take the action
    b the date by which the action should be taken
    c the date of the next meeting to review the situation.

6 The name and description of the signatory.

Memos

Memos are normally used for internal communications or for messages to representatives or agents in other parts of the country or the world. No salutation or complimentary close is needed.

Fig 3.4 shows a memo sent from the General Manager of White Bros to their Bristol agent.

Action slips

To reduce paperwork and typing, instead of a covering memo, an action slip, as illustrated in Fig 3.5 can be attached to documents asking for comments, noting, draft reply, etc.

Text-processing equipment

Most secretaries now use computers with word processing, database and spreadsheet packages, although there are many manual and electronic typewriters still in use. Computers are dealt with in more detail in Unit 3.5.

Electronic typewriters vary according to their size of memory and

```
┌─────────────────────────────────────┐
│ ACTION SLIP                         │
├─────────────────────────────────────┤
│ To  Martin          URGENT  ☑       │
├─────────────────────────────────────┤
│ Please:                             │
│ ☑ Draft a reply for my signature    │
│ ☐ Give me your comments             │
│ ☐ Circulate and return to me        │
│ ☐ Note and return to me             │
│ ☐ Take appropriate action           │
│ ☐ Note for your information         │
├─────────────────────────────────────┤
│ REMARKS                             │
│ Send a copy to the bank.            │
├──────────────┬──────────────────────┤
│ From:  KR    │ Date:  1/3/ –        │
└──────────────┴──────────────────────┘
```

Fig 3.5   Action slip

the facilities providing for text editing. An important feature of the electronic typewriter is that it allows work to be viewed before it is reproduced on paper, which makes correction so much easier. The more advanced machines offer many of the facilities to be found on word processors, ie their memories, VDU screens and inter-communication devices, but still retain the benefits of a typewriter capable of producing 'hard copy' directly from the keyboard. Although word processors are capable of most aspects of text processing and production, typewriters are usually more effective for 'one-off' envelopes and labels, and the completion of printed forms.

The top end of the market includes electronic typewriters with visual display screens incorporating many of the features that are found on microcomputers. The screen aids the typist in editing and processing text and, when a piece of work has been typed in its final form, it can either be automatically printed on paper and cleared from the memory or transferred to a floppy disk for permanent storage.

The features which may be found on electronic typewriters are:

- internal memories ranging from those holding a few hundred characters to those holding many thousands of characters
- visual displays or windows ranging from one line to full page for viewing text before printing
- backspace correction
- margin justification
- pitch selection and emboldening

- automatic facilities which include paper insertion, centring, carriage return, underscoring and decimal tabulation
- electronic dictionary for checking spelling errors
- links with other machines or a network; they may, for example, be used as a computer printer.

Dictation equipment

There are three main categories of dictation equipment:

1 Central dictation network systems used by large organisations which are either connected to a telephone system or to a separately wired circuit.

2 Desk-top machines.

3 Portable hand-held (pocket-size) recorders.

Digital dictation systems

Digital dictation systems, which dispense with tapes, may be used in organisations with a high volume of dictation. The equipment in this type of system is illustrated in Fig. 3.6.

The authors dictate via a digital dictation station or telephone directly onto the hard disk of a network server. The dictation is automatically distributed to typists according to priority, workload and the author's directions. The typist has voice as well as visual prompts on a screen denoting author, length and nature of dictation, priority given to the task and any special directions. The supervisor has instant overview of the system, user and department performance including:

- window style interface for easy monitoring of the total workload
- on-line visual display of dictation times, jobs in queue, calculated turnaround time
- management systems which compile job, author or transcription performance by department
- automatic archiving for reference purposes.

Voice recognition systems

The most recent developments in voice recognition systems, which replace the traditional keyboard for inputting text into a computer system, are discussed in Unit 3.5.

Fig 3.6 Digital dictation system

Questions

1 Your junior assistant, who fell in the street during the luncheon interval, has been taken to hospital with a broken wrist. Your employer asks you to write a letter for his signature sympathising with her, telling her 'not to worry', and inquiring whether she has left any particular items of work unfinished or unattended to. Write this letter.

2 Reply to the following invitation, stating that you are unable to attend:

Major and Mrs T R Davis request the pleasure of ... at a luncheon to be held at The Regent Hotel, Sparkton, on Wednesday 22 June 19 . . at 1200 hrs.
RSVP

The Blanktown Rotarians have pleasure in inviting

Mr & Mrs A Turner
·····························

to their St Swithin's Ball on Saturday 15th July 19 —

at

The Grand Hotel, Blanktown

from 8 pm to midnight

RSVP   Evening Dress   Buffet

---

3 Your employer has received the above invitation.

   a) Write a formal acceptance for him.
   b) Blanktown is 200 miles away from your employer's home. He asks you to make the necessary arrangements on his behalf. Describe the steps you would take.

4 Write a report for your Office Manager of a visit to an Office Machinery Exhibition held in your town. Make recommendations for the acquisition of suitable new items of equipment for your office.

5 Write memos from the General Manager to the Works Manager and Production Manager asking them to attend a meeting on 4 September, at 1000 hrs in the General Manager's Office, to discuss the proposed reorganisation of their departments. Tell them to discuss the matter with their deputies and bring along all factual information relevant to the subject.

6 What points would you wish to make to a new secretary on report writing? (*LCCI PSC*)

7 You are an audio-typist. When you transcribe, you expect to get certain instructions:

   a) at the beginning of the whole dictation
   b) at the beginning of each letter
   c) during the course of the dictation of a letter
   d) at the conclusion of either a letter or the whole dictation.

   Make a list of these instructions, divided as above, in a manner which you consider would help you most when transcribing.

8 Dictating machines have been introduced into your organisation. The representative of the firm supplying the machines has shown the staff how to use them. You are the only experienced audio-typist in the organisation and you are asked to write some simple instructions (which do not include the mechanical aspect of the machines) to guide the other transcribers. Write the rules covering the points of importance.

9 Mr Spencer and Mr Adams are busy surgeons.

   a) Mr Spencer dictates his letters to his secretary as and when he can. Sometimes he is not free to deal with correspondence for two or three days at a time.

   b) Mr Adams dictates his letters to a dictation machine. Sometimes he does this in his consulting room, when he is free; sometimes he dictates at home and leaves the tapes on his secretary's desk early in the morning on his way to the hospital.

   State the relative merits of each system of dictation from the points of view of both the employer and the secretary.

In-tray exercises

10 You are employed by the New Tech Office Services Bureau (Case Study 1). Please carry out the request in the telephone message overleaf.

11 You are employed by Mr Brian Dobson, Manager of 'The Secretairs' (Case Study 3).

   Sean Lawrance has asked you to reply on his behalf accepting this invitation:

Jan and Michael Stewart

have much pleasure in inviting

Sean Lawrance

....

to the first night of their group's concert

tour at the Mayfair Hotel. Grand Parade.

Eastbourne

on Monday 11 November 19-- at 7.30 pm

and afterwards for a celebration meal in

the Grosvenor Suite

RSVP 14 St Helens Gardens. London W10 6RM

Martin Please draft a letter for my signature KR

MESSAGE FOR

MRS ROBINSON

WHILE YOU WERE OUT

MR P SAUNDERS

OF. R Knight & Sons Ltd., 14 Rugby Road, Leamington Spa

TELEPHONE NO. 416712

TELEPHONED	✓	PLEASE RING	
CALLED TO SEE YOU		WILL CALL AGAIN	
WANTS TO SEE YOU		URGENT	

MESSAGE:

Mr Saunders would like your advice concerning a new

audio-typing system he has installed at his firm.

Mr Saunders has to travel to many branches throughout

the country, sometimes spending two or three days

away from the firm. When he is away he dictates

letters and reports on to tapes and posts them to

his office but he finds that his secretary has

difficulty in transcribing them accurately.

Mr Saunders wants to know if there are any tips you

can give him to improve his dictation technique and
what advice he should give his secretary.

DATE 10 December 19   TIME 0945

RECEIVED BY M. Clark

3.2 Business documents

Business transactions and communications are normally required in written form, to provide a record for both recipient and sender. The principal documents used in buying and selling transactions are explained in this unit in order to outline the information which must pass between the buyer and the seller and to show the purpose of the forms used and the uses made of these forms within the company. The examples relate to the sale of manilla computer files by Office Products Ltd to British Traders plc.

Requisition

Purpose   An internal request for goods to be purchased or drawn from stock.

Prepared by   Department requesting goods: eg Accounts
                   Filing Section
                   Purchasing company: British Traders plc

Distribution   1 copy to Buying Department

Example   Fig 3.7 (page 150)

Letter of inquiry

Purpose   Sent to a supplier to invite them to quote for goods to be supplied.

Prepared by   Purchasing company: British Traders plc,
                   Buying Department

Distribution   1 Supplier(s)
                   2 Buyer's file

Example   Fig 3.8 (page 151)

Quotation

Purpose   Gives full particulars of goods offered for sale including terms of payment and delivery. Similar information may be supplied in catalogues, price lists and estimates.

Prepared by   Selling company: Office Products Ltd, Sales Department

Distribution   1 Prospective customer (buyer)
                   2 Sales Department (file)

Example   Fig 3.9 (page 152)

REQUISITION			No. 40

Department **ACCOUNTS (Filing Section)**

Supplier's name (if known) _____

Address _____

Estimate Reference No **AB 129**
Capital/Revenue

Quantity	Details	Cat No	Price each
			£
100	Manilla computer files for unburst sheets (485 gsm) 20mm capacity for sheet size 389mm x 279mm Colour: blue Overprinted with BRITISH TRADERS plc		

Signature of Head of Department	Date
g Smith	3/1/ —

Fig 3.7 A requisition

Trade discount	An allowance from the invoice or list price of goods; it is deducted on the invoice and it does not depend on the time of payment. It is given as an allowance for a large order, an agent's profit, a trade allowance or as a correction of a list price.
Cash discount	An allowance made for the prompt settlement of an account within a stated period; it is deducted when payment is made.

BRITISH TRADERS plc

79 Bradford Street
Manchester
M10 7EY

Tel: 0161-205 5123
Fax: 0161-205 7891

4 January 199-

Our Ref: JB/jmh
Your Ref:

Office Products Ltd
Parkston Industrial Estate
Derby Road
Liverpool
LL19 2SP

Dear Sirs

With reference to your advertisement for office stationery in "Business Equipment Digest" I shall be glad if you will kindly quote us your most favourable terms for supplying:

> 100 manilla computer files for unburst
> sheets (485gsm) 20mm capacity for
> sheet size 389mm x 279mm
> Colour: blue
> Overprinted with BRITISH TRADERS plc

Please indicate your earliest date of delivery as we require the files as soon as possible.

Yours faithfully

J Browning

J Browning
Chief Buyer

Registered Company No 234651 England

Fig 3.8   Letter of inquiry

QUOTATION

OFFICE PRODUCTS LTD
Parkston Industrial Estate, Derby Road,
Liverpool LL19 2SP

Telephone: 0151-203 4116   Fax: 0151-321 9426

VAT No 159 6423 72

Company No
109091 England

BANKERS   Midland Bank plc
           Liverpool LL21 3SY

Quotation Ref: PR 1962   Dated: 6 January 199-

To:
     British Traders plc
     79 Bradford Street
     Manchester
     M10 7EY

     For the attention of Mr J Browning

In reply to your inquiry dated 4 January 199-
we have pleasure in quoting you for the
following:

     100 manilla computer files (Opal) for
     unburst sheets (485gsm) 20mm capacity
     for sheet size 389mm x 279mm in blue
     Overprinted with BRITISH TRADERS plc

                 £160.00

This price includes delivery by our van

Delivery date: 2 weeks on receipt of order

Trade discount: 15%

Terms of payment: Net cash within one month
                     after delivery
                     VAT at the standard rate

We look forward to receiving your order which
will receive our prompt attention

P. Jones
Marketing Manager

Fig 3.9   Quotation

ORDER

No 1234

From: **BRITISH TRADERS plc**

79 Bradford Street, Manchester M10 7EY

Tel: 0161-205 5123

Fax: 0161-205 7891

Date: 8 January 199–

To:

Office Products Ltd
Parkston Industrial
   Estate
Derby Road
Liverpool LL19 2SP

Please supply:

Quantity	Description	Your Cat No	Price £
100	Opal Manilla Computer Files (Sheet size 389mm x 279mm) Blue colour Overprinted: BRITISH TRADERS plc	Your Quotation PR 1962 dated 6.1.9–	160.00
	Carriage paid/~~forward~~		

Deliver by: Road/~~Rail~~ promptly to: the above address

J Browning
Buyer

Fig 3.10   Order

Order

Purpose	An external request for goods to be supplied.
Prepared by	Purchasing company: British Traders plc, Buying Department
Distribution	1 Supplier
	2 Goods Received Section (notification of goods to be received)
	3 Stores (stock control)
	4 Accounts (checking invoice)
	5 Buyer (file)
Example	Fig 3.10 (page 153)

Delivery note

Purpose	Accompanies goods as a record of delivery.
	An advice/dispatch note may also be used if goods are dispatched by post or rail to notify the buyer when goods have left the supplier.
Prepared by	Selling company: Office Products Ltd, Dispatch Section
Distribution	1 Goods Received Section
	2 Driver (for obtaining signature of recipient)
Example	Fig 3.11

DELIVERY NOTE　　　　No　483

From: **OFFICE PRODUCTS LTD**
Parkston Industrial Estate, Derby Road, Liverpool LL19 2SP

Tel:　0151-203 4116　　　　　　　Fax:　0151-321 9426

Delivered to:

British Traders plc
79 Bradford Street
Manchester
M10 7EY

Date of despatch:　**22 January 199–**

Number of packages	Description	Order No
4	Opal Manilla Computer Files	1234

Received in good order and condition　*but parcels not opened and inspected.*

Customer's signature　*T. Cox*

Fig 3.11　Delivery note

Goods received note

Purpose	Internal communication reporting arrival of goods.
Prepared by	Purchasing company: British Traders plc, Goods Received Section
Distribution	1 Buyer (notification of the arrival of goods)
	2 Accounts (checking invoice)
	3 Stores (stock control)
Example	Fig 3.12

GOODS RECEIVED NOTE   No   148

Supplier: OFFICE PRODUCTS LTD   Date: 22.1.199–

Quantity	Description	Order No
100	Opal Manilla Computer Files	1234

Carrier	Received by	Checked by	Bay No
OPL VAN	G Harris	L Warren	A15

Condition of goods: 3 parcels: Satisfactory
1 parcel (25 files) incorrect size

Distribution: Accounts
Storekeeper
Buyer

Fig 3.12   Goods received note

Invoice

Purpose	To charge the buyer with the cost of goods supplied; it is a source document for recording purchases/sales in accounting records.
Prepared by	Selling company: Office Products Ltd, Sales Department (Accounts Section)
Distribution	1 Purchaser (for checking against order and goods

received note, and entering in accounts)
2 Accounts (entering in accounts)
3 Stores (stock control)
4 Dispatch (for delivery note)
5 Sales (file copy)

INVOICE

No 1384

From: **OFFICE PRODUCTS LTD**
Parkston Industrial Estate, Derby Road, Liverpool LL19 2SP

Tel: 0151-203 4116   Fax: 0151-321 9426

VAT Registration No 159 6423 72   Date: 22 January 199-

To:
> British Traders plc
> 79 Bradford Street
> Manchester
> M10 7EY

Date of despatch:

22 January 199-

Terms: Net cash within one month after delivery

Completion of Order No   1234   dated   8 January 199-

Quantity	Description	Cat No	Price each £	Cost £	VAT rate %	VAT amount £
100	Opal Manilla Computer Files	PR 1962	1.60	160.00		
	Less 15% trade discount			24.00		
				136.00	17½	23.80
	Add: VAT			23.80		
				159.80		
	Carriage: by our van					

Fig 3.13   Invoice

Credit note

Purpose   To reduce the amount charged to the buyer for an overcharge, goods returned, short delivery, etc, as in the case of the example in which a parcel of 25 files was returned because they were of the wrong size.

Prepared by   Selling company: Office Products Ltd,
                 Sales Department (Accounts Section)

Distribution   1 Purchaser (for entering in accounts)
                 2 Accounts (entering in accounts)

CREDIT NOTE

No C183

From: **OFFICE PRODUCTS LTD**
Parkston Industrial Estate, Derby Road, Liverpool LL19 2SP

Tel: 0151-203 4116   Fax: 0151-321 9426

VAT Registration No 304373911   Ref: Invoice No 1384
                                   dated   22.1.9–

To: British Traders plc
      79 Bradford Street
      Manchester   Date: 25 January 199–
      M10 7EY

Quantity	Details	Price each £	Amount £	VAT rate %	VAT amount £
25	Opal Manilla Computer Files returned – incorrect size (Quotation PR1962 refers)	1.60	40.00		
	Less 15% trade discount		6.00		
			34.00	17½	5.95
	Add: VAT		5.95		
	Credit value		39.95		

Fig 3.14   Credit note

3 Stores (stock control)

4 Sales (file copy)

Example   Fig 3.14 (page 157)

Statement of account

Purpose   Advises buyer of the total amount due to be paid for the previous month's transactions and requests payment. It is a copy of the customer's account in the sales ledger.

Prepared by   Selling company: Office Products Ltd, Accounts Department

Distribution   1 Purchaser (requesting payment)

2 Accounts (file copy)

Example   Fig. 3.15 (page 159)

Computerised procedures for buying and selling

The following is a list of buying and selling office procedures which can be computerised.

- A word processor can be used to prepare letters of inquiry or any standard letters using texts stored on a disk. The suppliers' names and addresses can be merged from a mailing list file to a text file to provide automatic typing in one operation of both letter and address.

- All forms used in buying and selling can be completed on a word processor, since the machine tabulates to the correct positions on the forms and automatically reproduces any standard data.

- Suppliers' and customers' records can be filed on a computer disk, providing a rapid means of locating and printing details from them.

- To order goods by computer:

  a the operator keys in catalogue/part numbers to reveal on the terminal screen:

    1 a description of the item
    2 the preferred supplier and any other suitable suppliers
    3 the current price
    4 discounts allowable
    5 carriage charges
    6 normal delivery time

```
                          STATEMENT


 From      OFFICE PRODUCTS LTD
           Parkston Industrial Estate, Derby Road, Liverpool  LL19 2SP

 Tel: 0151-203 4116         Fax: 0151-321 9426


 To    ┌─────────────────────────────┐
       │ British Traders plc         │
       │ 79 Bradford Street          │
       │ Manchester                  │       Date  31 January 199-
       │ M10 7EY                     │
       └─────────────────────────────┘


 Terms  Net cash within one month after delivery
```

Date	Details	Ref No	Dr £	Cr £	Balance £
199–					
Jan 22	Goods	1384	159.80		159.80
25	Returns	C183		39.95	119.85

The last amount on the balance column is the amount owing

- -

Remittance Advice

Please detach and return this remittance advice when making payment

To   Office Products Ltd
     Parkston Industrial Estate, Derby Road, Liverpool, LL19 2SP

Cheque/cash for
in payment of statement dated

From:

Date:

If you require a receipt please insert 'R' here ☐

Fig 3.15   Statement of Account

  b the operator keys in details of the order placed to:

   1 record it in the purchase record file

   2 print the order at the end of the day

   3 sort orders by supplier to enable all the orders for one supplier to be printed on the same form.

- To prepare invoices and statements by computer:

  a The operator keys in the code number of the customer, to print out the customer's name and address on the invoice form.

  b The operator keys in the product code number and the quantity for each item ordered, to print out the type and quantity of goods ordered with their unit and total prices.

  c When the last item has been entered, the computer calculates and prints the gross total price of goods ordered, discounts, VAT and the net invoice price.

  d When all of the invoices for a day have been completed, the computer can print out:

   1 the daily total of sales and, if necessary, the total sales for each country, region or division

   2 the totals of each product sold

   3 the totals of each product remaining in stock after the day's sales.

  e At the end of the month the statements are printed automatically from the data entered into the sales record file when the invoices and credit notes were prepared.

- If terminals are 'on line' to a computer, the following tasks are carried out automatically:

  a when the order clerk keys in details of an order, the computer stores it on the purchase record file

  b when the goods-received clerk keys in details of goods received, the computer checks whether these agree with the data supplied in a on the purchase record file

  c when the accounts clerk keys in details from the supplier's invoice, the computer checks these with the data supplied in a and b on the purchase record file and then enters the results in the supplier's account.

Questions

1 It has been decided to purchase a new copier for your office, and the model has been chosen after a demonstration by a salesman.

a) State the names of the documents which will pass between your company and the supplier, from the placing of the order to the payment for the machine.

b) Make a list of the supplies which will have to be obtained before the machine can be put into operation.

c) For what types of work will the machine be most suitable?

2   You are employed at the New Tech Office Services Bureau (Case Study 1).

a) Using the price list issued by Office Products Ltd (pages xx and xxi), prepare a requisition dated 1 April and an order form dated 3 April for 50 Opal Computer Files for sheet size 241 mm × 279 mm (pink) and 20 Portable (blue) Filing Boxes for computer printout (size 76 mm × 368 mm × 248 mm).

b) Name some ways in which a prospective buyer might obtain all the information required from the seller before deciding to place an order.

3   You are employed at Office Products Ltd (Case Study 2).

a) The goods ordered in Question 2 are delivered by delivery van to New Tech Office Services Bureau on 10 April 199-. Complete a delivery note to accompany the goods.

b) Why is it necessary to prepare a delivery note?

c) How would the documentation in (a) differ if the goods were dispatched by post?

4   You are employed at the New Tech Office Services Bureau.

a) Complete a goods received note for the goods delivered in Question 3. The goods were received in a satisfactory condition, apart from a parcel of 10 portable filing boxes which had been damaged in transit.

b) Give reasons for the use by a company of a goods received note.

c) Name two other departments to which copies of the goods received note would be sent by the department receiving the goods.

5   You are employed at Office Products Ltd (Case Study 2).

a) Prepare an invoice to New Tech Office Services Bureau on 10 April 199- for the goods ordered in Question 2. Terms of payment are as stated on page xiv.

b) Prepare a credit note for New Tech Office Services Bureau on 13 April 199- for the filing boxes damaged in transit in Question 4.

c) Prepare a statement to be sent to New Tech Office Services Bureau on 30 April 199- requesting payment for the goods supplied.

d) Explain what advantages would be gained by using a computer to produce the documents in a, b and c and to record the accounts.

6   You are employed at Dobson Enterprises (Case Study 3). Mr Brian Dobson has asked you to write to Office Products Ltd for a quotation giving their best terms

for supplying an executive chair 530 mm×460 mm×470 mm with an adjustable tilt mechanism (colour: paprika).

7   You are employed at Office Products Ltd (Case Study 2). Reply to the letter of inquiry in Question 6 offering to supply the executive chair, as requested, Model Charisma, Cat No 23478. Price: £372 excluding VAT. Terms as given on page xx. Delivery: 3—4 weeks from receipt of order.

In-tray exercises

8   You are employed by Mr Brian Dobson, Manager of 'The Secretairs' (Case Study 3). Prepare an order for the calculator requested by Mr Dobson (see below) and, when the invoice arrives, check it and if it is correct make out a cheque to the supplier for Mr Dobson's signature. If, for any reason, the invoice (page 163) is unacceptable, return it to the supplier with a letter of explanation.

Jane

Please order a Casio 10-digit desktop calculator with 58 mm printer, which I have seen advertised by Office Products Ltd — Cat No 18923
        Price £54-70 plus VAT
They agreed to allow us a trade discount.*
                        BD

Atkins — The Stationers

INVOICE

No **1826**

From: **OFFICE PRODUCTS LTD**

Parkston Industrial Estate, Derby Road, Liverpool LL19 2SP

Tel: 0151-203 4116   Fax: 0151-321 9426

VAT Registration No 159 6423 72   Date: 10 June 199—

To:

> Mr Brian Dobson
> 172 Albemarle Street
> Mayfair
> London W1 2AX

Terms: Net cash within one month after delivery
       Postage free

Completion of Order No 29   dated 4 June 199—

Quantity	Description	Cat No	Price each £	Cost £	VAT rate %	VAT amount £
1	Casio 10-digit Calculator	18923	54.70	54.70		
	Less 10% trade discount			5.47		
				49.23	17½	8.61
	Add VAT			8.61		
				57.84		

Delivered on: 9.6.9—
           by: Post

9   This task is based at Pinder and Moore (see Case Study 4).

   a) Using the mail order price list for children's clothes (page 165) respond to the letter from Mrs Leaf (page 166) by completing the invoice.
   Calculate the total.
   Work out her discount of 12.5% if she pays the full amount before the end of the month. Total her bill.

   b) Explain the difference between a cash discount and a trade discount.
   (*PEI OP2*)

PINDER & MOORE

Children's Clothing Manufacturers

**45 The Strand
BRISTOL**

Tel/Telex No Bristol 37960
Fax No 24786

INVOICE/DESPATCH NOTE NO   54619   Date:

To:

Agents No:

Catalogue No	Description	No	Size	Price

Total price of goods _____

Less Agent's Discount of .... _____

TOTAL INVOICE PRICE _____

Terms: 30 days from Invoice Date

BACK TO SCHOOL

PRICE LIST

BOYS

	Catalogue No	Sizes (inches)	Price
Shirts (long sleeves)	27114	43/46	7.99 pack of two
		48/51, 53/55	8.99 pack of two
Shirt (long sleeves)	27115	43/46, 48/51	6.99 each
Trousers (polyester)	28444	23/24	7.99
		25/26/27/28	8.99
		29/30	11.99
V-neck Jumpers (plain knit)	28449	43/46	4.99
		53/55	5.99
		58/60	7.99
V-neck Cable Sweater	29771	43/46	11.99
		48/51, 53/55	12.99
		58/60, 62/64	15.99

GIRLS

Skirts (straight)	34444	48, 51, 53	8.99
		55, 58, 60	11.99
Skirts (pleated)	34721	48, 51, 53	7.99
		55, 58, 60	9.99
Blouses (long sleeves)	36671	39/41, 43/46	7.99 pack of two
		48/51, 53/55	8.99 pack of two
Blouses (long sleeves)	36672	39/41, 43/46	6.99
		48/51, 53/55	7.99
Cardigan long-line	34660	39/41, 43/46	10.99
		48/51, 53/55	11.99
		62/64, 67/69	14.99

Colours: Red, Royal Blue, Navy, Bottle Green, Grey.
             Shirts and Blouses are available in White, Pale Blue and Light Grey only.

Measurements: Order by height only except for boys' trousers which are in waist
                  measurements. See back of your catalogue for full details of sizing.

Agents No: 071- 345769

49 Fare Street
Midsomer Norton
Avon
BA2 467

Pinder & Moore
45 The Strand
Bristol

Dear Sirs

I would like to order the following children's clothes from your 'Back to School' leaflet for my customers.

BOYS:- 3 pairs of trousers cat no. 28444 sizes 23/24 } Grey
    1 pair "   "   " "   "   sizes 29/30)
    Pack of 2 shirts cat no.27114 size 53/55 - pale blue
    1 V-neck jumper " " 28449 "   53/55 - Navy
    " "   "   "   "   "   "   "   58/60 - Navy

GIRLS :- 1 pleated skirt cat no 34721 size 53 - Grey
    1 straight "   " " 34444 "   48 - Grey
    1 "   "   " " . "   " 60 - Grey
    3 packs of 2 blouses cat no.36671 size 41 - white
    1 long-line cardigan " " 34660 " 41 - Navy

Would you please also send me some order forms for future use as I have run out.

Yours faithfully

R Leaf (Mrs)

3.3 Pay and contracts of employment

Pay and contracts of employment are of great importance to all employees, but in particular this unit will help secretarial students preparing for the LCCI Private Secretary's Certificate examination to meet the requirements of the syllabus, ie to show a comprehensive knowledge and understanding of wages systems and procedures; PAYE income tax and principles of Social Security; and the principal provisions of current employment legislation.

Net pay, ie the amount you receive in your pay packet, is calculated as shown in Fig 3.16.

Note: The reference numbers refer to the items in the pay advice slip given in Fig 3.17.

The pay advice slip (Fig 3.17) informs employees of their pay entitlement and the adjustments which have been made for additions (overtime, bonus etc) and deductions (statutory and voluntary).

Statutory deductions

The employer is required by law to make these deductions from the pay of all employees, where applicable:

1 Income tax
2 National Insurance } variable deductions

Voluntary deductions

These deductions are not compulsory and are made only with the consent of the employee. They are fixed deductions and may include contributions to a social fund; national savings; holiday savings and a benevolent fund.

A variable deduction is one which must be calculated separately on each pay day and may vary according to the amount of gross pay received, whereas the fixed deductions remain the same and can be printed in advance on the pay documents, ie the payroll, the employee's pay record and the pay slip.

Calculating basic pay

Basic pay may be a fixed rate, such as an annual salary divided by 12

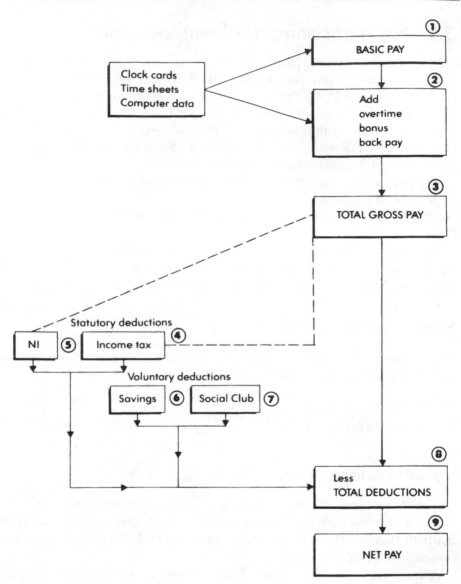

Fig 3.16 How net pay is calculated

for monthly payments or 52 for weekly payments, or it can be a variable rate calculated from clock cards, time sheets or computer data.

Modern time-recording systems not only record the time staff arrive and leave work but with the aid of a computer automatically calculate their wages. Each employee uses a personalised plastic key card to register attendance in a special terminal and this is fed directly into a

PAY ADVICE

Name		Works No
KAREN BROWN		120

Week no	Date	Code No
1	12 04.–	348L

		£
① Earnings: basic		160.00
	overtime	20.00
	bonus	--
②	back pay	–
	other	–
③ Total Gross Pay		180.00

Less deductions:		£
④	Income tax	25.11
⑤	National Ins.	13.49
⑥	Savings	10.00
⑦	Social Club	2.50
⑧ Total deductions		51.10
⑨ NET PAYMENT		128.90

Fig 3.17   Pay advice slip

computer system to provide such information as hours worked, staff attendance, lateness, overtime, etc. The system provides management and staff with a visual display of hours worked together with a printout of staff time data.

Pay as you earn (PAYE)

PAYE is the method used for deducting income tax from wages and salaries received from employment. The employees, under this system, pay their income tax as they earn their money. PAYE is applied to all who are employed, irrespective of age, and who receive an earned income which exceeds the allowable deductions, including personal reliefs.

The advantages of the scheme to the state are that taxes are collected regularly each week or month by employers from all their employees, thus relieving the Inland Revenue authorities of the task of collecting the money from the individuals. The employer sends a bulk cheque to the Collector of Taxes once a month. The state is also assured of receiving all income tax due, and under this system bad debts are unlikely to occur.

The employees benefit because the amount of tax they pay is related to their actual earnings and the weekly or monthly deduction of tax is adjusted to meet any variation in such earnings; they do not have the trouble of sending their contributions along to the Collector of Taxes, as tax amounts are deducted from their weekly or monthly pay packet.

The amount of tax to be deducted by the employer each pay day depends upon:

1 the employee's code number — listed on their tax deduction card, it represents their income tax allowances

2 their total gross pay since the beginning of the tax year*

3 total tax deducted on previous pay days in the current tax year.

Procedure for calculating and recording income tax and National Insurance contributions

The amounts of tax and National Insurance contributions to be paid on an employee's earnings are recorded on a deductions working sheet, known as Form P11 (see Fig 3.18 on pages 172 and 173). The procedure for calculating and recording these amounts is as follows:

1 Calculate the total amount of gross pay due to the employee and enter it in column 1a. (This is the sum on which contributions are based.)

2 Contributions may be calculated by using the contribution tables supplied by the Department of Social Security or by applying the appropriate percentage. The total of the employee's and employer's contribution calculated on the sum in 1 is entered in column 1b.

*Tax year runs from 6 April to 5 April.

3 Enter the employee's contribution in column 1c.

4 Columns 1d, 1e, 1f, 1g and 1h are used only for 'contracted out' employees, statutory sick pay and statutory maternity pay.

5 Enter gross pay in column 2.

6 Add the amount in column 2 to the total of all previous payments made to the employee since 6 April and enter the new total in column 3.

7 Calculate the amount of free pay to which the employee is entitled according to their code number and enter this in column 4. Reference is made to Table A (Pay Adjustment Table) in the tax tables.

8 Subtract the free pay in column 4 from the total pay to date in column 3 to arrive at the amount of taxable pay, which is entered in column 5.

9 Calculate the total tax due to date by reference to the amount of taxable pay in Taxable Pay Tables and enter this sum in column 6.

10 Subtract the amount of tax already deducted from the total tax due to date in column 6, to arrive at the amount to be deducted from the employee's gross pay on the pay day in question, and enter it in column 7. Sometimes, for example if the employee has worked a short week, the figure of total tax shown by the tax tables may be less than the tax already deducted; in that case the wages clerk must refund the difference to the employee instead of making a deduction and must enter the amount of refund in column 7 with the initial 'R'

Deductions working sheets

Each employee's deductions working sheet must show the code number by reference to which tax is calculated. If there is an amendment to the code number, the new number, together with the week or month in which it applies, should be entered in the space provided (see Fig. 3.18). The completed sheets have to be retained by the employer for at least three years after the end of the year to which they relate.

Employees starting and leaving

When an employee starts work for the first time, the employer deducts income tax under code BR, ie at the basic rate with no tax free allowances. The employee is required to complete a coding claim form P46 and send it to the tax office to inform them of other income and allowances. As soon as the employer receives the notice of coding

Deductions Working Sheet P11   Year to 5 April 19 ___

Employer's name	
OFFICE PRODUCTS LTD	Complete only for occupational pension schemes newly contracted-out since 1 January 1986. Scheme contracted-out number
Tax District and reference	
823 C/R B418 26 19B	**S** | **4** | | | | | |

National Insurance contributions*

For employer's use	Earnings on which employee's contributions payable 1a	Total of employee's and employer's contributions payable 1b	Employee's contributions payable 1c	Earnings on which employee's contributions at contracted-out rate payable included in column 1a 1d	Employee's contributions at contracted-out rate included in column 1c 1e	Statutory Sick Pay in the week or month included in column 2 1f	Statutory Sick Pay recovered. Only complete this column if you are claiming Small Employer's Relief 1g	Statutory Maternity Pay in the week or month included in column 2 1h	Month no	Week no
	£	£	£	£	£	£	£	£	6 April to 5 May **1**	1
	180	27 21	13 49							2
	180	27 21	13 49							3
	200	35 94	13 49							4
	200	35 94	13 49						6 May to 5 June **2**	5
	200	35 94	13 49							6
										7
										8
									6 June to 5 July **3**	9
										10
										11
										12
										13
									6 July to 5 Aug **4**	14
										15
										16
										17
									6 Aug to 5 Sept **5**	18
										19
										20
										21
									6 Sept to 5 Oct **6**	22
										23
										24
										25
										26
									6 Oct to 5 Nov **7**	27
										28
										29
										30
	Total c/fwd	Total c/fwd	Total c/fwd	Total c/fwd	Total c/fwd	Total c/fwd	Total c/fwd	Total c/fwd		

P11(1994)

Fig 3.18   Deductions working sheet Crown copyright, reproduced with the permission of the Controller of HMSO

Employee's surname *in CAPITALS*		First two forenames			
BROWN		KAREN			
National Insurance no.		Date of birth *in figures*	Works no. etc		Date of leaving *in figures*
		Day Month Year			Day Month Year
KT 34 26 31 B		18 09 75	120		

Tax code †	Amended code†	354L		
348L	Wk/Mth in which applied	5		

PAYE Income Tax

Pay in the week or month including Statutory Sick Pay/Statutory Maternity Pay 2	Total pay to date 3	Total free pay to date (Table A) 4a	Total 'additional pay' to date (Table A) *K codes only* 4b	Total taxable pay to date i.e. column 3 *minus* column 4a *or* column 3 *plus* column 4b 5	Total tax due to date as shown by Taxable Pay Tables 6	Tax due at end of current period Mark refunds 'R' *K codes only* 6a	Regulatory limit i.e. 50% of column 2 entry *K codes only* 6b	Tax deducted or refunded in the week or month Mark refunds 'R' 7	Tax not deducted owing to the Regulatory limit *K codes only* 8	For employer's use
£	£	£	£	£	£	£	£	£	£	
180 00	180 00	67 10		112 90	25 11			25 11		
180 00	360 00	134 20		225 80	50 48			25 37		
200 00	560 00	201 30		358 70	80 84			30 36		
200 00	760 00	268 40		491 60	111 21			30 37		
200 00	960 00	341 25		618 75	140 07			28 86		

* You must enter the NI contribution table letter overleaf beside the NI totals box - *see the note shown there.*

† If amended cross out previous code.

Ø If any week/month the amount in column 4a is more than the amount in column 3, leave column 5 blank.

Fig 3.18 Continued

back from the tax office, the wages clerk will make any adjustments for tax overpaid or underpaid.

When an employee leaves for whom the employer holds a deductions working sheet, a certificate on form P45 'Particulars of Employee Leaving' must be prepared, as described below.

Form P45

Parts 2 and 3 of the completed form P45 must be handed to employees when they leave, and Part 1 must be sent to the tax office immediately.

The employee should not separate the two parts. As soon as they begin their next employment they must give both parts of the form to their new employer so that the correct deductions of tax may be continued. The new employer should keep Part 2 and detach Part 3 and send it to the tax office.

If a new employee does not produce form P45, it may be because they have lost it, or because they have not been in any previous employment, or because they object to disclosing the figures to their new employer. In any such case, if the period of employment is for more than one week the employer should send form P46 at once to the tax office and prepare a deductions working sheet. Tax should then be deducted in accordance with the BR code specified for emergency use until further directions are received from the tax office.

Errors in deducting or refunding tax

It is very important that the entries on the deductions working sheets are made correctly, and a check of the additions and subtractions on the sheets is essential. If the employer finds, during the course of the year, that an error has been made in deducting tax in an earlier week or month of the year, the matter should be put right in the week or month in which the error is discovered.

When the payment made in a week was wrongly recorded, a line should be drawn through the original figure of pay in the week (but so that it can still be read) and the correct figure inserted. All other original entries should not be altered or erased but a mark should be made against them to indicate that the error has been discovered and put right in the later week.

Employer's Guide

A comprehensive *Employer's Guide* and a series of Guide Cards to PAYE are prepared by the Board of Inland Revenue and should be referred to when queries arise in connection with PAYE procedure.

The secretary and wages clerk should note all changes brought about by the Chancellor of the Exchequer's Budget speech proposals each year. Circulars are sent out advising taxpayers of the changes as they are made.

National Insurance

The National Insurance Scheme provides cash benefits in return for regular weekly or monthly contributions for unemployment; sickness, attendance allowance and invalidity; National Health Service benefits; industrial injuries disablement; maternity; children; guardian allowances; family credit and income support; one-parent benefits; widowhood; housing and council tax benefits; and retirement. It is quite separate from the National Health Service, which provides medical attention and treatment for everybody, whether they are insured or not.

Employees who pay into occupational pension or superannuation schemes which meet specific requirements can be 'contracted out' and pay lower contributions.

National Insurance contributions for employees are related to their earnings and are collected along with income tax under the PAYE procedure. Both the employee and the employer contribute to the scheme.

Employee's contributions are either:

a standard rate payable by most employees or

b reduced rate payable by certain married women and widows.

Employer's contributions are at the same rate regardless of whether the employee is liable to pay at the standard or reduced rate.

Liability for the contributions of both employers and employees is limited by upper and lower earnings limits. Where earnings do not reach the lower limit there is no liability for contributions from either employee or employer. The contribution rates and the upper and lower earnings limits are reviewed each year and the figures applicable to the next year are fixed by legislation. There is liability for contributions on any payment of earnings made to an employee from the date on which they reach the minimum school-leaving age, even though they may be still at school, and irrespective of whether the pay was earned before or after that date.

National Insurance contributions are always calculated on gross pay before all deductions are made. Normally this will be the same as the amount of pay entered on the deductions working sheet for income tax purposes. The employer is responsible for payment of both the employee's and the employer's contributions, but is entitled to deduct the employee's contribution from the payment of earnings on which that contribution has been calculated.

National Insurance numbers

The Department of Social Security allocates National Insurance numbers to all contributors to enable contributions to be correctly recorded on their accounts. Generally, young people will have a National Insurance number allocated to them shortly before they reach school-leaving age and will be given a National Insurance number card. Any person who has not been given a number must, when first becoming liable for National Insurance contributions apply to the Department of Social Security or to the local careers office if under 18. A new employee who is changing jobs will normally produce a form P45 on which their National Insurance number should have been entered by their previous employer.

Employer's guides

The local office of the Department of Social Security will give advice on all matters connected with National Insurance and the statutory sick pay and maternity pay schemes. Further details can be found in the employer's guides which are issued for each of these schemes.

Itemised pay statements

Under the Employment Protection (Consolidation) Act 1978 employees working between 8 and 16 hours a week have the right to be given itemised pay statements by their employers except in firms with fewer than 20 employees, where they have to complete a five-year qualifying period of continuous service. The pay statements must specify:

- the gross amount of pay
- the amounts of any fixed deductions and the purposes for which they are made
- the amounts of any variable deductions and the purposes for which they are made

- the net amount of pay and, where different parts of the net amount are paid in different ways, the amount and method of payment of each part-payment.

Contracts of employment

A contract of employment exists as soon as an employee proves his or her acceptance of an employer's terms and conditions of employment by starting work. Most larger firms provide a full written contract of employment but there is no statutory requirement for this to be done. However, under the Employment Protection (Consolidation) Act 1978, as amended by the Trade Union Reform and Employment Rights Act 1993, an employee must be given a written statement containing the main terms of employment within two months of starting work. This rule applies to employees working for at least eight hours a week in employment which lasts for one month or more.

The statement should contain the following points:

1 The names of the employer and employee.

2 The date employment began and whether any previous employment counts as part of the employee's continuous period of employment.

3 The remuneration and the intervals at which it is paid.

4 The hours of work, including a definition of normal working hours.

5 Details relating to holiday entitlement and holiday pay.

6 Provisions for sick pay and entitlement to sick leave.

7 Details of pensions and pension schemes and whether or not a pension's contracting out certificate is in force.

8 The length of notice of termination of employment which both the employer and employee must give.

9 The title of the job or a brief job description

10 For temporary posts, the period for which the employment is expected to continue or, if it is for a fixed term, the date when it is to end.

11 The place of work or, if the employee is required to work in more than one location, an indication of this and of the employer's address.

12 Details of the existence of any relevant collective agreements which directly affect the terms and conditions of the employee's employment.

13 Details of the employer's disciplinary and grievance procedures.

Whenever a change is made to any of the items included in a written contract of employment, employees are entitled to be given individual written notification as soon as possible and in any event within one month.

More detailed information is given in the Education and Employment Department's pamphlet *Written Statement of Employment Particulars.*

Trade Union Reform and Employment Rights Act 1993

This Act introduced several new provisions in employment rights. It

- Increases the rights of trade union members in relation to election and other ballots and gives them new rights concerning the conduct of their union's financial affairs and the deduction of union subscriptions from their wages.

- Requires postal balloting before official industrial action and gives employers additional protection against precipitate industrial action.

- Introduces a new Citizen's Right to enable individuals to bring proceedings to halt unlawful organisation of industrial action.

- Gives a minimum entitlement of 14 weeks' maternity leave for pregnant employees and protection against dismissal on maternity-related grounds.

- Gives employees new protection against being dismissed for asserting a statutory employment right.

- Introduces further improvements to other rights for employees including the right to written particulars of employment and to an itemised pay statement.

- Makes amendments to the constitution and jurisdiction of industrial tribunals.

More detailed information is given in the Education and Employment Department's *Guide to the Trade Union Reform and Employment Rights Act 1993.*

Termination of employment

The period of notice for termination of employment will normally be stated in the written contract or statement but, if not, there are statutory minimum requirements. An employee who has been employed for more than four weeks must give at least one week's notice. An employer must give at least one week's notice to an employee who has been employed for up to two years and one additional week for each year of employment above two years to a maximum of 12 weeks.

Questions

1 What is PAYE? Does it apply to everybody, and what are its advantages:

   a) to the state
   b) to the individual?

2 What is the purpose of PAYE, and to whom does it apply?

3 Under the PAYE system, on what does the amount of tax to be deducted depend?

4 Describe the action necessary in connection with PAYE when an employee changes his or her employment.

5 If an employee is absent through sickness, are they:

   a) entitled to any refund of income tax
   b) obliged to pay National Insurance contributions?

   What action should be taken, and by whom, in both these circumstances?

6 What action in relation to sickness benefit is necessary if you are away from your employment through illness?

7 You deal with the wages of the staff in your office. Two new employees start work. One has not been employed before, the other has come from another company. What documents would you expect them to bring with them and what action would you take with these documents?

8 Each year the company employs a number of 16 year–old secretarial trainees straight from school. As a representative of the Personnel Department, you have been asked to give a talk explaining the company's credit transfer system of salary payment, and the deductions which will be made. Make notes for your talk, in a format which will allow you to refer quickly to the points you wish to make. (See also Unit 8.2.) (LCCI PSC)

9 You started work four years ago when you were seventeen years old. During this time your employer has made the necessary deductions for National Insurance, superannuation contributions, and income tax from your wages. What benefits could you expect to receive in each of the following circumstances?

a) You are away from work for three weeks suffering from tonsillitis.

b) The firm for which you work closes down and you do not obtain other employment for two weeks.

10 a) What information would you expect to be given in a contract of employment?

b) How much notice should an employer give to terminate employment?

c) What deductions must be made, by law, from an employee's pay?

In-tray exercises

11   You are employed by the New Tech Office Services Bureau (Case Study 1).

Using current income tax and National Insurance tables, continue the entries on the tax deductions working sheet on pages 172–3 for weeks 6 to 10 as follows:

Week No	Gross pay	Code No
	£	
6	200	354L
7	200	354L
8	120	354L
9	200	354L
10	200	456H

12   You are employed by Office Products Ltd (Case Study 2).

Karen Brown asks you why she received less pay this week (week 2) in her pay packet (see pay slip on page 181) than she did last week (see Fig 3.17 on page 169) although her earnings were the same for both weeks. She also cannot understand why she has to pay National Insurance contributions each week. You are extremely busy today with a rushed job and cannot spend time with Karen to discuss this matter with her but you agree to spend some time tomorrow to answer her questions.

Prepare some brief notes for your discussion with her.

PAY ADVICE

Name	Works No
KAREN BROWN	120

Week no	Date	Code No
2	19.04.–	348L

		£
Earnings:	basic	160.00
	overtime	20.00
	bonus	–
	back pay	–
	other	–
Total Gross Pay		180.00

Less deductions:		£
	Income tax	25.37
	National Ins.	13.49
	Savings	10.00
	Social Club	2.50
Total deductions		51.36
NET PAYMENT		128.64

3.4 Reprography and paper handling

Reprography

The process of making copies or duplicates of documents for circulation is known as reprography. The principal methods of reproduction are:

- carbon paper and carbon-free paper, eg NCR
- duplicators
- copiers
- word processssors/computers.

Duplicators

Although there are still a few duplicators in use today, most organisations use high speed copiers capable of reproducing large quantities. .

The duplicating medium in the stencil process is ink which is fed through indentations made into a stencil and on to semi-absorbent paper.

The spirit process reproduces copies using an aniline dye which is transferred from the master to the copy paper by spirit.

In the offset-litho process, copies are reproduced in ink from a plate containing a 'greasy' litho image. The master, fitted round a plate cylinder, is dampened with water, which the greasy material refuses to accept, but which is retained by the non-greasy areas. The master also comes into contact with an inking roller, the ink being accepted by the greasy image area and repelled by the moistened areas. The image on the master, which has attracted the ink, is offset in negative form on to a rubber blanket which in turn is offset on to the copy paper in positive form.

Copiers

Duplicating and printing processes produce copies of documents, whereas copiers produce replicas of the originals. One of the great advantages of copying by machine is obtaining a number of good copies quickly and without the possibility of any keying errors being introduced.

Copiers range in size and performance from small desk-top copiers for personal use to high-capacity, heavy duty copiers for large-scale print operations and sophisticated colour reproduction.

At the top of the range are the 'intelligent' copiers which are capable of volume copying and accepting information directly from computers. The image of the original is converted into a digital electrical signal as the intermediate process instead of using a drum. This signal turns a laser on and off to reproduce the image, which can be processed, transmitted to other locations or stored for later recall. The machine is in two parts: a reader and a print unit, which work separately from one another, allowing one reader to be interfaced with up to three printers to produce 135 copies a minute.

Modern integrated digital copiers process information through a scanner which manipulates the data. They process, store, transmit, call up and edit information, as well as acting as printers for a computer and fax machine. Documents can now be created on personal computers and produced in hardcopy form at the press of a button, using remote laser printers.

The copier which is illustrated in Fig 3.19 is a high capacity copier designed for those who do a wide variety of copy jobs, make a large number of copies every month and work with many sizes of copies and originals.

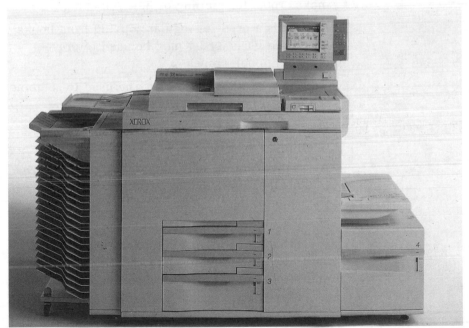

Fig 3.19   A high–capacity copier

The following factors should be considered when selecting a copier:

Price and method of purchase	Consider the benefits of outright purchase, leasing and rental schemes
Size	The quantity and nature of copying must be considered when determining the size of copier required
Speed	This ranges from 20 copies per minute to 135 per minute, although colour copiers are much slower
Document feed	This can be manual, semi-automatic or fully automatic
	Multi-page documents can be loaded and copied automatically, allowing for single copies to be taken from a stack of up to 100 documents without interrupting the copying flow
	A recirculating document feeder allows for copying double-sided originals
	Some machines are able to copy from bound documents without repositioning them for left- and right-hand pages, and a variable margin shift makes room for binding or hole punching
	If there is a need for regular copying from books, an angled glass feeder may be used to prevent damaging book spines
	An image overlay feature may be used to combine the images from two originals
Paper feed	Uses magazines, trays or cassettes with paper quantities ranging from 250 to 4000
	An automatic tray-switching device provides continuous long-run copying, because when one paper tray empties the machine automatically switches to another one
	A computer continuous stationery feeder automatically feeds fanfold stationery into the copier and prints the data out on separate A4 sheets
	A self-diagnostic facility senses the correct size of paper cassette to bring into operation when an original is placed on the platen

Paper size	Most copiers handle originals and copies of A3–A5 paper sizes but the range can extend to A2–A6
	It is possible to have a copier fitted with a document sensor which automatically measures each original and selects the appropriate enlargement or reduction to create uniform-size copies from mixed-size originals
Image editing	This includes: mask and trim push-button facilities for cutting out unwanted material; image shift for relocating parts of an original from one position to another; reversing out graphics or text, ie white on black instead of black on white
Reduction and enlargement	Different ratios of reduction and enlargement of images may be provided; these may be preset to provide reduction or enlargement from one standard paper size to another
Memory	The copier can be programmed to carry out routine tasks such as reduction, enlargement or collation; sets of programmed instructions may be stored in the memory so that they can be recalled at a later date by operating a pre-set key, or for storing images of originals
	A step-by-step fluorescent message display panel can guide the user through the copying process using a touch screen control panel
Finishing functions	Automatic collation to provide sets of documents ready for stapling or binding – if collating is a major requirement, consider how many bin sorters you need: these range from 10 to 40
	Automatic jogging
	Automatic folding
	Automatic stapling
	Automatic stitching/adhesive binding
Colour reproduction	Colour copiers are available using a range of different processes such as electrophotographic, digital, photographic/laser, thermal transfer and encapsulation using light-sensitive paper – the user must consider whether the extra cost of a colour copier is advantageous

	Colour highlighting of copies can be done in four different colours
Control of use	By issuing users with code numbers or charge cards, which are essential to activate the copier, the machine can record the number of copies made by each user
Maintenance	Toner/developer cartridges and drum cartridges can be replaced simply and cleanly
Multi-functions	Machines are now available which combine the functions of copying, printing and faxing (see Fig 3.20). It has the ability to fax images from books and magazines without copying them first
Overhead transparencies	Preparation of overhead transparencies by copying originals directly on to film instead of paper
Uses	Reproducing copies of printed documents, legal documents, insurance policies, statistical returns, diagrams and drawings, overhead transparencies, extracts from books and magazines, and incoming letters required for several departments, and printout copies required for filing

Guidelines for copying

A checklist of what you should know about your copier

- The warm-up procedure at the beginning of the day.
- How to insert copy paper.
- How to prepare originals for reproduction.
- How to insert the originals and set the machine up for copying.
- How to replace the toner cartridge.
- Techniques of image editing.
- Appropriate quality required in copies produced.
- Copyright restrictions (see page 189).
- The methods used for sorting, collating and binding copies.
- How to prepare overhead projector transparencies.
- The method used to control the use of the copier.
- Ways of ensuring economic use of the copier.
- Safety, security and confidentiality procedures.

Fig 3.20 A multi-functional copier, fax and printer

- How to plan and monitor work schedules to meet the deadlines set. The procedure for clearing paper jammed in the machine.
- The procedure for reporting faults and arranging for a mechanic to attend.

- Day-to-day maintenance in accordance with the operating manual.
- The closing-down procedure at the end of the day.

Desktop publishing

Desktop publishing (DTP) is the term used for a computer application which combines text and graphics in order to produce camera-ready copy, ie in final form ready for printing. It is a multi-functional process integrating the use of a scanner, a computer (with a hard disk), a laser printer and specially-designed software combining text creation, editing and graphics (see Fig. 3.21). A scanner is an electronic copying device for transferring images directly from source documents to the computer memory or screen, providing complete accuracy and reliability. These images can be enlarged, reduced or edited before being combined with the text.

Desktop publishing (Fig 3.22) is ideal for producing forms, letter headings, advertising copy, price lists and catalogues, brochures,

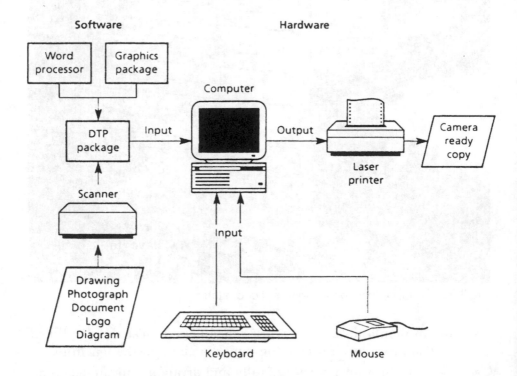

Fig 3.21 Desktop publishing diagram

Fig 3.22 Desktop publishing

bulletins, in-house journals, technical manuals, handouts, 35 mm slides and overhead projector transparencies. It can be used to advantage for:

- Producing high-quality printed documents combining text and graphics to enhance a company's reputation. This does, however, depend on the training and ability of the staff employed on the work.
- Providing a cheaper means of producing artwork, compared with typesetting, as well as reducing expenditure incurred in overruns.
- Producing more up-to-date documents and publications because of the easier access to in-house facilities.
- Editing disks of previous issues of price lists, catalogues, etc, to provide a simple and speedy means of updating them.
- Allowing users to create their own 'in-house' styles of text and graphic presentation.
- Providing a quick turnaround of printed material without having to rely on external printers.
- Reducing security risks as copy does not have to leave the premises.
- Storing and retrieving documents for use at a later date to avoid holding large stocks which would be costly and would occupy valuable office space.

Copyright law
Under the 'fair dealing' provisions of the Copyright, Designs and

Patents Act 1988 you are permitted to make one copy of an agreed maximum amount of any published material for the purposes of research, private study, criticism, or review, but you are not permitted to copy a substantial part of the work. In addition, for the purposes of review, sufficient acknowledgement must be made. In order to copy a substantial part of a work, ie more than a single chapter or article of a publication, or to copy for any purpose outside the 'fair dealing' provision, it is necessary for you first to obtain the permission of the copyright holder (usually the publisher or author) or you must have taken all reasonable steps to find out the name and address of the copyright holder and have been unsuccessful. You must make at least three attempts at regular (say one-monthly) intervals before you can be regarded as having made 'all reasonable attempts' to contact the copyright holder. If you do not succeed, you must indicate this in your publication or review in the form of an acknowledgement along the following lines:

'Unfortunately, I have been unable to trace the copyright holder(s) of the following material (*list material*) and would welcome any information which would enable me to do so.'

The main provisions of the Act and Regulations should be brought to the notice of staff using copying facilities.

Paper handling equipment

Binders
These are used for fastening multi-page documents and booklets. Several types are available but the most commonly used are spiral binders and flat comb binders. In the spiral method the pages are punched and a plastic spiral binder is threaded into the holes to hold the pages together. Flat comb binders are made up of two plastic strips which are placed on either side of the pages and heat-sealed to provide a permanent binding. (See Fig 3.23.)

Bursters
These machines cut or 'burst' sprocketed continuous stationery at the perforations into single sheets, neatly trimmed and ready for the post. They can handle a variety of forms of different sizes and thicknesses and stack them in strict sequential order. (See Fig 3.24.)

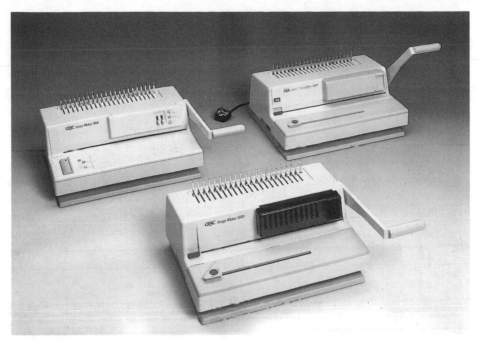

Fig 3.23 Plastic comb binders

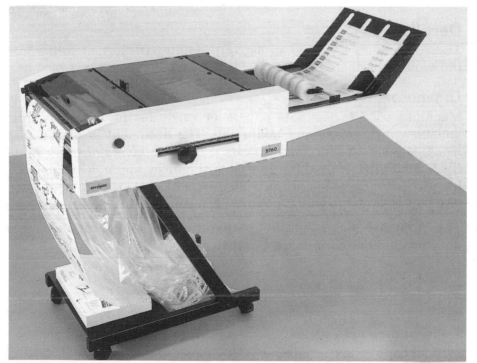

Fig 3.24 A burster

Fig 3.25 A decollator

Decollators

These machines are used to separate multi-part sets of forms into individual sheets and to dispose of the carbons. (See Fig 3.25.)

Laminators

Machines used to laminate papers or cards for protection against moisture, dirt, grease and tampering. The document is placed in a machine where a heat process seals it between layers of transparent film. Lamination is used for noticeboard notices, valuable documents, identity cards, sales literature, book or record dust jackets, menus and any papers or cards which require protection against wear and tear.

The principal stages in the preparation of circulars and other documents required in large quantities

Task	Equipment which may be used	See also page
1 Preparation of draft text	word processor	202
2 Final copy of text produced incorporating amendments*	word processor	202

3 Checking of final copy with draft copy		
4 Reproduction of the copies required	copier	182
5 Collation of papers into sets in the correct order	collator	54
6 Vibrate papers into alignment ready for stapling	jogger	54
7 Stapling	stapler	54
or		
Binding with a plastic comb or strip	binder	190
8 Addressing envelopes or labels	addressing equipment	47
9 Mailing	various	47

*Computerised typesetting may be used for formatting text into columns for the production of newspapers, magazines and books.

Questions

1 With the increased workload, Mr and Mrs Ashworth, partners of a small family printing business, are considering purchasing a new copier. The current copier has been in use for a long time and is quite basic in comparison to new models available. Mrs Ashworth has handed you the following note:

> I think we need some details on paper about new copiers. Can you put together a brief report? I need to know what sort of benefits, if any, we are likely to get from a large, fully-automated copier.

2 a) Explain in detail how you would obtain one copy of an article printed in a business journal.
  b) What restrictions, if any, are placed on making copies of published articles?

3 What considerations influence a company's choice of reprographic system?
  (*LCCI PSC*)

4 You have been made responsible for a new copier which is to be used by

personnel from other departments. Draft instructions, in the form in which they are to be displayed in the office, for the use and care of the copier.

5 You have been left the following note by Mrs Chandler:

> Liz,
>
> I keep receiving very convincing leaflets in the mail trying to persuade us to move over to Desk top Publishing – I really think the time has come to give it some serious thought.
>
> Since the offset litho machine now needs replacing, this seems the ideal time to investigate the possibility of replacing this with a high-quality copier and a Desk top Pub. (DTP) facility.
>
> Can you prepare a summary sheet for me to take to the meeting next week with the MD covering:
>
> (a) What's DTP? (I expect he'll ask me for a simple explanation!)
>
> (b) How we can use DTP for "in-house" printing, eg documents.
>
> (c) He's bound to ask for disadvantages. Are there any?

6 Comlon International plc, a fruit and vegetable wholesaler, is about to launch a staff newsletter for all employees within the UK and abroad.

a) What advantages could the launch of the newsletter bring to Comlon?

b) What items might such a newsletter contain?

c) How should the newsletter be produced and distributed effectively and economically? (*LCCI PSC*)

7 State the most appropriate equipment to use for each of the following tasks, giving reasons for your choice:

a) Completion of 30 form letters with a mixture of standard and variable details.

b) Immediate circulation of an incoming letter to be seen by four different departments.

c) Preparation of a notice of meeting and agenda for dispatch to 100 members of the Staff Association.

    d) Preparation of 50 photo-identity cards for use by staff.

    e) Preparation of a 10-page handout with product illustrations for a sales conference to be attended by 60 customers and agents.

8 Your company is planning a sales drive which will include a personalised mail shot to all customers drawing attention to the new products.

    a) Suggest the most appropriate way of producing a 3-page letter. Justify your suggestions.

    b) Describe how your supportive literature might be prepared.

    c) Select the 6 items that would be helpful to the mailroom in sending off this mailshot. (*PEI OP2*)

9 State with reasons the equipment you would use in the following situations.

    a) Production of many complex diagrams in a variety of sizes to be incorporated into reports.

    b) Protection of frequently used fact sheets.

    c) Safe keeping of petty cash.

    d) Facility to input copy into desktop publisher.

    e) The binding of a report with many pages. (*LCCI PSC*)

10 How would you deal with the following:

    a) the production of a standard letter to franchise holders selling vegetarian food

    b) the typing from brief notes of a highly confidential memo to go to the Company Secretary

    c) the distribution of a monthly magazine to Company Directors? (*LCCI PSC*)

In-tray exercise

11 The New Tech Office Services Bureau (Case Study 1) has decided to extend the firm's range of activities by investing in a modern colour copier and facilities for desktop publishing.

    You are required to prepare a draft leaflet advertising these new services. Explain what additional help the bureau can now provide for small companies and stress how important it is to use top quality, professionally-produced paperwork to influence their customers.

3.5 Information technology

Information technology embraces all aspects of integrated office systems for controlling the production and processing of information in text, data, image and voice. In the automated/electronic office, word processing and data processing systems are linked in an integrated information processing network. Computers, word processors, copiers, fax and telex terminals are linked to each other and to a central network controller to provide rapid exchanges of information without the need for paperwork. Office workers can have terminals which communicate with the terminals of other employees, customers, suppliers, banks, etc. Messages pass from one terminal to another and are held in memory banks for the storage and retrieval of records and correspondence, and electronic mail could make the mailroom, as we know it today, obsolete. The integrated network system within an organisation can also be linked to the national and international public telecommunications networks, as illustrated in Fig 3.26, to provide instant communication between the computers of different organisations.

Information technology through its use of microcomputers is having a big impact on the way offices function and consequently on the role of the office worker.

Computers

It is now common practice for office workers to have access to personal computers on their desks. This enables them to operate the keyboard to write their own letters and messages, gain access to records stored on the computer, make calculations using stored and input data, update the records with new data and use e-mail.

The physical parts of a computer, including the central processing unit and disk storage, visual display unit, keyboard and the printer, are known as *hardware*, whereas the programs which tell the hardware what to do are called the *software*.

In most cases the personal computer will be part of a wider network in which it is linked to a network controller or central file server where all data is stored, retrieved and updated. Messages may be sent from one terminal to another, held in memory and called up by the staff on their terminals. In this way filing can be transferred from the filing cabinet to the computer memory. When information from a file is needed, it is simply called up on a VDU and, if a paper record

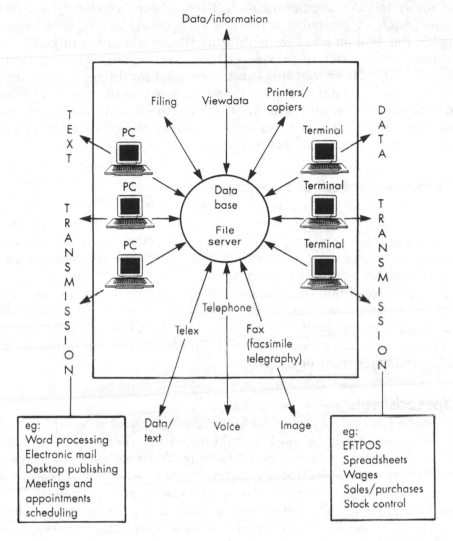

Fig 3.26 Information processing network

(known as a *hard copy*) is required, it is produced on a printer.

The file server may also be linked to external services, eg other computers, telex, the Internet, videotex or other commercial databases, in order to provide access to sources outside the organisation.

Databases

A computer system is made up of files and records as in a manual office system. A computer file is a collection of records for a particular topic, such as personnel staff records, whereas a computer record holds the data on one item within the file, eg a member of staff.

Information relating to several files may be brought together to form a database so that this can be accessed for different uses, such as manpower planning, wages and salaries, staff bonuses, sales commissions, cost analysis, etc. It allows the data to be sorted and selected in a variety of ways using different 'fields', eg staff names, departments, invoice numbers, job numbers.

Software applications packages

These are applications programs which are written for a particular function such as word processing; database (which may include sales, purchases and wages systems); spreadsheet; contact management; or management information system (including meetings and appointments scheduling). They are stored on the hard disk (see page 202) and loaded into the computer's memory each time they are used. There are many business software packages on the market which can be bought 'off the shelf'. They are of a general nature and conform to standard practice, although some packages are tailored to the needs of a particular trade or industry.

Spreadsheets

A spreadsheet program, which is in the form of a computerised analysis sheet, can be used to make rapid calculations to help with financial planning and decision-making. A spreadsheet displays a matrix of cells identified by columns and rows. The screen is a window through which any part of the matrix may be viewed. Data and formulae are entered to give a rapid means of forecasting and financial planning. For example, it can reveal the effects of an increase in wages or raw materials on the cost of finished products, profit margins, etc. Hard copy of the spreadsheet figures can be printed out at any stage. Spreadsheets are particularly useful if amendments have to be made quickly or there is a need for columns of figures to be updated regularly, as recalculations can be done automatically.

A computer screen is illustrated in Fig 3.27 showing a typical spreadsheet application. Note that it includes column headings (referred to as labels) with the different elements of the calculation; side or row labels for each year; and 'cells' of data within the chart, identified by the column letters and row numbers, eg G5.

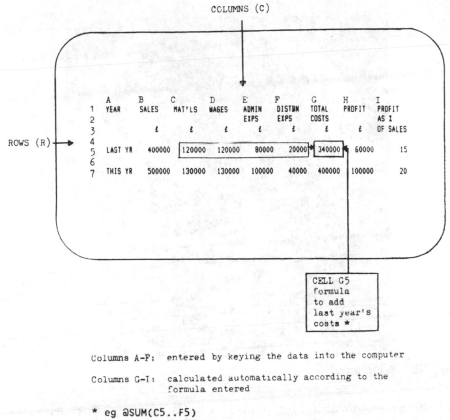

Columns A-F: entered by keying the data into the computer

Columns G-I: calculated automatically according to the
              formula entered

* eg @SUM(C5..F5)

Fig 3.27   Computer screen showing spreadsheet

Laptop computers (or notebooks)

It is common for business executives to make use of laptop computers, as illustrated in Fig 3.28, which they carry around with them and use in meetings in this country and abroad. This provides them with access to vast amounts of information, previously transferred from their office computer to the hard disk of a laptop computer. These portable laptops can be fitted with a modem to enable them to communicate with a head office network and read their e-mail or access data from different sources, including company databases and the Internet.

It is important for security reasons that networks are 'password' protected.

The Internet

The Internet, or the information superhighway as it is sometimes

Fig 3.28   A laptop computer

called, is a means of linking homes, schools, libraries, businesses, etc to a worldwide fibre-optics communications network. This huge online computer network service provides access to databases with vast sources of information and electronic mail (e-mail) between suppliers and customers. It is estimated that 40 million or more people are linked to the Internet and almost a third of UK businesses.

Any computer user can use the Internet Service by subscribing to a commercial online service or establishing a link via a local Internet access service provider. The commercial online services provide e-mail links to the Internet Service and to each other. Gateways to other Internet applications including the World Wide Web are offered in some cases. Calls are usually accessed with a local phone call and charges are made for hourly connect fees and each e-mail message distributed. If a local Internet access service is used, eg Netconect, the user accesses the Internet by a local phone call and pays a standard monthly fee. Companies also provide software for accessing the World Wide Web. It is now possible for any computer user to send e-mail via the Internet to almost anywhere in the world where there is a computer linked to the network or a telephone link.

Computer Video Conferencing

Computers can now be fitted with videoconferencing to allow for users to transmit images of themselves to other users equipped with the same facilities and to view the person they are communicating with on their own screen.

Speech Recognition

IBM's Voice Type Dictation System has been released and it is one of the first practical voice recognition systems to provide an alternative to the keyboard for inputting text and data by speech into a computer. It uses a large active vocabulary and sophisticated language models to analyse spoken words and turn them into text on a personal computer screen.

The voice type kit consists of a microphone headset, speakers, a small adaptor card and the software package.

Every new user has to begin by doing an enrolment session which involves reading 150 sentences in order to create a personalised voice model. The software uses these voice samples it has recorded to build up the new user's personal voice print. It is necessary for the person dictating to use discrete speech with a minimal pause between words but it is claimed that average users can dictate from 70 to 100 words a minute.

The program has a 32000 word vocabulary, and up to 2000 additional words of the user's choice can be added. Correction of words, such as previously unused proper names or misrecognised words, is made easy by the voice-play back facility which allows the user to hear what was dictated. Text can be transferred from the dictation window to a word processor or any OS/2 Windows or DOS program that supports the adaptor card.

Speech recognition is still in its early stages of development and it is too early to assess its effect on traditional methods of text processing. Its introduction will no doubt have far-reaching implications but keyboards are nevertheless likely to be the normal method of input for most applications in the foreseeable future. It is suggested that with the Voice Type Dictation System secretaries will have more time to devote to the more rewarding aspects of their jobs and that they will wish to use it to produce their own material and correct their manager's reports.

Computer applications

Computers are capable of handling and manipulating data for a wide range of office procedures. In a sales ledger application, for example, the computer is able to compare the amounts of invoices with the credit limit of customers. In stock control, comparisons of stock levels can be made with predetermined minimum figures, automatically drawing attention to the items which require reordering.

Other typical computer applications include payroll, bought ledger, production planning, costing and budgetary control, sales forecasting, market research and cash flow.

Desktop publishing
See page 188.

Word processing

Word processing has been developed from typewriting, using computer technology to automate many of the procedures involved in the production of messages, letters, reports, forms, lists, etc. As a result, the operator is freed from time-consuming and repetitive tasks. There are a variety of word processing software program disks to run on most computers.

Word processing equipment can be arranged, or configured, in a variety of ways depending on whether it is a single unit or part of a network linking several workstations. The screens usually display either a full page or half a page of text. The text can be stored on hard disks (a compact, high-capacity hard disk unit, permanently in the computer) or floppy disks (flexible magnetic disks available in different sizes). Most word processors currently use 3.5" floppy disks (capable of storing the text for 400 A4 pages).

Word processing software
Word processing software programs are normally capable of:

- Editing text on the screen by inserting new material and deleting unwanted material and using justified or ragged margins.
- Underscoring, emboldening and centring text automatically.
- Moving words, sentences, paragraphs and columns to other parts of the page.
- Numbering paragraphs and pages automatically.
- Aligning decimals automatically in columns and tabulations.
- Formatting columns, eg newspaper or parallel style columns.
- Using different font styles and sizes with laser printers to produce high-quality work.

- Incorporating graphics (drawings and graphs) with text.
- Producing a composite document from previously stored standard paragraphs.
- Preparing mailing lists, eg merging names and addresses with a circular letter and printing labels.
- Sorting text alphabetically and numerically.
- Producing an index and table of contents automatically.
- Printing one page of a document while the operator is typing the next.
- Verifying the spelling of words – a program will check words and highlight any that do not comply with a dictionary of commonly-used words. Some systems will check that words are correct in context and also suggest where phrases may be stated more concisely.
- Adapting the keyboard for typing in a foreign language.
- Storing standard formats in templates or style sheets, ie forms, report layouts, cv's, agenda.
- Producing desktop publishing applications.
- Producing tables for ruled documents.

Word processing applications

Common applications for word processors include:

a automatic typing of standard or form letters merged with a mailing list to provide top copies of letters to selected names and addresses

b updating price lists, telephone directories, mailing lists, parts lists, etc, where amendments can be inserted without retyping all of the matter

c typing the drafts of reports, minutes, articles, etc. Once the draft has been typed, amendments can be made and the machine automatically reformats the pages without any further retyping and checking.

Choosing a computer

Key factors when considering the purchase of a computer are:

- Analyse the nature and quantity of work to be undertaken, bearing in mind both current and future needs. This will normally be incorporated in a feasibility study. It is advisable to budget for as much memory capacity as possible.

- Decide which configuration is required, such as:

  a stand-alone (a single self-contained computer)
  b shared resource (two or more workstations sharing the same printer and possibly storage devices)
  c local area network (for connecting computers and telecommunications in one network)
  d wide area network, ie the Internet.

- Consider the need for compatibility with equipment already in use.

- Bear in mind the costs involved in:

  a hardware (the physical parts of the computer)
  b software (the programs and operating manuals)
  c furniture
  d accommodation
  e materials (stationery, disks, ribbons, toner, etc)
  f training of users and authors and redeployment of staff
  g maintenance of equipment and software packages.

- Arrange for demonstrations of various makes and seek advice from other users of the equipment.

- Consider the changes in office procedures which must be made.

- Consult and keep staff informed of your proposals.

- Consider the advantages and disadvantages of purchasing equipment outright, leasing and rental schemes – bearing in mind obsolescence and the rapid changes in technology.

- Consider the range of equipment on offer:

1 Microcomputers

Microcomputers have 4, 8 or 16 Megabytes (Mb) of Random Access Memory (RAM). A minimum of 4 Mb is required when working with Windows but 8 Mb will make it operate at a faster rate.

2 Backing storage

All microcomputers are now fitted with a hard disk. It is advisable to buy one with a capacity at least twice the size of your estimated needs.

Application programs are supplied on floppy disks or on CD-ROM and can only be run on a hard disk. A CD-ROM drive provides the opportunity to access research material, eg past copies of *The Times*, encyclopaedias, computer-based training programmes, etc.

3 Tape drive

A tape drive is used to make a back-up copy of the hard disk at the end of every working session. This is an important security technique.

4 Printer

The choice of printer determines the quality of print:

- Dot-matrix printers with 9, 18 or 24 pins are still in use for impact printing of multi-part forms, but the quality is not of a high standard.

- Ink-jet printers print line by line at 150 to 270 characters per second.

- Laser printers print the whole page at once with a range of different type-faces. High quality work is produced at a speed of between 6 and 12 A4 pages per minute.

5 Software

Microcomputers normally have MS-DOS and Windows loaded on to the hard disk. The nature of the work to be undertaken will determine the number and type of software packages needed, but as a general rule you will need to select an integrated software package which includes wordprocessing, database, spreadsheets, e-mail and sometimes a presentation package and a diary. If your work is mainly involved in displaying documents, forms, brochures, etc, you will need a desktop publishing package, and if you require financial and accounting applications, an accounting package will be needed.

Maintenance and care of equipment

Guidelines for the day-to-day care and maintenance of electronic equipment:

1 Keep a copy of the operating manual with the machine and follow the instructions given for regular cleaning.

2 Do not smoke, drink or eat when operating the equipment.

3 If the machine has to be moved, be sure to disconnect it from the electrical supply.
   Note: It may be necessary to 'park' the hard disk before moving the machine.

4 Keep a log record of any intermittent faults which occur and the dates and times when maintenance engineers call to attend to the equipment.

5 Have access to a maintenance service for remedying faults, but before calling in a mechanic for a breakdown CHECK:

    a that the power supply is on

    b that fuses in the equipment are working

    c that there are no faults in the connecting cables and plugs

    d the operating manual 'trouble shooting' for useful tips on tracing the fault.

If, after taking these steps, there is still a fault with the equipment, call for the services of a maintenance engineer.

Care of floppy disks

Do

- Keep floppy disks in their wallets, when not in use, to protect them from dust
- Return disks to their wallets after use and store them upright in the disk box supplied
- Label each disk with a description of its contents
- Insert disks carefully into the disk drive, without forcing them, to avoid damage
- As a safeguard against damage or loss, keep a back-up (duplicate) of any disk containing important data, eg all master program disks should be copied and the masters stored in a secure place
- Use a write protect tag on a system disk to prevent data from being added to it

Do not

- Bend, fold or scratch disks
- Touch the exposed portion of a disk
- Write directly on to the disk wallet
- Store disks near a hot radiator, fire or heat of the sun
- Use disks which have not been checked for viruses
- Remove disks when the drive light is on
- Leave disks around on the top of a screen, printer, telephone and other electronic equipment (sources of magnetism) which could corrupt them

Questions

1 An induction conference for new secretarial staff, from all the hotels in the group, is to be held in London next month at the company's main hotel, the Thames Garden Hotel. Miss Stephenson (your employer) particularly wants to ensure that new staff make maximum use of the word processing equipment installed in the hotels. She intends to give a talk on this theme and has asked you to outline the main uses of the word processing equipment in the hotels and how this equipment could be used to enhance the facilities offered for conferences.

2 You are employed as secretary to Mr Brian Webb, Purchasing Manager (Fruit) of Comlon International plc (a food wholesaling business). New, integrated word processing/ spreadsheet/database packages have just been installed on your own and Mr Webb's microcomputers.

   a) How would you expect to make use of the spreadsheet and database elements of the package?
   b) In which ways would you expect Mr Webb to make use of the word processing element of the package? (LCCI PSC)

3 You are employed as secretary to Mr John Whitmore, Personnel and Training Director of Comlon International plc (publishing group). John Whitmore has recently been supplied with a portable personal computer.

   a) What would you expect to be the major uses of the portable personal computer?
   b) How is its use likely to affect the nature of your work over the next 12 months? (LCCI PSC)

4 You are employed by Comlon International plc, manufacturers of fashion goods. You have overheard the marketing executives refer frequently to spreadsheets and graphics.

   a) State what you understand by the terms 'spreadsheets' and 'graphics'.
   b) Describe uses of a spreadsheet and of graphics which would be helpful to the efficient working of Comlon. (LCCI PSC)

5 You work for Mr Paul Wood, Operations Director (Cleansing and Security Services) at Comlon International plc.

   a) Comlon has networked computers. Briefly describe the function of the following software packages:

   i database
   ii spreadsheet
   iii diary
   iv word processing
   v desktop publishing

b) Describe how Comlon could make use of two of these packages. (*LCCI PSC*)

6 Your Office Manager has asked you to attend a business equipment exhibition and examine some of the latest machinery and systems. Prepare a report of your visit, giving details of four items of recent development.

7 Discuss the ways in which the automation of offices today is affecting secretarial staff. (*LCCI PSC*)

8 You have been asked to make arrangements for a one-day staff development programme for secretarial staff at Head Office to update them on word processing software. Outline:

a) arrangements
b) the programme
c) the equipment required. (*LCCI PSC*)

9 What use would a spreadsheet program be for the comparison of sales over specified periods? Describe how this information could be presented in an easily read format. (*LCCI PSC*)

10 What are the advantages of computerised speech recognition? How will it affect the work of secretaries?

In-tray exercise

11 You are employed by Mr Brian Dobson, Manager of 'The Secretairs' (Case Study 3). Reply to the following message which Mr Dobson left on the dictating machine for your attention and refer to In-tray exercise 11 (page 245).

I am pleased to see that you have made a start with the arrangements for next year's concert tour and that you have booked hotel accommodation for the first concert — just another 14 hotels to be booked! It's going to take you quite a time to type all those letters. Would a word processor speed up this task? I had been thinking that we might get a microcomputer for the accounts. Could the same machine do word processing? I think it would also be very useful if we could computerise the year planner and then the members of the group could be given updated copies whenever changes occur. Is this a possibility? Do you think we can justify the cost of buying a computer? What else could it do for us? Are there any 'hidden' costs apart from the cost of the machine itself? Please give me your ideas on this proposal and suggest what steps we should take to select a suitable machine.

Maintaining a healthy, safe and effective working environment

4.1 Health and safety in the office

To maintain healthy and safe conditions in the office, employees are required to:

- keep their immediate work area (including equipment, fixtures and fittings) free from hazards
- recognise and report promptly any potential hazards
- report and record accidents accurately, completely and legibly, in accordance with laid down procedures
- follow operating instructions for the use of equipment and fixtures
- use approved and safe methods for lifting and handling heavy or bulky items
- observe regulations and guidelines when using keyboards which involve exposure to VDU screens.

The health and safety of office employees is protected by legislation and in particular by the Health and Safety at Work Act 1974 and regulations arising from it which were brought into use in 1993, including:

1 Management of health and safety at work.

2 Workplace health, safety and welfare (relating to many of the provisions of the Offices, Shops and Railway Premises Act 1963).

3 Provision and use of work equipment.

4 Personal protective equipment.

5 Display screen equipment.

6 Manual handling operations.

Health and Safety at Work Act 1974

Under this Act the employer must provide:

- a safe place of work with safe access and exit
- safe equipment (including efficient maintenance)
- safe systems of work
- a safe working environment (as specified in the Workplace (Health, Safety and Welfare) Regulations 1992 — see below
- safe methods for handling, storing and transporting goods
- first-aid facilities governed by the Health and Safety (First Aid) Regulations 1981
- reports of accidents
- instruction, training and supervision of safe practices
- consultation with a view to making and maintaining effective arrangements for promoting health and safety
- where appropriate, a written statement on health and safety and the means of carrying out that policy.

Duties of employees

All employees have a duty to:

1 take reasonable care for the health and safety of themselves and of other persons who may be affected by their acts or omissions at work

2 follow safety practices

3 co-operate with their employer in promoting and maintaining health and safety

4 refrain from interfering with or misusing anything provided for health and safety of themselves or others.

Safety precautions extend beyond the office, as office employees are sometimes required to visit other parts of the organisation, such as warehouses, workshops and stores. They are then subject to the dangers entailed in the operation of, for instance, fork-lift trucks and cranes and the movement of heavy goods. The fact that office staff are infrequent visitors to these workplaces can easily add to the risks of injury unless they are especially careful and conscious of the dangers.

Workplace (Health, Safety and Welfare) Regulations 1992

Under these regulations and related codes of practice the employer must provide:

- **Maintenance of equipment**

  Regular maintenance (including, as necessary inspection, testing, adjustment, lubrication and cleaning) must be carried out at suitable intervals.

  Any potentially dangerous defects must be remedied and access to any defective equipment prevented.

  A suitable record should be kept to ensure that the system is properly controlled.

- **Ventilation**

  Effective suitable provision of ventilation must be provided

- **Temperature**

  There must be a reasonable temperature in workrooms, ie at least 16 degrees Celsius unless much of the work involves severe physical effort in which case the temperature must be at least 13 degrees Celsius.

  Thermometers should be available at a convenient distance from every part of the workplace to enable temperatures to be measured, but these need not be provided in each workroom.

- **Lighting**

  There must be suitable and sufficient lighting. This should be sufficient to enable people to work, use facilities and move from place to place safely and without experiencing eye-strain.

- **Cleanliness**

  Every workplace and the furniture, furnishings and fittings must be kept sufficiently clean. Floors and indoor traffic routes should be cleaned at least once a week.

- **Office space**

  There must be sufficient floor area, height and unoccupied space for the purposes of health, safety and welfare. In a typical office, where the ceiling is 2.4 m high, a floor area of 4.6 m^2 (for example 2.0×2.3 m) will be needed to provide adequate space of 11 m^3. Where the ceiling is at least 3.0 m high the minimum floor are will need to be 3.7 m^2 (for example 2.0×1.85 m).

Offices may need to be larger, or to have fewer people working in them, than indicated above, depending on such factors as the contents and layout of the office and the nature of work undertaken.

- **Seating**

A suitable seat must be provided for each person at work in the workplace whose work includes operations of a kind where the work can or must be done sitting. Workstations should be arranged so that each task can be carried out safely and comfortably. Seating in offices should provide adequate support for the lower back and a footrest should be provided for any worker who cannot comfortably place their feet flat on the floor.

- **Sanitary conveniences**

Suitable and sufficient sanitary conveniences must be provided at readily accessible places.

- **Washing facilities**

Suitable and sufficient washing facilities must be provided at readily accessible places. They should include a supply of clean hot and cold water.

- **Drinking water**

An adequate supply of wholesome drinking water must be provided for all persons at work in the workplace.

- **Accommodation for clothing**

Suitable and sufficient accommodation must be provided for clothing.

- **Facilities for rest and meals**

Suitable and sufficient rest facilities and places for employees to eat meals should be made available

Further details are given in the Approved Code of Practice and Guidance for the Workplace (Health, Safety and Welfare) Regulations 1992 published by HMSO for the Health and Safety Commission.

Fire Precautions Act 1971

This Act governs fire safety in all places of work. A fire certificate must be obtained from the fire authority and this relates to the provision of means of escape, fire fighting equipment, fire alarm systems, etc.

Safe working practices

Codes of practice

1 Equipment

- Read and comply with operating instructions.
- Know how to stop electric supply in an emergency.
- Avoid having a trailing flex from a socket to a machine.
- Arrange regular care and maintenance of equipment (see guidelines on page 205).
- Report faulty or damaged equipment without delay.
- Check that dangerous parts of machinery are fitted with guards, especially paper-cutting machines.
- Place equipment securely on desks and tables.
- Use a trolley to move heavy machines and equipment, but do not attempt to lift very heavy weights. When lifting heavy items from the floor, there is less strain if you bend your knees and keep your back straight.
- Load and position filing cabinets safely to prevent:

    a the cabinet toppling over because of a heavy top drawer
    b drawers obstructing a passage way.

- Use a step-ladder when reaching files or other objects in a high position.

2 Premises

- Plan the layout of the office so as to reduce the danger of accidents.

- Position furniture and equipment in safe positions.
- Ensure that corridors, stairs, etc, are safe and free from combustible storage materials and other obstructions.
- Make suitable arrangements for heating water and preparing hot drinks, preferably away from the workstation.

3 Fire precautions

- Keep all fire exits clear to ensure that they are immediately available for use in an emergency.
- Make sure that you know what to do should a fire break out, ie:
    a how to operate the fire alarm
    b how to use fire-fighting equipment if required to do so
    c where to assemble outside the building
    d which is the shortest escape route to the assembly point and what other routes might be used if the shortest route is blocked.

    A specimen instruction notice is given in Fig 4.1 for fire/evacuation procedures and the action to be taken if you discover a fire.

- When dealing with a fire:
    a if a person's clothing is on fire, wrap a blanket, rug or similar article closely round them and lay them on the ground to prevent flames from reaching the head
    b if electrical appliances are on fire, switch off the current before dealing with the fire
    c shut the doors and, if possible, the windows of the room in which the fire is discovered.
- Keep fire doors closed, except in situations where the Fire Brigade has given permission for the doors to be held open by an automatic device.
- Do not allow smoking in any part of the building where there is a risk of fire.
- Make sure that bulk quantities or large cans of highly flammable correcting and cleaning fluids are locked away in a well-ventilated storeroom or metal cabinet when not in use.
- Insist upon combustible materials, such as papers and envelopes, being placed in waste bins and that they are removed regularly for disposal.
- Ensure regular maintenance and checking of fire alarms and fire extinguishers.

FIRE/EVACUATION PROCEDURE

Instructions to staff

Action to be taken in case of fire or other emergency

Assembly point: **FRONT CAR PARK**

If you discover a fire:
1 Immediately operate the nearest fire alarm call point
2 Attack the fire, if possible, with the appliances provided but without taking personal risks — ensuring a clear escape route is available at all times

On hearing the fire alarm:
3 The Receptionist on duty will call the Fire Brigade immediately
4 Leave the building and report to the person in charge of the assembly point at the place indicated above, where a roll call will be taken
5 The senior person or authorised deputy on the affected floor will take charge of any evacuation and ensure that no one is left in the area

- USE THE NEAREST AVAILABLE EXIT
- DO NOT USE THE LIFT
  (unless specifically provided and indicated as a means of escape for persons with disabilities)
- DO NOT STOP TO COLLECT PERSONAL BELONGINGS
- DO NOT RUN OR PANIC
- IF YOU HAVE VISITORS, ESCORT THEM TO THE ASSEMBLY POINT
- DO NOT RE-ENTER THE BUILDINGS FOR ANY REASON UNTIL THE SAFETY OFFICER OR THEIR REPRESENTATIVE GIVES YOU PERMISSION

(Notice for display in premises having a simple alarm system — to be displayed on noticeboards in all rooms and by each fire alarm point)

Fig 4.1　Fire instruction notice

- Arrange regular fire drills for all personnel.

4 First aid

Be aware of the need for safety at all times and know:

- How to contact the named first aider when an accident or illness occurs.

- Where the nearest first aid box and facilities are kept.

- How to send quickly for a doctor or an ambulance in major accidents or illnesses (see emergency telephone procedure on page 119).

- How to help an injured person by:

  a making the casualty as comfortable as possible (but do not attempt to move them until you know what is wrong)

  b ensuring that the casualty can breathe freely by allowing plenty of fresh air into the room

  c disconnecting the electric power as quickly as possible in the case of an electric shock

  d keeping the casualty warm by wrapping them in blankets or coats for treatment of shock.

- That first aid treatment, apart from the above procedures, should only be applied by qualified first aiders.

- That an accident report form (as in Fig 4. 2) should be completed in accordance with the organisation's policy.

The Health and Safety (First-Aid) Regulations 1981 place a general duty on employers to make adequate first-aid provision for their employees if they are injured or become ill at work. Employers must also inform their employees of the first-aid provision made for them. The approved code of practice published by the Health & Safety Commission gives practical guidance for employers in meeting the requirement of the regulations.

Health requirements for VDU operators

Potential health problems which may arise from the operation of VDUs include:

ACCIDENT REPORT FORM

Report of an accident or injury to a person at work or on duty and/or a dangerous occurrence
This form must be completed in all cases of accident, injury or dangerous occurrence and submitted to the Safety Officer

Injured person's:
Surname B R E A K W E L L   Forenames BARBARA

Title *~~Mr/Mrs~~/Miss~~/other (state)~~ Date of birth 14 . 10 . 74
Home address Flat 9, 200 King Street, Manchester M2 4WD
Position held Keyboard Operator
*Employee/~~Student/Contractor/Visitor~~

Date and time of accident   21 November 199-
                                     15 00 hrs

Particulars of injury/incapacity

  Electric shock

Activity at time of accident/injury
  Preparing mail for post
Place of accident/injury
  Mailroom
Give full details of the accident and any injury suffered and
explain how it happened   Made contact with a loose
wire which had come away from the plug of the
franking machine, causing an electric shock
What first-aid treatment was given? and state of
Mouth-to-mouth resuscit- unconsciousness
ation to restore breathing.
Was the injured person taken to hospital? If so, where?
  Yes - Manchester General Hospital
State names and positions of any persons who were present
when the accident occurred
  Paul Brooks, Mailroom clerk

Signature of person reporting incident   P Brooks
Date of report 21 November 199-
* delete those inapplicable

Fig 4.2 Accident report form

Possible remedies

1 Eyestrain caused by glare and reflections from the screen

- sustained keyboarding may lead to a build up of fatigue but regular short breaks throughout the day should prevent this from happening
- avoid siting the VDU in a brightly lit area where the lights are reflected in the screen; but the light must be adequate for reading the copy and the screen image
- do not look directly at windows or bright lights
- use task lighting specially designed for VDU operation — avoid unshielded fluorescent lights
- use the brightness controls to suit the lighting conditions in the office
- keep the screen clean, removing dirt and 'grease' finger marks from it
- try moving the screen, desk or source of reflections
- consider using an anti-glare screen filter
- operators wearing glasses or contact lenses may have to have them corrected to the range of focus required

2 Stress caused by boredom and slow computer response time

- Job variation and rotation will help to relieve this

3 Posture fatigue

- use adjustable chairs to provide the correct seat height and back-rest positions — see page 11 for British Standard Institution specifications
- adopt a comfortable and relaxed keying position
- adjust the detachable keyboard and tilt swivel facilities on the screen to suit your own needs

4 Screen flicker

- as a VDU ages, it is inclined to develop

more faults such as drift and jitter of the images and it is possible that the brilliance control will need turning up

- screen flicker may affect epileptics but it should be possible to avoid excessive flicker by adjusting the VDU controls
- regular servicing is essential to correct deterioration of the visual image

5 Unsatisfactory working environment:

space

- make sure that there is adequate space for you and the workstation so that you can move your arms and legs freely (see minimum space requirements on page 212). Your desk should be able to take whatever documents are handled. The use of a copy holder may help to avoid awkward neck movements

ventilation
light
heat

- check that these are set at comfortable levels. As electronic equipment may dry the air, make provision for the circulation of fresh air or a humidifier

noise

- consider methods of sound proofing if noise is a distraction

The Health and Safety (Display Screen Equipment) Regulations 1992, published by HMSO for the Health and Safety Executive, came into force on 1 January 1993 to implement minimum safety and health requirements for work with display screen equipment. Under these regulations employers are required to:

- Analyse workstations of employees covered by these regulations and assess and reduce risks.
- Ensure workstations meet minimum requirements. Employers have until the end of 1996 to upgrade existing equipment (unless immediate action is necessary to reduce risks). Equipment used for the first time must comply immediately.
- Plan work so there are breaks or changes of activity.
- On request, arrange eye and eyesight tests, and provide spectacles if special ones are needed.
- Provide health and safety training.

- Provide information for employees on what steps have been taken to comply with the regulations.

Questions

1 List five hazards in the use of machines in the office and state the precautions to be taken against these.

2 You notice in your diary that the next fire drill is due shortly. Compile a notice to be sent to all offices, clearly stating that there will be a fire drill some time next week (but do not mention the date). List at least seven general points to be considered when evacuating buildings.

3 Comlon International plc is shortly to combine offices in three buildings at Heathrow into one large complex. Because of the widespread use of VDU-based equipment, special consideration is to be given to the office environment. Using the three headings OFFICE LAYOUT, ATMOSPHERIC CONSIDERATIONS and FURNITURE AND FITTINGS, explain the features which you would expect to be incorporated into this modern office environment. (LCCI PSC)

4 You are employed as secretary to Mr James Baker, the Export Sales Director. Mr Baker has received a memo from the staff of the Export Department, complaining about conditions. A meeting is to be held with the staff and, in the absence of the Export Manager, Mr Baker would like to know whether or not the current law is being broken in the following situations:

a) Miss A complains that no soap is supplied in the staff cloakroom.
b) Mr B says the office is never warm enough, the temperature only reaching 64°F (18°C).
c) Miss C says that she has backache after keyboarding all day — she has an ordinary chair, the same as the clerks.
d) Miss D, the filing clerk, says she frequently has to carry, from the archives at the end of the building, files which are very heavy.
e) Miss E says that when her friend who does the collating was away, she decided to 'have a go'. She had never used the collator before and hurt her fingers badly when trying to release the paper which jammed .
f) The staff do not like the new open plan office: there is no privacy and it is difficult to hear when dealing with overseas telephone enquiries.

Prepare notes for Mr Baker's guidance.

5 Mrs Neelum Khan, the Reprographics Technician, received burns to her right hand and arm yesterday. She works in the Reprographics room and has an assistant, Tom Woods, who saw the accident. The room contains an offset-

litho machine, two photocopiers, a computer and printer, a guillotine and a collator.

Apparently Mrs Khan had been cleaning the offset–litho with a cloth soaked in blanket wash which she had thrown into the waste paper bin. Bill Brown had been smoking and discarded his cigarette end in the waste paper bin. The cloth ignited in the bin and Mrs Khan tried to put out the flames by covering them with the lid of a box. This was not successful and she was burned.

Please complete the following tasks:

a) Draft a report of the accident.
b) As a result of the above accident you make an inspection of the Reprographics Department with Mrs Khan. Complete the Inspection Form and include four possible hazards you could encounter with the actions which would be required to remedy the hazards. Include recommended timescale for carrying out the action, ie number of days.
c) Draft a FIRE NOTICE to include what members of staff should do if they discover a fire and if they hear the fire alarm. (PFI OP2)

6   By what means can Comlon:

a) seek to prevent or reduce the risks of fire within its offices?
b) minimise damage to the building and injury to staff in the event of fire? (LCCI PSC)

7   The safety record of your company has deteriorated with a resultant increase in absence.

a) The Personnel Manager asks you to draft a memo reminding employees of their responsibilities in respect of safety.
b) Describe four actions that can be taken to improve safety in the office, indicating what types of accident would be prevented.
c) Describe five ways of avoiding the problems associated with VDUs. (PEI OP2)

In-tray exercises

8   You are employed at Office Products Ltd (Case Study 2). Reply to the Personnel Manager's message overleaf:

9   You are working at New Tech Office Services Bureau (Case Study 1) and witness an accident which occurred at 1000 on Friday 1 September 199– in the General Office. John Rogers of 146 Campion Road, Leamington Spa (– date of birth: 18.09.76) accidentally walked into a filing cabinet drawer which had been left open. He suffered a deep gash to his right leg and

TELEPHONE
MESSAGE FOR _Maxine_

IN YOUR ABSENCE A CALL WAS RECEIVED

FROM _P Henderson_   TIME _1730_

ACTION

Will you please draft a notice on safety
for circulation to all office staff and
I will sign it.
Remind staff of their obligations under
HASWA and point out tactfully three
instances of hazardous behaviour which
you have noticed recently.

MESSAGE
TAKEN BY _D.H._   DATE _19-10- —_

immediately fainted. Mrs Robinson was called and she managed to revive him and apply a bandage to the wound. John was later taken to the Warneford Hospital for further treatment. He was working as a temporary clerical employee engaged on a large-scale VAT assignment.

Complete a report form for this accident.

4.2 Security and confidentiality

Secretaries have a responsibility to ensure the security and confidentiality of all the information and documents that pass through their hands. Data relating to personnel, such as their ages, salaries, medical history, etc, plans for the future development of the organisation and other sensitive information must be protected from unauthorised access by staff and visitors. It is essential that those who deal with such sensitive information and records should be aware of their responsibilities and constantly alert to any attempts made to breach confidentiality and leak information. Any suspicious circumstances must be reported to higher authority.

Safeguards for maintaining confidentiality

- Follow and implement security and confidentiality procedures at all times.
- Never leave confidential records lying around when you leave your office — be sure to lock them away when they are not in use.
- Place confidential records in a folder so that they are not immediately visible to an onlooker.
- Classify and control confidential, private or secret records by marking them accordingly.
- Position your desk in such a way that visitors to your office will not be able to read confidential documents while they are being processed — if this information is displayed on your word processor screen, it may be necessary to scroll it away temporarily when visitors are present.
- Supervise visitors so that they are never left alone at any time in your office or your employer's office.
- If confidential documents have to be reproduced on a copier, it may be desirable for the secretary to do this to ensure that the contents are not disclosed to others.
- If asked for confidential information by an unauthorised person, use tact and diplomacy to evade the question and explain that you have no authority to supply such information and that enquiries should be made elsewhere.
- Take care when supplying confidential information on the telephone that the caller is authorised to receive it.

- Avoid confidential telephone information being overheard by others — this may entail ringing back when you are alone in your office or transferring the call to a more private office.
- Any confidential or secret documents no longer required should not be put in the waste paper bin but destroyed in a shredder or incinerator.
- Take as much care over confidential computerised data and recorded data on dictation machines as you would with documents.
- Inform your manager immediately of any breaches of security you see or which are brought to your attention.

Security of computerised data

Special precautions must be taken to safeguard computerised data against loss or corruption and this may entail:

- keeping back-up duplicate copies of disks in a secure place
- arranging for personal passwords to be used by the staff authorised to have access to the computer, the passwords being changed at regular intervals
- using codes, known only to the users, for document files
- using write-protect tags on system disks to prevent data from being altered or added to them.

Data Protection

The Data Protection Act 1984 establishes rights for individuals to have access to their own personal data held on computer files. The Act contains the following principles which govern the processing of personal data:

1 Data must be obtained fairly and lawfully, ie people must not be misled as to the use to which information they supply about themselves will be put.

2 Data must only be held for registered and lawful purposes. Data users are required to register the personal data they hold with the Data Protection Registrar.

3 Data must only be used and disclosed for the purposes registered.

4 Data must be adequate, relevant and not excessive for its purpose.

5 Data must be accurate and, where necessary, kept up to date.

6 Data must be held for no longer than is necessary.

7 Individuals must be allowed access to data about themselves at reasonable intervals and without undue expense and they must be provided with a copy of it in an intelligible form. Where appropriate, the data must be corrected or erased.

8 Data users must take appropriate security measures to prevent unauthorised access, disclosure, alteration or destruction of personal data and against its accidental loss or destruction.

The Act gives an individual, ie data subject, the following rights:

1 To be informed whether or not a data user has personal information about him/her, eg an application form for employment should contain a signed statement by the applicant saying: 'I understand that if I am appointed, personal information about me will be computerised for personnel and employee administrative purposes including analysis for management purposes and statutory returns.'

2 To receive, within 40 days of the request, a copy of this information expressed in terms intelligible to him/her.

3 To seek a court order to enforce the data user to comply with this request if the data user refuses to do so.

4 To seek compensation for any damage and distress he/she may have suffered if the data held by the data user is inaccurate, misleading, lost, destroyed or disclosed without the data user's authority.

5 To have inaccurate data rectified, erased or supplemented by a statement of the true facts if a court is satisfied that it is inaccurate or that the data subject has suffered damage by reason of the disclosure of the data.

Suspicious postal packets and bomb threats

See special security procedures on page 441 for handling suspicious postal packets and on page 262 for handling bomb threats by telephone.

Guidelines for the security of valuables

1   Cash

- Check sums of money carefully when receiving and paying them.
- Lock any cash held in the office in a cash box and keep it in a safe.
- Never leave the office unattended with the cash box unlocked.
- Ensure that every payment of cash is supported by a voucher or receipt.
- Pay money into the bank as soon as possible after receipt to avoid the security risk of holding money on the premises.
- If large sums of money have to be transported to and from the bank, security agency staff will normally be employed. If the office staff have to undertake this task, two people should go, using a specially designed cash-carrying case and, if regular journeys are made, vary the route taken.
- Spot checks should be made regularly on any transactions involving the transfer of money and any discrepancies brought to the attention of the Manager.

2   Equipment

- Maintain an inventory, ie a written record of all equipment held, and include serial numbers and any distinguishing marks.
- Mark all items of equipment by engraving them or by writing on them with an ultra-violet marking pen so that they are easily identifiable.
- If any item of equipment has to be borrowed, record the name of the person borrowing it in the inventory.
- Make a regular 'stock-taking' check of equipment and investigate and report any deficiencies.

Security of buildings

Security of premises can be controlled by restricting access to authorised personnel and adopting some of the following procedures:

- Issue all employees with photo-identity cards to be worn at all times.

- Use coded electronic cards incorporating pre-programmed number combinations or computerised cards for staff to operate door locks, allowing only those authorised to enter premises — cards may carry an employee photo ID which is photographically or digitally reproduced.
- Issue visitors and contractors with passes to be worn at all times.
- Maintain a visitors' book and also keep a record of all permanent and temporary passes issued.
- Arrange for visitors to be met and returned to the reception office by their hosts.
- Employ security officers to control the admission of visitors and contracting staff.
- Use a closed-circuit television for surveillance of buildings — a time-lapse video system offers 24-hour surveillance, and the input from up to 16 video cameras can be recorded on one tape, providing up to seven days' recall.
- Install public address equipment throughout the building to enable emergency announcements to be made to all occupants.
- Use a Central Alarm Monitoring Station with a round-the-clock manned national communications centre, as in Fig 4.3, to provide monitoring and management services for controlling both electronic systems and security of premises — a computer system reports and logs all system transactions. Any alarm or default is automatically brought to the attention of the CAMS operators, who ensure a swift and efficient response by the firm's security staff.

Questions

1 The organisation you work for handles top secret information which could be of use to unscrupulous competitors. Naturally businessmen from other companies must visit your offices but what arrangements could be made to minimise the security risk presented by visitors? (*LCCI PSD*)

2 In your work as a private secretary you sometimes deal with very confidential matters. How can you:

  a) ensure that persons who come into your office do not see this confidential work while it is being typed

  b) ensure that filed copies of this work remain inaccessible to unauthorised persons

Fig 4.3   Central alarm monitoring station for security

c) deal with colleagues who ask you direct questions about this work? (*LCCI PSC*)

3 You are secretary to the senior partner of your company. His duties include the recruitment of new staff, in consultation with other partners or senior staff concerned with particular appointments. A new audiotypist tells you she is disturbed to realise how much her fellow–typists in the firm appear to know already about her personal background. Suggest how this information might inadvertently have been disclosed and how the situation could be avoided in the future. (*LCCI PSC*)

4 Mr Patrick Moreland, Operations Director of Comlon International plc, is concerned about the leak of confidential information to which several members of staff may have had access.

a) How would you deal with this matter?
b) What steps could be taken to try to prevent any further leaks? (*LCCI PSD*)

5 It has been decided by Comlon to hold seminars throughout the country and invite manufacturers of security products to display their goods.

Choose six possible items that may be on display and briefly describe their use. (*LCCI PSC*)

6 Much of your work in the Personnel Department is of a confidential nature. How would you seek to minimise the likelihood of any 'leaks' or unauthorised access to confidential information? (*LCCI PSC*)

7 Since the company is a small, friendly, family business, many customers are in the habit of walking in and out of the factory quite freely. Recently, however, the company has been handling increasing amounts of confidential work and there is now concern that some control should be kept over who is in the factory.

Mr Ashworth, a partner in the business, has made it clear that it will be the new receptionist's responsibility to filter customers and deter them from wandering into the printing factory. You know that some of the older customers will still consider it their right to walk straight in unannounced, as they have always done.

Prepare some guidelines:

a) for the new receptionist
b) for all factory/office staff

8 You are employed as Secretary to Diane Chandler (Public Relations Manager) and Michael Hadfield (Sales Manager) of Praxitoys, a toy manufacturing company.

a) You travel to work on the same train as Clare, the new junior secretary. This morning you hear her talking openly about one of the new toys which is to be launched on the promotion tour. You know that details are to be kept confidential.

What action will you take?

b) You are also aware that gossip and general slackness in security measures are increasing amongst junior staff. You realise that this is a matter which should be referred to Personnel but also realise that since the problem originated in your department you have a responsibility to take some initiative in the matter. You decide to draft some 'SECURITY DO'S AND DONT'S' to present to Mrs Chandler which could be issued to staff.

Prepare these guidelines which you will discuss with Mrs Chandler.

9 There has been a spate of thefts from Comlon recently. Prepare a memorandum to administrative staff setting out preventive measures to be undertaken by themselves and Comlon. (*LCCI PSC*)

In-tray exercise

10 You are employed at the New Tech Office Services Bureau (Case Study 1). Reply to Mr Wood's memo given on page 230.

Martin,

As a good proportion of our reports contain sensitive commercial information about customers' profit margins, expansion plans, etc, the Company ought to be more security conscious- especially as we are now extensively using computers and disks. I have a staff meeting at the end of the week and I intend to raise the issue of confidentiality and my concern about it then. Please compile a report on precautions and safeguards we might employ to ensure security of confidential information. Thanks.

G W

Office procedures, work schedules and targets

5.1 Planning and monitoring procedures

Careful planning of work schedules is important to make sure that the workload is controlled, monitored and spread evenly, that priorities are established and all deadlines and targets met.

Planning guidelines

- Begin by drawing up a checklist of all the activities involved in a task, arranging them in the order in which they should be carried out, and noting especially any deadlines for completing parts of a task as well as the date when the total task should be completed. Fig 5.1 is an example of a checklist for organising conferences, as supplied for secretaries at the Industrial Society. (See also the checklist for arranging travel abroad (page 326 with deadlines for carrying out the tasks.)

- Complete tasks in order of priority, planning each day's work as follows:

  1 URGENT, ie top priority — must be done today.
  2 NOT SO URGENT BUT IMPORTANT — try to do it today.
  3 NOT URGENT AND LESS IMPORTANT — could wait for another day if time does not permit for it to be done today.

- Plan well ahead to allow adequate time for each stage of the work schedule. Enter reminders of work to be done at different stages in the office diary (Fig 5.2 in Unit 5.2).

231

- Ensure that the work schedule is sufficiently flexible to allow for any unexpected circumstances, eg the unforeseen absence of the manager or secretary, or a delay in receiving data and materials.
- Make effective use of planning aids such as diaries, computerised desk diary planners, year planners, follow-up systems, etc.

The organisation of courses and conferences

Checklist

- *Programme* Title/content
Drafting/approval
Printing/proof reading
Distribution
Publicity — internal
            — external

- *Venue* Select and book accommodation
Catering arrangements:
    morning coffee
    sherry
    lunch
    afternoon tea
Cloakroom facilities
Flowers
Direction signs
Confirm final numbers

- *Speakers* Invitation/appointment
Send programme
Travel arrangements
Hotel accommodation
Equipment requirements
Letter of thanks with fee

- *Financial* Calculate course/conference fee
Determine minimum number of delegates required for viability
Check for viability of bookings
Record/bank receipts
Record/prepare cheques for expenses

- *Aids* Order: microphones
      lectern

projector and screen
tape/video recorder
Set up equipment
Return equipment to supplier

- *Delegates*   List of names and companies
Folders
Badges
Hosting arrangements

- *Literature*   Book stand
(if required)   Order forms
Invoice for books ordered

- *Press*   Invitations
(if required)   Press release
Table

- *Staff*   Briefing
Prepare staff accountability
Debriefing

Fig 5.1 Checklist for organising conferences

Target setting and monitoring

When targets, or objectives as they are often called, are carefully defined and communicated they can have the effect of motivating employees to work more effectively and with greater purpose. The NVQ competences quoted on page xiii are examples of targets which are appropriate for secretaries, eg manage appointments successfully to enable business to be conducted efficiently, or in the case of text processing to produce and present approximately 1500 words in 2.5 hours on a keyboard, under workplace conditions. The performance criteria for monitoring and controlling the achievement of agreed targets, as specified in the Administration NVQ, is:

1 Valid and accurate control mechanisms are maintained in accordance with organisational procedures.

2 Work outcomes are reviewed, analysed and evaluated against agreed targets.

3 Reasons for deviations from planned targets are identified and, where necessary, reported to appropriate persons.

4 Corrective actions are implemented, without delay, within limits of own authority, and relevant people informed.

Guidelines for target setting and monitoring

- Be clear about your own work role and the targets set in your job description.
- Write agreed targets in terms of quality, time and quantity.
- Agree the timing and performance criteria for each of your responsibilities.
- Where possible stick doggedly to your work schedules and do not allow yourself to be sidetracked from your targets.
- Identify the circumstances when it is necessary to deviate from planned targets and be aware of the steps necessary to re-schedule the planned activities.
- Understand the scope and limit of your own authority for taking corrective actions.
- Agree and understand what is expected of you in evaluation processes and staff appraisal schemes.
- Agree with your Manager an appropriate staff development programme as a result of your appraisal.
- Establish systematic procedures for reviewing and evaluating work outcomes against set targets.

Developing, implementing and monitoring office procedures

Various office procedures are outlined in this book, such as buying and selling (Unit 3.2), wages (Unit 3.3), stock (Unit 7.1), methods of payment (Unit 8.2) and travel (Unit 10.1). The performance criteria for developing these and other procedures, as supplied in the Administration NVQ specification is:

1 Procedures meet identified needs and conform to legal and regulatory requirements.
2 Designs and specifications for procedures are developed in conjunction with users.
3 Benefits and costs are formulated and agreed with decision makers.

4 Specialist advice is obtained, when required, and acted upon, where appropriate.

When designing a new procedure or examining the effectiveness of an existing one ask the WHAT, WHERE, WHEN, WHO, HOW questions, as follows:

Purpose	WHAT is done?	Is it necessary?
		Does it achieve its objective?
		Should it be modified?
Place	WHERE is it done?	Is this the right place?
Sequence	WHEN is it done?	Is this the right time?
		Does it meet the target date?
Person	WHO does it?	Why that person?
Means	HOW is it done?	Is it the best method?
		Would some other method be better?
		Should it be integrated with other procedures?

An efficient office procedure will normally incorporate the following features:

- meet the needs of all users
- conform to legal and regulatory requirements
- incorporate controls to avoid fraud, inaccuracies and delays
- use good form design
- be economic in terms of use of equipment, materials and staff time
- be flexible and adaptable to accommodate changing needs
- avoid unnecessary manual checking, paperwork and data input
- where appropriate, use existing data systems in order to meet the need for standardisation of procedures.

These features should be considered when assessing and evaluating the effectiveness of a procedure to meet its purpose.

Questions

1 Among the targets set for Mrs Henderson, Personnel Manager of Office Products Ltd (Case Study 2) is:

'Contribute, along with other senior executives, to achieving the corporate objectives of ensuring that the company's administrative procedures are more efficient and cost-effective than in previous years.'

Assume that you are secretary to Mrs Henderson and prepare five targets which you would set yourself to assist her in achieving this objective.

2   Peter Jones, Production Manager of Pinder and Moore (Case Study 4) has been set the target of developing and contributing towards the implementation of more efficient and cost-effective production and administrative procedures. Discuss how the Production Manager may achieve this target.

3   You work for Ms Gillian Davies, Manager (Hotels), Comlon International plc which operates a coach hire business worldwide with a division based in the United Kingdom offering coach tour holidays throughout Europe.

In order to maintain a uniform standard of accommodation for customers purchasing coach tour holidays Comlon International plc has purchased three hotels. The Classic in Rome and the Palace in Madrid have been refurbished and will be officially opened in March 199- as the Comlon Classic and the Comlon Palace respectively. The Olympia in Athens is being refurbished and it is expected that the official opening of the Comlon Olympia will take place in July 199-.

The Chief Executive, Andrew Johnston, and the Chairman, Leonard Brooker, will be present at the opening ceremonies for which the dates are:

Comlon Classic   Wednesday 9 March 199-
Comlon Palace   Thursday 17 March 199-

The Manager (Hotels) is responsible for supervising the arrangements in conjunction with the local hotel manager. You have been asked to make the arrangements for inviting guests to the official opening of the Classic Hotel in Rome in March 199-. List in chronological order what should be done.
(LCCI PSC)

4   In response to the Office Manager's request for suggestions for controlling costs, prepare a memo outlining how costs could be controlled for:

a) telephone calls
b) reprography. (PEI OP2)

5   The Company's insurances and tenancies are periodically renewable. What methods could you use to ensure renewal on time? (LCCI PSC)

6   Refer to Case Study 1 relating to New Tech Office Services.

a) Identify any typical activities which Martin might encounter in his work (routine and non-routine).
b) How often must these activities be done (eg daily, weekly, monthly, quarterly, yearly)?

c) Make a list of daily activities and assess their priorities, ie jobs which *must* be done; jobs which *should* be done; jobs which *could* be done.

In-tray exercise

7 As a member of your local branch of a secretarial association, in your free time you are asked to assist the Branch Secretary in organising a Gala Dinner to celebrate the centenary of the London Chamber of Commerce Commercial Education Scheme. It has been agreed that the Grand Comlon International Hotel will be the most suitable venue for the event.

The Branch Secretary asks you:

a) i   to make *all* the arrangements with the hotel on her behalf;

ii to trace two former members who gained the Diploma Top Secretary awards in previous years, who have moved away and have lost touch with the local branches. If traced, the ladies are to be invited as guests for the occasion;

iii to arrange a small exhibition to celebrate the centenary in the hotel foyer for the week prior to the dinner; and

iv to arrange publicity for the event.

How would you tackle these problems?

b) Draft a suitable letter to send to branch members inviting them to the dinner. (*LCCI PESD*)

5.2 Managing appointments

This unit is involved in the successful management of appointments to enable business to be conducted efficiently. (NVQ Element 3.3.)

It is important that appointments are managed with the intention of meeting the organisation's objectives, as well as being arranged according to the availability of the persons concerned.

Booking appointments

When booking appointments, the secretary should:

- keep in mind the routine office matters with which the executive probably prefers to deal at certain times of the day
- allow the necessary travelling time between appointments
- provide sufficient time for discussion with their executive and for dealing with the mail
- avoid making appointments immediately the executive returns after being away from the office
- remember that meetings can extend beyond their estimated finishing time, and allow for this by mentioning the difficulty, if necessary, to the person requiring an appointment — unless it is so important that the executive would wish to leave the meeting to keep the appointment
- as a rule appointments are made by telephone. On the same day write a letter or fax confirming the telephone conversation. A copy of the letter or fax will be made, providing a permanent record of the conversation and booking for the file. A note of the action taken should then be given to the executive for information
- if a caller requests an appointment and a date and time are agreed, make a note of the caller's name, address and telephone number, in case contact has to be made to amend the date or time
- if writing to an hotel, address the letter to 'The Manager' (hotel addresses and descriptions are given in the publications listed on page 26)
- when negotiating appointments, assess priorities and suggest alternatives if conflicts arise
- when declining an appointment, be polite and firm. If appropriate, offer alternatives, agree options within the time constraints and confirm decisions reached

- if making social appointments which include the executive's partner, either during the day or the evening, make sure that each appointment is convenient to both parties before accepting on their behalf
- if an appointment has to be cancelled because of illness or other unforeseen circumstances, telephone an apology and arrange another appointment.

The diary

As a secretary, you cannot be expected to remember the large number of details necessary in the day-to-day working of the office, including your executive's engagements and appointments and future planning of your duties. You should make a note in your diary, not only of every engagement and appointment arranged for your executive, but of work to be done on future occasions. You will normally be expected to keep two diaries up to date — your executive's and your own — and any entries which affect your executive should be entered in both diaries.

A desk diary can be used as a reminder of:

- work deadlines
- appointments and meetings
- files to be followed up
- staff absences — holidays, etc.
- social engagements.

When making entries in the diary, the secretary should:

- be systematic:

   1 **At the beginning of the day** refer to the diary and take the necessary action on all entries, eg prepare the papers and files for appointments, meetings and correspondence (follow up).

   2 **During the course of the day** keep in mind and prepare for the various activities, making amendments, additions and deletions to the diary as required.

   3 **At the end of the day** ensure that all items have been dealt with or, if necessary, transferred to a future date.

- Write entries clearly and concisely with a pen, including essential details of appointments, time and place.

Secretary's Diary

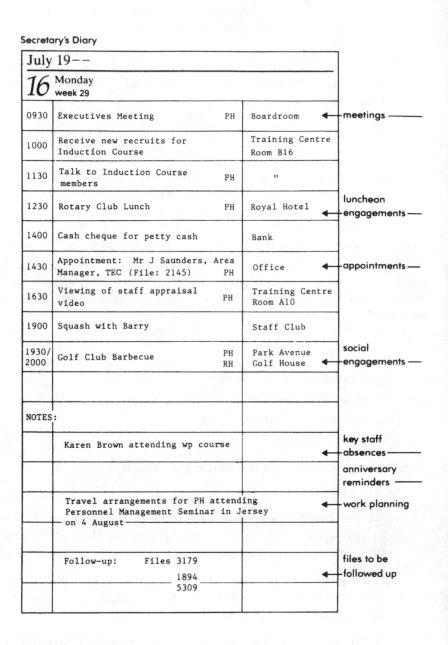

July 19−−				
16 Monday week 29				
0930	Executives Meeting	PH	Boardroom	◄ meetings
1000	Receive new recruits for Induction Course		Training Centre Room B16	
1130	Talk to Induction Course members	PH	"	
1230	Rotary Club Lunch	PH	Royal Hotel	luncheon ◄ engagements
1400	Cash cheque for petty cash		Bank	
1430	Appointment: Mr J Saunders, Area Manager, TEC (File: 2145)	PH	Office	◄ appointments
1630	Viewing of staff appraisal video	PH	Training Centre Room A10	
1900	Squash with Barry		Staff Club	
1930/ 2000	Golf Club Barbecue	PH RH	Park Avenue Golf House	social ◄ engagements
NOTES:				
	Karen Brown attending wp course			key staff ◄ absences
				anniversary reminders
	Travel arrangements for PH attending Personnel Management Seminar in Jersey on 4 August			◄ work planning
	Follow-up: Files 3179 1894 5309			files to be ◄ followed up

Fig 5.2a Secretary's diary

Executive's Diary – Mrs Pauline Henderson (Personnel Manager)

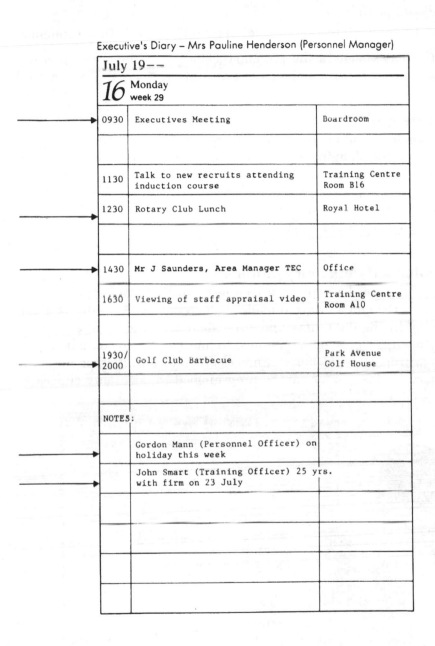

July 19––		
16 Monday week 29		
0930	Executives Meeting	Boardroom
1130	Talk to new recruits attending induction course	Training Centre Room B16
1230	Rotary Club Lunch	Royal Hotel
1430	Mr J Saunders, Area Manager TEC	Office
1630	Viewing of staff appraisal video	Training Centre Room A10
1930/ 2000	Golf Club Barbecue	Park Avenue Golf House
NOTES:		
	Gordon Mann (Personnel Officer) on holiday this week	
	John Smart (Training Officer) 25 yrs. with firm on 23 July	

Fig 5.2b Executive's diary

- Enter provisional appointments in pencil, and use a pen when they are confirmed.
- Enter the appointments for each day in the correct time sequence.

A typical day's page in the secretary's diary and the corresponding entries in the executive's diary are given in Fig 5.2, parts a and b.

Plastic year planners

Large plastic calendars provided with spaces for every day of the year can be used for planning appointments, meetings and other business activities. By this means it is possible to see at a glance a year's activities and to plan engagements methodically on one single sheet. Self-adhesive coloured signals can be used to highlight significant dates. Fig 5.3 illustrates a year planner.

Computerised desk diary planner

A desk diary can be kept on a computer so that the entries can be seen on a VDU and a printout made when required. An entry is made by keying in the date, time and brief details of the item, and if an appointment is cancelled or changed to another time or date it can be removed from the 'memory' and re-entered on another date, if necessary. The computer can be programmed to reject any entries at

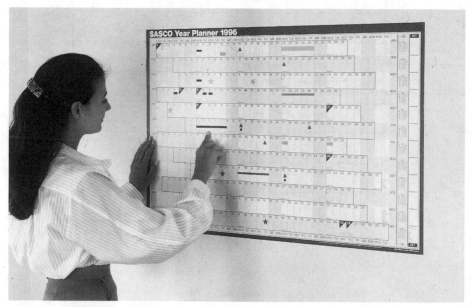

Fig 5.3 Year planner

certain times of the day or even whole days when the employer does not wish to have appointments. An appointment which occurs several times during the year at regular intervals can be entered once with the relevant dates and is automatically entered on each of the dates. Also annual events such as wedding anniversaries can be automatically entered in the diary for subsequent years. Each day's entries can be viewed at the beginning of the day and, for planning purposes, it is possible to view a month's entries. All forthcoming events, reminders and 'unavailable' days can be displayed up to a maximum of 30 days.

A computerised system, such as this, is particularly good for following up correspondence and for reminders of work to be done on particular dates, such as the preparation of an agenda for a meeting.

Computerised diary programs can be used to co-ordinate dates for meetings if the executives of a company all keep their diaries on computer. When it is necessary to call a meeting of the executives, the secretary can call up the program on the computer and enter the likely duration of the meeting. The computer searches the diaries of each of the executives and gives a choice of times and dates when all are free to attend. The secretary can then select one of the options and the diaries are automatically updated with the selected meeting date and time.

Questions

1 Your employer has a great many business and social engagements. Assume that you are responsible for his appointments diary; what are the chief factors to be borne in mind? (*LCCI PESD*)

2 Discuss means by which you can ensure:

a) that your employer keeps all the appointments made for him, and

b)that he deals with all matters that he has put aside for attention on specific dates.

3 When your employer returns from her holiday, she will want to know what has taken place in her absence, and what appointments you have made on her behalf. How would you prepare this information for her?

4 An employer has a desk diary and so does his secretary. What are the advantages of each having a diary?

5 Explain how you would deal with the following situation. Your employer is at a meeting in another town for the day. A customer telephones you and asks to

make an appointment to see your employer in one week's time. You have no record of any appointments on the proposed day in your desk diary but your employer has taken his own diary with him to the meeting. The customer would like to know definitely within the next twenty-four hours.

6 As you enter your office this morning Polly, a girl in her first secretarial job, in the Advertising Department, is waiting for you in tears and clearly very upset. She explains she is afraid to face her manager this morning because of a number of incidents yesterday afternoon. She had returned twenty minutes late from lunch only to find her manager at her desk, talking on the telephone, searching through a mass of mail and papers spread over her desk, and a visitor impatiently waiting in his office. In angry tones her manager was telling the caller he was certain a contract was sent to him two days ago, although he can't find the copy. Polly now admits to you that she had forgotten to enter the visitor in the diary because she left work early the previous evening, and on the way to work today discovered the contract, which should have been posted two days ago, in the bottom of her shopping bag. You now have to advise her urgently

a) how to cope with the problem of facing her manager and starting work on time today

b) what action she should take to avoid any repetition of similar incidents in the future.

Explain briefly the points of advice you give her.

7 For a 1000 appointment two visitors arrive but the name of only one person is recorded in your diary.

a) Explain how you would cope with this situation.

b) How would you avoid this occurring in the future? (*LCCI PESD*)

8 a) Explain how you would use an electronic diary to schedule internal meetings.

b) What are the advantages and disadvantages of the electronic diary? (*LCCI PSC*)

9 You work for Mr Edward Hayes, Director, Sales and Marketing, Comlon International plc.

Mr Hayes is at a meeting with the Head Designer. How and why would you deal with the following situations?

a) The Managing Director's secretary rings to say Mr Jacobson wants to see Mr Hayes urgently.

b) Francis Warren (Director, Head Buyer) calls in to the office to talk with Mr Hayes.

c) Alan Abbot rings to arrange to visit and discuss whether Comlon will require a stand at a forthcoming trade show. (*LCCI PSC*)

In-tray exercises

10 You are employed at the New Tech Office Services Bureau (Case Study 1) and are responsible for arranging appointments for Mrs Robinson and Mr Wood. The following appointments should be arranged for the week commencing 1 March:

You should note that Mrs R likes to keep 0900–0930 free every day to deal with the mail and discuss matters with you, while Mr W normally deals with his correspondence and outstanding matters from 1400–1430 daily.

Mr R Jackson of Jackson, Jones & Jarvis of 49 Castle Street, Warwick has requested an appointment with Mrs R as early as possible in the week — it will take about 2 hours.

When Mr W returns from the Office Equipment Exhibition he would like to hold a meeting with the Office Manager and yourself to discuss the new products on show.

Mr R Murgatroyd, Solicitor, would like both Mrs R and Mr W to go to his office at Regent House to sign the leasing agreement for the new branch offices.

Arrange an appointment for Mr W at his opticians, Leightons, 234 The Parade. Mr W will be away from home on 6 and 7 March working on his yacht at Hamble.

Joan Barnes, typist, has requested an appointment with Mrs R to discuss her job prospects.

a) Select suitable days and times for the above, having regard to the appointments already arranged in the diaries on page xvii and enter the appointments in both partners' diaries.

b) Confirm in writing the appointments made with Mr R Jackson and Mr R Murgatroyd.

11 You are employed by Mr Brian Dobson, Manager of 'The Secretairs' (Case Study 3).

a) Select suitable dates for the group's concert tour of UK towns and cities and enter them on the year planner (page xxiii), bearing in mind holiday dates, the US tour which has already been booked for April and the dates requested on page 246. Try to reduce travelling as much as possible by arranging each week's programme with towns in the same region. Allow adequate time for travelling between towns. Leave the weekends free for recording sessions and TV/radio engagements which may be required.

b) Write a letter reserving accommodation for the group in a good class hotel for the first concert which you have planned.

Concert town/city	No. of days	Dates requested
Aberdeen	1	
Belfast	3	Leave until June
Birmingham	3	
Blackpool	2	
Brighton	1	
Cambridge	1	
Edinburgh	3	
Exeter	1	
Glasgow	3	5—7 March
Liverpool	2	
Llandudno	2	
London	5	6—10 February
Manchester	3	
Scarborough	1	During 2nd week in May
Swansea	2	

12 You work for the Personnel and Training Department of Madison Confectionery Ltd of Holland Place, Reigate, Surrey, RH42 1PQ.

You have just been promoted from the post of Receptionist/Telephonist to Administrative Assistant (a new post) and are responsible to the Personnel and Training Officer in whose name all letters and memos are prepared.
Staff include:

John Green   Personnel & Training Officer
Mary Mason   Office Manager
Carol Baker   Training Assistant

There is a management post vacant and the following applicants have been invited for interview on the first day of next month:

Sonia Brown, Hugh Black, Carmen White and John Smith.

Your offices are close to The Royal Hotel, Hookwood Road, Reigate, Surrey, RH43 2PQ.

The four applicants invited for interview will need accommodation on the night before the interview and breakfast the following morning. A provisional booking for rooms with bath or shower has been made at the Royal Hotel by telephone.

a) Write a letter of confirmation; ask for details of the cost and that the Hotel Manager sends the bill to the Personnel Officer.

b) Prepare a programme for the day which should include the time of interview for each candidate.

All candidates should arrive by 10 am for a preliminary discussion, lasting about 45 minutes, with John Green. They will then be shown round the offices and factory. Lunch has been booked in the staff restaurant for 12.15. Formal interviews begin at 2 pm and each interview is expected to last about 45 minutes. Candidates will be seen in reverse alphabetical order and will be free to leave after the interview as they will be contacted by telephone the following day with the result.

c) Suggest sources of reference that the applicants might refer to in preparation for the day. (*PEI OP2*)

Note: This task is also included in Unit 1.1 as aspects of personnel are dealt with in that unit.

Interpersonal skills and relationships

6.1 Working relationships, qualities and responsibilities

Interpersonal skills for secretaries are involved in:

- establishing and maintaining effective working relationships
- supervising and supporting junior staff
- identifying and solving problems using judgement and initiative
- influencing others and negotiating successfully with them
- communicating effectively with others to co-ordinate administrative procedures.

The secretary's role

An important element of the private secretary's success and value to the executive lies in skill in dealing with people, and in creating an impression which will enhance the organisation's reputation. The responsibilities are enormous, for the secretary is the executive's personal organiser, generally deciding whom they see and to whom they speak, what matters receive their urgent personal attention, and what can be redirected to others.

The secretary should provide a vital link between the executive and their various contacts, ensuring that communications are effective and that the required action is taken. The secretary is the executive's personal representative and in this key role should be relied upon to create a favourable impression with contacts within and outside the organisation. Secretaries cannot play a full part unless they are given a full and clear understanding of their executive's role and objectives and the part these play in the organisation as a whole. In addition, secretaries need to know clearly what is expected of them in assisting the executive to achieve his or her objectives.

The role of the executive secretary has been defined in a brochure of the European Association of Professional Secretaries as one who has sufficient knowledge of their executive's activities and the sphere of work to be able to have a considerable amount delegated to them. They are able to make decisions, give instructions and represent the executive on business occasions.

The role of the secretary has changed with the advent of word processing equipment and improvements in reprographic processes and the increased production which results from these developments. At a simple level, the improvements in electrostatic copying have revolutionised the production of paperwork. Much of the drudgery of routine typing has been eliminated from the daily routine of the office, although it may be argued that this work is not the prerogative of the senior secretary. The computer terminal has also given the secretary quick access to data. The secretarial office with interactive word processing terminals, facsimile terminals and microprocessors for word, text and data processing has had a marked effect on the secretary's role. However sophisticated systems may become, they will never succeed in replacing the competent secretary who can use initiative, co-ordinate the activities of an office, and carry out what is in effect a public relations and human relations role both within and outside the organisation.

The secretary's qualities

The qualities of a private secretary can be divided into two categories: business attributes and personal attributes

Business attributes

- Secretarial and language skills
- Organising skills
- Efficiency
- Reliability
- Responsibility
- Discretion

- Initiative
- Tact and diplomacy
- Punctuality
- Loyalty, commitment to the job
- Anticipation of needs
- Appearance
- Personality and a sense of humour
- Adaptability, willingness to learn
- Desire to add to knowledge of job
- Interest in business
- Courtesy
- Resilience under pressure
- Enthusiasm

The secretary's responsibilities and limitations

When the executive is away, the secretary is the 'guardian' of the office, responsible for the administration of such matters as the mail (internal and external), the telephone calls and the visitors. In this capacity the secretary has to decide what matters are urgent and important and should be dealt with by the executive's deputy; what matters can be dealt with personally, as approved by the executive; and what matters should await the return of the executive. These are the decisions which the secretary must learn to make wisely, and under no circumstances should the secretary attempt to act as the executive's deputy.

If the secretary is in doubt concerning the action to take, the executive's deputy should be consulted. The secretary has an important part to play in supplying information concerning the executive's current business matters, bearing in mind the need for confidentiality and security. The secretary also knows where and how to contact the executive if the need arises. If the executive telephones the office, the secretary is there to supply information or to implement any action which is required to be taken. When the executive returns, the secretary is expected to brief him/her on all of the important developments which have occurred during their absence, and it is usual for these to be typed in summary form. Copies of important correspondence written either by the executive's deputy or by the secretary should also be retained in a folder for the executive to see.

The secretary's job description

An example of a typical job description is given in Fig. 6.1 on page 252.

The secretary's day

The secretary's day seldom follows a set pattern and no two secretarial posts are alike, but the following list of activities is representative of a typical day in the life of a secretary.

At the beginning of the day

- Collect the executive's mail from the mailroom, open and date stamp it, and attach it to the relevant files.
- Refer to your diary to ascertain your executive's and your own engagements for the day; locate relevant files and papers in connection with these and bring forward any files requiring action.
- Place all incoming mail and files (brought forward) in your executive's 'in-tray' .
- Access and print out any messages in the computer 'mailbox'.
- Draw the attention of your executive to any urgent items in the mail or in the day's activities.
- Check that the entries in your diary correspond with those in your executive's diary.
- Update calendars, visual control boards, computer data, etc.
- Read journals, reports, etc, and mark any items which will be of interest to your executive.

During the day

- Receive dictation from your executive and transcribe it. A regular time will normally be set aside for this during the day.
- Arrange for copying of documents to be undertaken as required by your executive.
- File yesterday's correspondence.
- Receive and make telephone calls.

JOB DESCRIPTION

Job title: Private Secretary to Marketing Manager

Department: Marketing

Accountable to: Marketing Manager

Accountable for: Marketing Department's junior secretarial staff (3)

Overall objectives:

1 To promote the marketing function of the company by providing an efficient and effective secretarial support service to the Marketing Manager.

2 To ensure a satisfactory secretarial service for second line Marketing Department Managers by the supervision and co-ordination of junior secretaries.

Main responsibilities:

1 Receive dictation and transcribe it, using a word processor, compose correspondence and summarise reports. Use the computer system to transmit electronic mail.

2 Receive and prepare incoming mail and, at the end of the day, deal with the Marketing Manager's outgoing mail.

3 Receive and entertain visitors.

4 Handle telephone calls and transmit messages by fax or telex.

5 Keep the Marketing Manager's diary; arrange his appointments and engagements; assist him in planning his day to ensure the most effective use of his time.

6 Make the Marketing Manager's travel arrangements.

7 Ensure that all correspondence and enquiries have been processed and actioned where necessary and that all records are filed accurately for speedy retrieval. Administer an effective follow-up system.

8 Organise and attend meetings.

9 Organise the Marketing Manager's office, maintaining wall-charts and statistical data.

10 Supply information, using teletext and database services and reference books; circulate information as directed by the Marketing Manager.

11 Control the Marketing Manager's petty cash, bank transactions and expense claim forms.

12 Supervise junior secretarial staff and administer their induction training, job allocation, appraisal, disciplinary and complaint procedures.

13 Organise conferences and special events, as required.

14 Control stationery and office materials for the Marketing Manager's Office.

15 Comply with the company's health, safety and security regulations.

Date: 1 January 199–

Fig 6.1   Job description

- Receive and entertain visitors.
- Use the computer for sending messages to staff, including dates of meetings.
- Arrange appointments and enter them in both diaries; make any necessary travel arrangements.
- Make arrangements for meetings and, if required, attend them in the capacity of secretary, taking the minutes.
- Organise and undertake work as required by your executive.
- Deal with bank transactions and draw cash, as required, for purchases.
- Complete expenses forms from receipts and vouchers.
- Deal with any tasks allocated (in your diary) for today.

At the end of the day

- Refer to your diary and notify reception of any visitors expected tomorrow.
- If your executive has to be away from the office early in the morning, supply any itinerary required and relevant papers.
- Ensure that all correspondence has been signed, enclosures attached and the envelopes prepared for dispatch.
- If your executive intends to work late, make sure that they have all the information they require.
- Clear your desk and lock up all pending files and papers.

The secretary's relationship with the executive

The qualities which go to make the ideal relationship between the executive and secretary are:

- The secretary must ensure that all the work that leaves the office is accurate, so that the executive is relieved of the duty of examining every document.
- The secretary must be able to deal diplomatically with any telephone inquiries, and the executive must be able to trust the secretary to treat all matters in the office as confidential.
- The secretary must be able to convey the essential facts contained in reports and journals, so that the executive does not have to study them personally in detail.

- The secretary should understand that it may be necessary to stay late if there is an urgent job to be done; nevertheless, the executive should not always expect the secretary to be in the office after hours when the work is not of an urgent nature.
- There must be a clear understanding about the scope of the work the secretary should undertake in the executive's absence and the executive should be perfectly satisfied that the secretary can cope with the work which may arise when the executive is not there.
- The secretary should be kept fully informed of all that the executive is doing so that the secretary can be of most use to the executive.
- Executives should appreciate that the secretary will need to attend training courses for updating their skills and for career development.
- The executive must be able to rely on the secretary's punctuality in attending the office, meetings and other functions.
- There should be a sense of humour on both sides.
- The secretary should set a high standard of conduct and efficiency for the rest of the office staff. Being always neat and tidy in appearance will enhance the reputation of the organisation.
- The executive must allow the secretary to use initiative to solve problems.

The secretary's relationships with staff at all levels

Secretaries have a special relationship with their immediate executives because they work closely together in a 'partnership' to achieve the objectives required of the executive's position. There may be several executives in the organisation and there may be more senior executives or directors to whom the secretary's executive is answerable. While the secretary has a loyalty to their executive, they must also have a loyalty to the organisation employing them, and the organisation in this context is the whole of the executive staff. The secretary should, therefore, seek to serve the organisation to the best of their ability. The executive is a member of the management team and their secretary has an important part to play in the successful operation of this team. The secretary must understand and appreciate the role of each executive and by their co-operation play their part in contributing towards the overall efficiency and smooth-working of the organisation. Co-operation and respect are important in establishing successful relationships between secretaries and their seniors.

Good relations with the other members of the secretarial staff are also crucial in creating a happy and trouble-free environment. As a secretary, many of your communications are with other secretaries, eg you may have to cancel or change an appointment or request urgent information or documents and there is no doubt that cordial and friendly relationships contribute to the successful outcome of such contacts. It is in your relationships with colleagues that you must guard against divulging confidential information. In your conversations with staff at all levels you should refrain from entering into gossip and wasting valuable time in the office. When meeting executives or other members of staff for social activities, you should not be tempted to enter into conversations about your work, as it is a wise rule to isolate business activities from social or personal activities. If, for example, your executive hears that a business matter has been divulged by you at an activity outside the office, there would be a loss of confidence in your ability to be discreet and the relationship would suffer as a result.

If secretaries have a personal grievance they should follow the procedure laid down in their contract of employment, which will probably mean discussing it with their immediate superior. It is unlikely to help the secretary to solve the problem if they choose to air their dissatisfaction with their colleagues or with other executives and it may create other problems by affecting the relationship with their executive.

Juniors are influenced by the standards set and the attitudes of their seniors and the secretary has a responsibility to set a good example which the juniors in the department will wish to emulate. A good working relationship is a contributory factor in gaining the full support and cooperation of the junior staff. In this relationship the secretary may be working in the capacity of a supervisor and it is important to be explicit when allocating tasks and to be clear about the standards and production times expected. The secretary should encourage the junior by praising their work when it is good. On the other hand, if the work is not up to the standard expected, the secretary, using their qualities of tact and diplomacy, should point this out to the junior and help the junior to improve their performance. The ideal relationship is one in which the junior staff work harmoniously with the secretary and have no inhibitions about seeking help and discussing their problems.

The secretary must appreciate that, however well-qualified the juniors are, they will be inexperienced and will take time to acquire proficiency in the tasks allotted to them, especially under pressure. The new entrants require a thorough induction so that they are made aware of such matters as the functions of the firm; its structure and organisation; its lines of communication; office rules and security regulations; welfare, medical and first-aid facilities and amenities; grievance procedure and arrangements for consultation; conditions of service; training, further education and career development. A tour of the organisation will usually be included in the induction programme. An induction programme enables new recruits to understand the conditions and purpose of their job in relation to the whole organisation and to appreciate their relationship with colleagues and seniors. It also enables them to settle into the new environment quickly and become more effective in their work.

Questions

1   You are secretary to a marketing executive who spends much of her time away from the office. There are times when you have no idea where she is and what she is doing as she changes her plans without telling you and also makes appointments without noting them in her diary or informing you about them. This causes confusion and embarrassment for you when appointments have to be re-arranged because of double-bookings. What action could you take to improve the situation?

2   You are responsible for two junior secretaries in your department (Jane and Sarah). Jane started taking days off from work for dubious reasons. Sarah complained that, as a result of these absences, her workload was becoming excessive and she was having to work late on most days. You gave Jane a number of official warnings but they were not effective. Discuss what action you should take in these circumstances.

3   'A high salary is not always the means of producing the best effort.' Expand this statement. (*LCCI PSC*)

4   'A secretarial post calls for much initiative because it is possible for a good private secretary to save her employer a great deal of time by the quick anticipation of his requirements and possible future action.' Justify this statement. (*LCCI PSC*)

5   How would you expect the nature of your work to differ if you were:

   a) secretary to Mrs Kate Robinson and Mr Gerald Wood (Case Study 1)
   b) secretary to Mrs Pauline Henderson (Case Study 2)
   c) secretary to Mr Brian Dobson (Case Study 3)?

6   The Director of Human Resources is in Singapore. You need to contact him urgently to inform him about a major incident which has taken place at the Southampton factory. Ms Flood, Human Resources Manager, is en route to the factory.

   What action would you take before and after contacting the Director? (LCCI PSC)

7   Your workload has increased considerably over the past 18 months. The Personnel Manager has suggested an assistant secretary should be recruited to help you.

   a) State the personal qualities you would look for in an assistant.
   b) Give suggestions as to how your workload could be split to ensure you are fully aware of the current situation at any time. (LCCI PESD)

8   One of the Sales Clerks was chatting to you in the lift this morning. Her young daughter is thinking of beginning a secretarial course in September. However, they are uncertain of the career opportunities available to someone pursuing a secretarial career and she asked you if you could outline a typical career structure for a person who is 'secretarially-trained', mentioning briefly what duties each job would entail and any qualifications necessary.

   List, in a hierarchical way, the possible job positions one can have in a secretarial career. State any technical qualifications necessary for each job listed and give a brief outline of the work responsibilities involved for each post.

9   The Office Manager has been drafting job descriptions for the posts at the new office in Birmingham. One of the posts is PA to the Director (Midlands Area) with additional responsibility for the supervision of secretarial office staff. The salary scale has just been approved — £10 100 to £12 200.

   The organisational structure for the new office is going to include one Director (Midlands Area), an Office Manager (with overall responsibility for a Chief Clerk, Sales Clerk, Filing Clerk and Cashier), a PA/Supervisor of the Secretarial Office (responsible for Shorthand-typist, Telephonist-Receptionist and a YT trainee) and a Sales Manager (responsible for 2 Sales Representatives).

   a) Prepare an organisation chart for the Birmingham Office from the information given, clearly showing managerial relationships.
   b) Using the proforma overleaf, complete a job description for the PA/Supervisor of the Secretarial Office. List at least five duties/responsibilities.

JOB DESCRIPTION

Job title

Location

Salary scale

Reports to

Responsible for staff

Job summary

Main duties and responsibilities

Date

In-tray exercise

10 You are employed at the New Tech Office Services Bureau (Case Study 1) and are required to take the necessary action in the note received from Mrs Robinson:

```
MARTIN
_____

We must soon start recruiting staff for our new branch at Redditch.

Can you let me have an idea of the qualifications and qualities the

secretary will need to cope with the varied secretarial work at

the new branch.

Please also draft a press advertisement for this post.

Thanks

K ROBINSON
```

6.2 Receiving visitors

The first impression visitors gain of an organisation is influenced by the manner in which they are received at the reception office. The office itself should be attractively furnished and designed in every way to impress the visitor, and the receptionist must possess the necessary personal qualities and business skills to greet all callers pleasantly and efficiently.

Visitors with appointments

At the beginning of each day the reception office should be notified of all the appointments made and the movements of executives, so that the receptionist is able to act without undue hesitancy when visitors arrive.

On arrival, visitors are usually asked to sign a visitors book or enter particulars of their visit in a register of callers (see Fig 6.2). This provides a useful permanent record of all visitors to the company. A

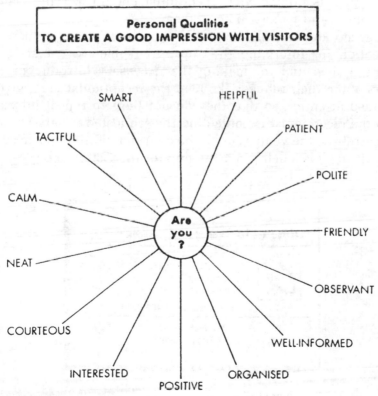

DATE	NAME OF CALLER	FIRM	TIME OF ARRIVAL	REFERRED TO
19 - - Jun 1	PL Jones	K & S Smith Ltd	0930	R Evans
" 1	R C Ware	} North Eastern	10 15	C Gillespie
" 1	V Coleman	} Finance Ltd		
" 1	C Giles	Giles & Porter Bros	1500	M Norton
" 1	E Chapman	Felgate Motors Ltd	1530	R Evans

Fig 6.2   Register of callers

visitor from another company may introduce themselves by offering the receptionist a business visiting card such as the one in Fig 6.3 which provides their name, company and position.

If no card is offered, the receptionist should ask the visitor for these details and make a note of them.

The receptionist should retain the card as it provides the relevant information for informing the appropriate member of staff of the visitor's arrival and for making the necessary introduction. When visitors make their requests known, the receptionist must give them undivided attention so that they do not have to repeat information. While the receptionist is contacting the requested member of staff or their secretary, the visitor should be seated and offered some reading matter. If there is a delay in arranging for the visitor to be seen by the

Fig 6.3   Business visiting card'

member of staff, it is polite to apologise to the visitor and explain the reason for the delay.

The member of staff, or their secretary, may collect the visitor from the reception office, or the receptionist may be expected to accompany the visitor to the appropriate office. In this case the visitor must be escorted politely and efficiently. If no one is present on arrival at the office, the receptionist must refer the visitor to the secretary or wait with the visitor until the person arrives. Under no circumstances should callers be shown into an executive's room before the executive has been informed. When introducing the visitor, the receptionist must clearly announce the visitor's name, title and company. The visitor's name should be given before the name of the executive, but when introducing a man and a woman, it is courteous to announce the woman's name first.

If a secretary is required to meet a caller in the executive's absence, a note of the meeting should be typed and given to the executive for information on their return to the office.

Receiving parcels

While goods received for production will normally be delivered to the Goods Received section, parcels for other departments are usually delivered to the reception office. They may be accompanied by a delivery or consignment note. The person delivering the parcel will normally require a signature to acknowledge its receipt. Before signing, the receptionist should check that:

- the parcels are addressed to their organisation
- the number of packages is correct, as stated on the delivery note
- parcels are not damaged in any way — any damage must be noted on the delivery note returned to the driver, as well as on the copy retained.

Emergency services

The receptionist has a vital role to play in the communications for emergency services, such as sending for ambulances and reporting fires, bomb alerts, etc.

The procedure for making an emergency telephone call is given on page 119.

If an offensive, indecent or menacing telephone call is received, it is advisable to cut off the caller immediately without giving the organisation's name in the usual way. If such calls continue, the receptionist should inform the security officer and the police.

If a telephone call is received stating that a bomb has been planted on the premises, as much information as possible should be obtained from the caller, such as:

- location of the bomb
- the time it is expected to go off
- any circumstances concerning the motive for the bomb
- the identity of the caller.

It is important to make as many notes as possible of the conversation and try to detect the nationality and any accent of the informer. Immediately after the call, the following steps should be taken:

1 Inform the security or safety officer and the police (dial 999)

2 Assist the security or safety officer to take the necessary precautions until the police arrive to take charge of the situation

Fire wardens, trained in bomb search techniques, should be assigned to search particular areas, eg corridors, toilets, fire escape staircases. It is essential that all escape routes from the building have been thoroughly searched prior to the evacuation being authorised.

First aid

In connection with first aid, the receptionist is required to know:

- where the nearest first-aid box and facilities are situated
- how to contact the organisation's named first-aider when an accident or illness occurs
- how to send quickly for a doctor or an ambulance in sudden illnesses or major accidents
- the organisation's procedure for reporting an accident.

Questions

1 In view of the rapid increase in the number of visitors to Pinder & Moore (Case Study 4) in recent months the Managing Director wishes to improve the reception procedures and to tighten up on security. Draft guidelines on dealing with the following:

a) callers with an appointment
b) casual callers
c) difficult and angry callers
d) company security measures (*PEI OP2*)

2 You are asked to be responsible for the reception area during the absence of the full-time receptionist.

a) Explain the duties that might be performed by the receptionist in taking responsibility for the security of the reception area. Give examples where appropriate.

b) Explain the advantages of a telephone answering machine to Salter Snacks. Describe the features available that might assist Sarah when her work takes her away from the office.

c) Prepare a message to be recorded on the telephone answering machine

d) You overhear the following conversation. Make constructive comments.

Reception, 'Hello.'

Caller, 'Is that Salter Snacks Ltd?'

Reception, 'Yes it is.'

Caller, 'Can I speak to Tony Brown please?'

Receptionist, 'He's not in today.'

Caller, 'It is rather urgent.'

Receptionist, 'Could you ring back tomorrow?'

Caller, 'Well I'm only in this country for a few days and I wanted to talk about purchasing some of your products.'

Receptionist, 'I could try the Assistant Sales Manager for you.'

Caller, 'Thank you.'

Receptionist (After a few minutes), 'She's not in her office either. Why don't you ring her this afternoon?' (PEI OP2)

3 The reception area is being updated. Reception duties vary according to the size of an organisation.

a) Briefly describe four important differences in the duties of a receptionist in a large and in a small organisation.

b) How can the reception area be used to promote the products of the Company? (LCCI PSC)

4 Reception duties form part of many secretarial posts and some callers do not have appointments. Describe the secretary's role in:

a) receiving callers with appointments

b) dealing with callers without appointments (LCCI PSC)

5 On 5 June 199-, the following people called at the reception desk of Grosvenor Engineering plc.

Mr Roger Brook of B & C Electronics saw the Managing Director at 10.15 am. At 11.05 am Miss V Davids requested an appointment with the personnel department on private business.

The marine department received Mr C Kavil of A Peters plc at 4.00 pm.

Mr G T Robinson came at 9.30 am for an appointment in the diesel department. (He is a representative of Tabco plc.)

Mr D Samuels of Fitzroy Ltd arrived at 2.00 pm for an appointment in the sales department.

Enter the particulars of these callers in the order in which they arrived, in a register of callers. Use the 24-hour time system.

6 An important, but very impatient, man calls to see your employer, who can see him either in an hour's time or on another day at a time to be arranged. Explain how you would deal with this caller.

7 What action do you consider could be taken in your company in the following situations reported by the receptionist:

a) A parcel of printer ribbons has arrived by post. It is addressed to your company but was not ordered by any member of staff.

b) A number of petty thefts by intruders have been reported in neighbouring firms.

c) No reply is being received from certain departments when contacted on the intercom during the middle of the day.

d) Delay is being caused to callers saying they have appointments, by the receptionist having to verify details from the departments concerned. (LCCI PSC)

8 Describe items and information you think it would be useful to include in a day's induction course for a new receptionist to enable her to perform the work efficiently as soon as possible. (LCCI PSC)

9 Comlon International plc has booked a stand at EXPO '9-, a major event to be held in Birmingham. Some secretaries have been chosen to attend the event to provide back-up to the main sales team. Their main tasks will be greeting clients, assisting with the running of the stand (including provision of refreshments), and ensuring that details of prospective clients are recorded in a systematic way. Draft a memorandum briefing the secretaries on their duties and appropriate behaviour for the day. (LCCI PSC)

10 Mr X calls at your office to see your employer, who has forgotten about the appointment and is now lunching at his club with an important overseas client. How would you deal with the situation?

In-tray exercise

11 You are employed at Office Products Ltd (Case Study 2). A new relief receptionist has been appointed and you are required to supply her with a

rapid guide to information which she may require during the course of her duties as receptionist/switchboard operator. Complete the boxes on the right–hand side with the names of the reference sources for the information listed below:

Reception Office
Sources of Information

1 Internal telephone numbers for staff.

2 Staff positions and their sections and departments.

3 Names of last week's callers.

4 Telephone number of one of yesterday's visitors.

5 Names of today's callers who have arranged appointments.

6 Details of the company's products.

7 Names and addresses of local hotels and places of entertainment.

8 Information to direct visitors to other parts of the town.

9 Telex numbers of other companies in the town.

10 Fax numbers of other companies in the town.

11 Dialling codes for telephoning countries abroad.

UNIT 7 Materials and equipment

7.1 Office supplies, furniture and equipment

Carefully selected furniture and equipment can make an important contribution to the morale of staff and can also be the means of increasing business efficiency and making the most effective use of space. Unsuitable furniture may have serious repercussions on the health and welfare of staff, which may ultimately result in a high level of absenteeism and staff turnover.

The secretary's office will normally contain the following items of furniture and equipment:

Desk

Typist's chair and additional chairs for callers

Word processor

Filing cabinets with appropriate folders and files and/or microfilm equipment

Stationery cupboard or container

Wastepaper basket

Bookcase with appropriate reference books

Telephone for external and internal communications

Clock

Wallboard for charts and plans

Safe with cash box and books

Fire extinguisher

Dictating machine, print calculator, office copier, fax, computer terminal, etc, as required.

Furniture

Furniture for the modern electronic office should be of the purpose-built systems type in order to provide for the needs of staff operating such equipment as VDUs, word processors, computers, microfilm equipment, etc. Provision also must be made for cabling which should be as unobtrusive as possible. Wiring channels can be incorporated in desks so that telephones and task lighting can be positioned in convenient places, thereby eliminating trailing cables.

Modern designs also provide for the needs of staff working in groups and sharing inter-related equipment. Such multiple workstation configurations facilitate the collaboration of staff in joint projects and the furniture easily interfaces with computing equipment. The terminal desks can have keyboard extensions for efficient and comfortable operation and a feature of the printer table is a paper feed slot in the table with a paper storage shelf below.

Several finishes are available for office furniture but the choice is basically wood, plastic or metal.

The secretary's office will usually be located in one of the following situations:

- a separate 'cellular' office adjoining the executive's office
- a work area in the executive's own office
- a work area in an open-plan office

The schedule for the Health and Safety (display Screen Equipment) Regulations 1992 sets out minimum requirements for office desks and chairs, as follows:

Work desk or work surface

- The work desk or work surface shall have a sufficiently large, low-reflectance surface and allow a flexible arrangement of the screen, keyboard, documents and related equipment.
- The document holder shall be stable and adjustable and shall be positioned so as to minimise the need for uncomfortable head and eye movements.
- There shall be adequate space for operators or users to find a comfortable position.

Work chair

- The work chair shall be stable and allow the operator or user easy freedom of movement and a comfortable position.

- The seat shall be adjustable in height.
- The seat back shall be adjustable in both height and tilt.
- A foot rest shall be made available to any operator or user who wishes one.
- The British Standards Specification BS 5940:1980 gives the following measurements for typists' chairs:

  a Height of seat from ground 393.7 mm (15.5 in) adjustable to 495.3 mm (19.5 in)
  b Back to front of seat not less than 330.2 mm (13 in)
  c Width of the seat 406.4 to 431.8 mm (16 to 17 in)
  d Back-rest height from seat level adjustable between 203.2 and 304.8 mm (8 and 12 in)
  e Depth of back-rest 127.0 to 152.4 mm (5 to 6 in)
  f Width of back-rest not greater than 304.8 mm (12 in).

These characteristics are designed to ensure that the typist sits comfortably on the chair, with the small of the back supported by the back-rest and with the feet resting firmly on the floor.

Stationery

Office statonery (or consumable office supplies) comprises the materials which are used in the administration of office work. These include typewriting paper (bond for top copies and bank for carbon copies), computer printout paper, writing paper, shorthand notebooks, envelopes, labels, postcards, carbon paper, typewriter/printer ribbons, paper clips and fasteners, laser toner, copier supplies, files and folders, floppy disks, string, adhesive tape, pencils, pens, erasers, compliment slips, memo forms, petty cash vouchers, telephone message pads, and supplies of various office forms, etc.

International paper sizes

Here are examples of some of the common uses for the different sizes of paper (see Fig. 7.1):

A3 legal documents, balance sheets and financial statements

A4 business letters, reports, minutes, agenda, specifications, bills of quantities, estimates, quotations, invoices

A5 short letters, memos, invoices (small), credit notes, statements

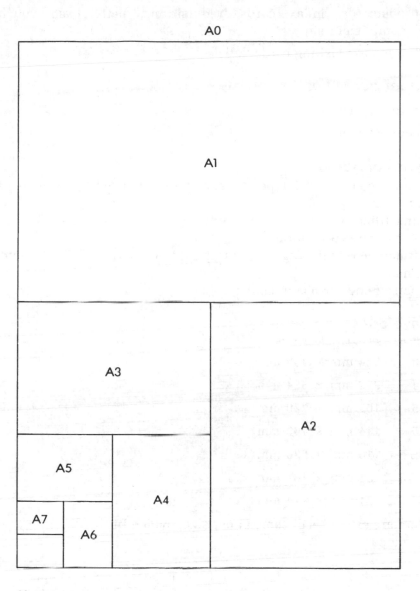

Sizes

A0 = 841 mm×1189 mm	A4 = 210 mm× 297 mm
A1 = 594 mm× 841 mm	A5 = 148 mm× 210 mm
A2 = 420 mm× 594 mm	A6 = 105 mm× 148 mm
A3 = 297 mm× 420 mm	A7 = 74 mm× 105 mm

Fig 7.1 International paper sizes

A6 postcards, index cards, requisitions, petty cash vouchers, compliment slips

A7 business visiting cards, labels

Paper quantities

Quire   25 sheets

Ream   500 sheets

Types of paper

Bond a good quality type of paper which is used for headed paper and 'top-copy' work.

Bank (flimsy) a cheaper and lighter grade of paper used for carbon copies and sets of forms.

Airmail very thin (lightweight) paper for correspondence sent by airmail.

Copier bond for use in copiers.

Envelopes

International envelope sizes

C3   324 mm × 458 mm

C4   229 mm × 324 mm

C5   162 mm × 229 mm

C6   114 mm × 162 mm

DL   110 mm × 220 mm

C7/6   81 mm × 162 mm

C7   81 mm × 114 mm

Here are examples of some paper sizes which fit the different sizes of envelope:

Envelope	Paper unfolded	Paper folded once	Paper folded twice
C3	A3	A2	A1
C4	A4	A3	A2
C5	A5	A4	A3
C6	A6	A5	A4
C7/6			A5

Types of envelope

Banker the opening is on the longer side.

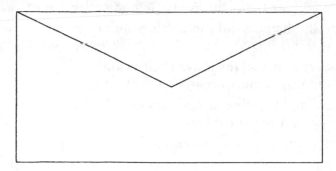

Pocket the opening is on the shorter side.

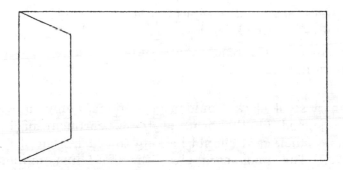

Window contains a 'window' opening with transparent material covering it, dispensing with the need for the typist to type the name and address on the envelope.

Aperture as above but with an uncovered address panel.

Stock control

It is important to maintain a satisfactory stock-control system, as stationery and other office supplies must always be available when they are required, and they must be kept in good condition in the stationery storeroom.

Guidelines for stock control of office consumables:

- Appoint one person to be in charge of issuing and ordering office consumables.

271

- Allocate a central storeroom for housing stocks of stationery and other supplies.
- Allocate regular times for the issue and collection of supplies.
- Arrange the items neatly in cupboards or on shelves with clear labels at the front.
- Place heavy items on the lower shelves and arrange the items used frequently in the most accessible positions.
- Store any highly-inflammable materials in sealed containers and preferably in a metal cabinet.
- Prohibit smoking in the storeroom.
- Adopt a FIFO (first in first out) system for issuing stock, to avoid deterioration.
- Check that every issue is covered by a requisition, authorised by a supervisor.
- Enter every issue and receipt on a stock control card, keeping a watchful eye on stock levels.
- When stock levels reach the re-order level, order up to the maximum figure.

The stationery stock clerk should issue stationery only on receipt of a requisition signed by the head of the department of the office concerned. A stock card should be kept for each item of stationery (see Fig 7.2). The stock card gives the maximum, minimum and reorder stock levels. When the balance in stock has been reduced to the re-order level, the stationery stock clerk knows that a further quantity of stock has to be ordered. The clerk is guided in the amount of the order, as the total of the balance in stock and the new order must not exceed the maximum stock figure (stated on the card). A record is kept of the receipt of stock from the suppliers and the issues of stock to departments.

A computer can be used to maintain stock records, with the minimum and maximum levels stored in its memory. When receipts and issues are entered on the keyboard, the balance of stock is automatically updated and the screen shows the operator when the re-order level has been reached, thus indicating the need for re-ordering.

Effective systems for controlling stationery are very important, as the efficiency of an office depends very largely upon the availability of suitable materials as and when they are required by members of the staff.

STATIONERY STOCK CARD

ITEM: A.4. White. Bank. Paper.... MAXIMUM STOCK: 50. reams...

.... MINIMUM STOCK: 20. reams...

STOCK REF NO............... P.112.... RE-ORDER LEVEL. 30 reams....

DATE	RECEIPTS			ISSUES			BALANCE IN STOCK
	Quantity Received	Invoice No	Supplier	Quantity Issued	Reqn No	Dept	
1.1.19 –							35
14.1.19 –				15	x14	Accounts	20
20.1.19 –	30	19263	Elite Paper Co				50
27.1.19 –				3	x 29	Sales	47

Fig 7.2 Stationery stock card

Every piece of paper or envelope used unnecessarily adds to the cost of running the business, and the utmost care must be taken by all staff to ensure that stationery is used economically.

Questions

1   It is required to secure greater economy in the use of stationery in your office. You are asked to investigate the present position and submit a report of your findings together with suggestions. (*LCCI PESD*)

2   The desks, tables and chairs in your typists' office are being replaced by new ones. You are asked to make a report for the Office Manager on suitable modern equipment. What would you recommend him to buy? He has asked you to set out your reasons clearly.

3   You have been promoted from the typing pool to become secretary to the Manager, who has never before had his own secretary. An additional small room has been acquired for you. It is newly decorated but is empty. Make a list of the furniture and equipment you will need.

4   Memorandum   To: Company Secretary
                            From: Managing Director via Personal Secretary

I am disturbed at the state of affairs existing in relation to our stationery stocks. I find that no one person is responsible for ordering and dispensing stationery; instead, when any item cannot immediately be found, any of the senior staff telephone further orders. Tables, shelves and floor in the stockroom are piled high with mixed stationery; many packets have their wrappers torn open allowing contents to be soiled and creased. I would recommend that we institute a control system right away and I submit the following ideas for your consideration:

Complete this memorandum. (*LCCI PESD*)

5 You are in charge of the Department's stationery requirements.

a) What is the importance of stationery stock control?
b) What system would you use and why? (*LCCI PSC*)

6 a) Rule up a stationery stock record card for A5 bond paper and make the following entries:

Maximum stock: 50 reams Minimum stock: 20 reams
1.3 Balance in stock: 45 reams
8.3 Issued 10 reams to Sales Department
10.3 Issued 12 reams to Typing Pool
22.3 Bought 25 reams from L P Stevens & Co Ltd
1.4 Issued 8 reams to Purchases Department
12.4 Issued 10 reams to Typing Pool
23.4 Issued 10 reams to Works Department

When re-stocking this item on 30 April, what quantity would you order?
b) Explain the importance of the maximum and minimum figures in connection with stock-taking.
c) What do you understand by (i) a ream, (ii) A5?

In-tray exercises

7 You are employed by Office Products Ltd (Case Study 2) and responsible for controlling the stationery supplies in the company.

a) From the stock requisitions on page 275 select those relating to A4 bond paper white 74 gsm (ref A4HW) and record the items in date order on a stock control card. Twenty-three reams were in stock before the entries were made.
b) Make out a purchase requisition to the Purchasing Department ordering a suitable quantity of A4 bond paper white, 74 gsm to make up the stock (– maximum stock figure is set at 50). This paper is normally supplied in multiples of 10 reams. Sign the requisition and date it with today's date; the requisition reference is ST493.

STOCK REQUISITION

To: Stores   No: P 164

From: Purchasing   Date: 24ᵗʰ June 19-

Quantity	Ref	Description
3 Reams	A4 CH	A4 - Bond Paper White 74 gsm (Headed)

Authorization: P Wilder

STOCK REQUISITION

To: Stores   No: AD 73

From: Advertising   Date: 23ʳᵈ June 19-

Quantity	Ref	Description
6 Reams	A4 HW	Bond Paper A4 White 74 gsm

Authorization: B S Brophy

STOCK REQUISITION

To: Stores   No: A 11

From: Accounts   Date: 24ᵗʰ June 19-

Quantity	Ref	Description
2	A4 HW	Reams A4 White Bond Paper 74 gsm

Authorization: D. Cooper

STOCK REQUISITION

To: Stores   No: S 45

From: Marketing   Date: 20ᵗʰ June 19-

Quantity	Ref	Description
4 Reams	A4 HW	Bond Paper A4 White 74 gsm

Authorization: A. M. Mitchell

STOCK REQUISITION

To: Stores   No: S 46

From: Marketing   Date: 22ⁿᵈ June 19-

Quantity	Ref	Description
4 Reams	A4 BW	A4 Bank Paper White
4 Reams	A4 LW	A4 Bond Paper White 61 gsm

Authorization: A. M. Mitchell

STOCK REQUISITION

To: Stores   No: AD 72

From: Advertising   Date: 21 June 19-

Quantity	Ref	Description
3 Reams	A4 LW	A4 Bond Paper White - 61 gsm
2 Reams	A4 CH	A4 Bond Paper White 74 gsm (Headed)

Authorization: B S Brophy

STOCK REQUISITION

To: Stores   No: W 15

From: Wages   Date: 22ⁿᵈ June 19-

Quantity	Ref	Description
2 Reams	A4 HW	A4 Bond Paper White 74 gsm
1 Ream	A4 BW	A4 Bank Paper White

Authorization: A.T. Thomas

STOCK REQUISITION

To: Stores   No: P 163

From: Purchasing   Date: 23ʳᵈ June 19-

Quantity	Ref	Description
5 Reams	A4 LW	A4 Bond Paper White 61 gsm
3 Reams	A4 HW	A4 Bond Paper White 74 gsm

Authorization: P. Wilder

275

8 You are employed by the New Tech Office Services Bureau (Case Study 1) and are required to deal with the following message left by Mrs Robinson on the dictating machine:

Will you please supply me with lists of furniture, equipment and office consumables which we shall require for the secretary's office at the new branch.

9 This task is based at Pinder and Moore (see Case Study 4).

At present Pinder & Moore's stock control system is still done by a stock control clerk hand writing control cards, and although the stock control is centralised it takes time to keep up with stock movements and consequently items are frequently unavailable especially at the beginning of the new school year.

a) Write a short report explaining ways of updating their stock control systems using new technology.

b) In the report mention how the various agents and branches could be involved.

c) Explain the terms 'maximum' and 'minimum' stock levels. (*PEI OP2*)

Financial control

8.1 Control of cash

A petty cash account is used for recording small items of business expenditure or the private expenditure of the executives. An agreed sum of money is allocated to the petty cashier out of which all incidental cash payments are made. At the end of the month or other period of time, the amount spent is refunded, thus restoring the allocation to the original amount. The original amount is called an 'imprest' or 'float'. This method of keeping the petty cash is known as the 'imprest system'.

The three stages in the procedure for the imprest system are:

1 A sum of money estimated to be sufficient to cover the month's expenditure is allocated to the petty cashier.
2 During the course of the month the petty cashier uses this money for paying for small purchases.
3 At the end of the period the petty cashier receives a sum of money to cover the expenditure, thus bringing the total cash back up to the original amount.

Whenever cash is paid out, a voucher or receipt should be obtained, which means that at all times the total of the cash plus the current month's vouchers should equal the amount of the imprest. The vouchers should be numbered as they are received and filed in numerical order. A specimen petty cash voucher is given in Fig 8.1.

In a business the petty cash account is a subsidiary of the cash account and it relieves the cash account of the many small items of cash expenditure which are so necessary for day-to-day organisation.

The following procedure is used for petty cash:

1 When cash is paid from the cashier to the petty cashier:

PETTY CASH EXPENSE	DATE: 6 March 19 -		
REQUIRED FOR:		VAT AMOUNT	TOTAL AMOUNT INCLUDING VAT
Window cleaning		2 | 10	14 | 10
PAID BY: J. Potts	TOTAL	2 | 10	14 | 10
CHARGE TO: Admin .	AUTHORISED BY: L. Brown		

Fig 8.1   Petty cash voucher

Cr Cash account (enter the amount in the credit column)
Dr Petty cash account (enter the amount in the debit column)

2 When a petty cash payment is made:
Cr Petty cash account

3 At the end of the period:
Dr Ledger Accounts with the totals of each of the petty cash account analysis columns.

4 When a trial balance is taken out, the petty cash balance must be debited.

An example of a petty cash account is given in Fig 8.2 in answer to the following question:

Enter the following transactions in the petty cash account of Roberts Designs plc, showing the analysis under the headings of Postage, Stationery, Travelling Expenses, and Office Expenses:

19—
Feb   1   Received £60 for petty cash float
            Bought postage stamps for £3.50
       5   Paid fares £3.20
       6   Paid £14.10 for cleaning office windows (£2.10 VAT included)
       10   Paid £1.80 for tea
       11   Paid for envelopes £4.70 (70p VAT included)
       15   Bought postage stamps for £3.80

18 Paid £1.50 for bus fares

20 Paid £9.40 for a stapler (£1.40 VAT included)

23 Paid £2.49 for postal order

27 Bought postage stamps for £3.00

28 Paid office milk bill £3.00

Mar 1 Received total amount of expenditure for February

The arrangement of the columns in the petty cash account is important and the columns, numbered for reference purposes, in Fig 8.2 represent:

1 Date of cash received or balances brought down.

2 Details of cash received.

3 Folio column, ie the reference number of the double entry. In this instance the item of £60 cash paid to the petty cashier can be seen on cash account, page 1.

4 Total amounts of cash received.

5 The date payment is made.

6 Details of the payment made.

7 The receipt or voucher number entered.

8 The total cash paid out.

9 Various analysis columns (each column represents an account in the ledger).

The analysis columns can be varied to suit individual requirements. Each column represents an account in the ledger, and at the end of a month or other period the total in the column is transferred to the ledger account. The total of the analysis columns should equal the main total (no 8). The following points should be noted in the example given:

a The £60 received on 1 February was debited 'Cash'.

b When postage stamps were bought on 1 February, the amount of cash was taken out of the petty cash box and an entry made on the credit side of the account, first of all in the total column and then in the analysis column 'Postage'. Every item of expenditure is entered twice, once in the total column and once in the respective analysis column.

c On 28 February all the money columns were totalled up; the analysis columns were underlined and the ledger account numbers, eg L2, written below the totals. The amount of the total column was

PETTY CASH ACCOUNT OF ROBERTS DESIGNS plc

Debit													Credit
①	②	③	④	⑤	⑥	⑦	⑧			⑨			
Date	Details	Fo	Total	Date	Details	V N	Total £	Postage £	Stationery £	Trav Exp £	Office Exp £	VAT £	
19 Feb 1	Cash	CA1	60 00	19 Feb 1	Stamps	1	3 50	3 50					
				" 5	Fares	2	3 20			3 20			
				" 6	Cleaning	3	14 10				12 00	2 10	
				" 10	Tea	4	1 80				1 80		
				" 11	Envelopes	5	4 70		4 00			0 70	
				" 15	Stamps	6	3 80	3 80					
				" 18	Fares	7	1 50			1 50			
				" 20	Stapler	8	9 40		8 00			1 40	
				" 23	Postal Order	9	2 49	2 49					
				" 27	Stamps	10	3 00	3 00					
				" 28	Milk	11	3 00				3 00		
							50 49	12 79	12 00	4 70	16 80	4 20	
				" 28	Balance	c/d	9 51	L1	L2	L3	L4	L5	
			60 00				60 00						
March 1	Balance	b/d	9 51										
" 1	Cash	CA2	50 49										

Fig 8.2   Petty cash account

	A	B	C	D	E	F	G	H	I	J	K	L	M	N
1		Jan	Feb	Mar	Apr	May	Jun	Jul	Aug	Sep	Oct	Nov	Dec	Totals
2		£	£	£	£	£	£	£	£	£	£	£	£	£
3	Postage	14.00	12.79											26.79
4	Stationery	10.20	12.00											22.20
5	Travelling expenses	6.27	4.70											10.97
6	Office expenses	8.14	16.80											24.94
7	VAT	2.10	4.20											6.30
8														
9	EXPENDITURE TOTAL	40.71	50.49											91.20
10														
11	IMPREST	60.00	60.00	60.00	60.00	60.00	60.00	60.00	60.00	60.00	60.00	60.00	60.00	
12														
13	CASH BALANCE c/f	19.29	9.51											

Fig 8.3　Petty cash spreadsheet

deducted from the debit side (cash received) and the difference (known as the balance) entered below the total spent, namely £50.49. The debit and credit side totals were added up and entered on the same line. The balance of cash in hand, £9. 51, was carried down to the debit side below the total.

d On 1 March the amount spent, namely £50.49, was received to restore the 'imprest' to £60.

Control procedures

The control of accuracy and security of office cash requires:

- regular checking of the petty cash account and cash to ensure that the vouchers and cash held in the cash box equal the imprest
- prompt attention to any discrepancies which are identified
- strict adherence to cash handling security procedures, such as locking the cash box and keeping it in a safe place
- all petty cash vouchers to be sanctioned by authorised officials.

Planning and controlling expenditure

Careful planning and control of expenditure is important for establishing expenditure limits as well as ensuring that there are sufficient funds to meet expenses. Financial budgets, forecasts and cash flow statements all need to be regularly monitored and any variations from planned expenditure identified. Spreadsheets, as referred to on page 198, will normally be used to record and monitor such budgets, including petty cash. A spreadsheet for the petty cash account in Fig 8.2 would be as illustrated in Fig 8.3.

In cell C9 of Fig 8.3 a formula has been placed to tell the computer to add up all the figures in the column from C3 to C7 and in cell C13 the monthly total of expenditure is subtracted from the imprest in cell C11 to arrive at the balance of cash in hand. Cells N3 to N7 add up each of the individual monthly totals (Cells B3 to M3) to provide a total to date for each item of expenditure and cell N9 tells the computer to add up all the figures in the column from N3 to N7 to provide a total of all items of expenditure. Every time an entry is made the monthly and grand totals change, as well as the balance of cash in hand, providing an instant and effective method of controlling expenditure of petty cash.

Questions

1 On the 1st of the month, £250 was handed to you by the cashier to open a petty cash account. Using the imprest system, and in analysis form, enter the following transactions. Balance the petty cash account on the last day of the month, and carry down the balance.

			£	VAT included £
March	1	Postage stamps	5.00	
	2	Laundry of towels	14.10	2.10
	3	Date stamp and pad	8.75	1.30
	4	Postal order	0.90	
		Fax rolls	17.62	2.62
	5	Office cleaning	30.00	
	8	Aerogrammes	1.80	
	9	Laser toner	24.80	3.69
	10	Adhesive tape	0.94	0.14
	16	Refills for ballpoint pens	2.35	0.35
	19	Office cleaning	30.00	
	24	Mr Brown's expenses in Manchester	14.24	
	26	Office cleaning	30.00	
	29	Dusters	12.40	1.85
	31	Milk account	14.60	
		Window cleaning	16.45	2.45

2 From the information in the following petty cash book (which is kept on the imprest system) answer the questions given below.

Dr Cash received £	Date 19—	Details £	Totals £	Postage £	Office exps £	Stationery £	cr VAT £
4.08	Jan 1	Balance					
45.92		Cash					
	3	Postage	4.50	4.50			
	5	Stationery	9.40			8.00	1.40
		Coffee	4.20		4.20		
	6	Postage	7.25	7.25			
	7	Postal order	1.05	1.05			
		Pot plant	8.00		8.00		
	8	Stationery	5.87			5.00	0.87

a) What is the amount of the petty cash float?

b) What was the balance of petty cash at the end of the period?

c) How much was spent in Postage during the period?

d) How much was spent in Stationery during the period?

e) What was the total amount spent during the period?

f) How much must the petty cashier receive at the end of the period to make up the float?

g) Use a spreadsheet to prove the accuracy of your answers for a) to f).

3 Why would you expect to find two signatures on a completed petty cash voucher?

4 In a petty cash book, why are payments entered twice, once in the total column and again under an appropriate heading?

5 You have recently started a new job and among your duties is that of responsibility for the petty cash. This has previously been kept in a somewhat haphazard fashion, payment being made on production of odd pieces of paper, and your new employer has asked you to devise an acceptable system. Explain fully how you will do this and draw up six specimen entries. The company is a small one consisting of twelve employees, two of whom make several calls in the London area. (*LCCI PSC*)

6 You are a secretary in a small company and are responsible for some cash handling. Explain to your junior how she should deal with the following while you are away on holiday:

a) Remittances received in the incoming mail

b) Cash and cheques that she must pay into the bank

c) Acknowledging the receipt of a) and b), with guidance on when this is or is not necessary

d) Balancing the petty cash account (imprest system) and reopening it (*LCCI PSC*)

7 You are secretary/PA to Mr Matthew Davies, Sales and Marketing Director of John Peter Ltd, and a Junior Secretary, Katy Jones, has recently been appointed to assist you.

On Monday you managed a brief chat with Katy before her departure on a week's holiday. At the beginning of May, Katy had been made responsible for keeping the petty cash for the department. During your chat with her she confided to you that despite reading her Office Procedures textbook on petty cash she was finding it difficult to put theory into practice and had not yet begun to enter details in a petty cash book. Until now all information of purchases had been written on pieces of card, with the money for petty cash left loose in a drawer. You had felt concerned and had advised Katy that the purchase of a petty cash box with a voucher pad was necessary for security reasons.

To give Katy a start, you suggested that you purchase and begin the petty cash book during her absence. In addition, you offered to compile a note, postcard size, of the procedure to follow when keeping petty cash on the imprest system. Katy could then place this note in the petty cash box for reference purposes.

Compose this note for Katy and use all the information given below to complete the petty cash book from the beginning of May. Balance and restore the imprest on 12 May. Complete and number the petty cash vouchers for purchases made by you on 15 May. Sign and leave these vouchers for Mr Davies' written approval and provisionally enter these details in the petty cash book.

> Mon 1/5 Cash £55; 3/5 Stamps £14.50;
> 4/5 Coffee £3.95; 9/5 Leaving gift
> £17.25 including £2.60 VAT; Taxi fare
> £2.25; 12/5 Milk bill (2 weeks) –
> total of £8.30; Typing ribbon £4.90
> including 73p VAT; Urgent letter
> (Special Delivery) £2.07;
> 12/5 Rec'd from Basil, Chief Cashier,
> cash to restore imprest to £55 again.
>
> 15/5 Purchase of pc box £7.95 inc £1.18 VAT
> and pc voucher pad £3.25 inc 48p VAT
> (expenditure verbally approved by Mr D)

8 a) What checks must be carried out to ensure that a petty cash voucher is accurately completed?
   b) Give three reasons why the balance shown in the petty cash book does not agree with the float in the petty cash box.
   c) Give six headings for petty cash book analysis columns. (*LCCI PSC*)

In-tray exercise

9 You are employed by Mr Brian Dobson, Manager of 'The Secretairs' (Case Study 3).

   You are required to make the following cash purchases for Mr Dobson during the current month:

   a greetings card
   60 first–class postage stamps
   6 electric light bulbs

packet of filter coffee
2 theatre tickets (£18 each)
3 aerogrammes
2 international postal reply coupons
4 minicassettes for pocket recorder
a ream of A4 bond typing paper
a spray of flowers
a bottle of sherry

You keep a record of these purchases in a petty cash account and maintain an imprest of £100 which is restored at the end of each month by cashing a cheque. At the beginning of the current month you have a balance of cash of £100. Prepare petty cash vouchers for the above items and enter them in your petty cash account with appropriate analysis columns. Restore the imprest at the end of the month and make out a cheque for this amount for Mr Dobson's signature.

8.2   Methods of payment

The following methods of payment may be used in a business transaction:

- cash (including registration and COD)
- postal orders
- overseas postal and international payments
- girobank
- cheques
- credit transfers
- credit cards
- standing orders
- direct debits
- bills of exchange

Cash

Coins and notes may be sent through the post provided they are registered. See page 64 for details of registration. A trader may use cash to settle accounts when a representative calls, as is frequently done in a small retail business. Offices normally use cash to make small payments necessary for the running of their business, and a petty cash account is kept of these amounts. Wages and salaries may also be paid in cash.

Postal orders

Postal orders are a convenient method of remitting small sums, up to the value of £20 by post. They are issued by the Post Office for various amounts between 50p and £20. In addition to the face value, a poundage is charged.

Up to 49p in postage stamps may be attached to postal orders to increase their value.

The sender should complete the name of the payee and the office of payment on the postal order. The postal order may be crossed to ensure that payment is made only through a bank. A counterfoil is attached to it, and should be completed and kept for reference (see Fig 8.4).

The payee must sign the postal order and present it for payment at

287

Fig 8.4 A postal order

a post office unless it has been crossed, in which case it should be signed and paid into the payee's bank account.

A postal order is valid for six months from the last day of the month of issue. After the expiration of that period, the order should be sent to the local Royal Mail Customer Services Centre. If, after the necessary inquiry, payment is authorised, commission equal to the poundage will be charged.

International payments

International payments may be made all over the world through the Post Office. British postal orders may be sent for payment in a number of countries, details of which are given at post offices. Payments to most countries may otherwise be made through Girobank at the post office using the form 'Sending Money Abroad'. Payments in cash may be deposited at almost any UK post office; payments in cheque form should be sent direct to Girobank. A standard fee is charged for each transaction, no matter how great the sum being sent. Payment abroad is made by Girobank in the most appropriate form for the country of destination.

Girobank

Girobank plc is a subsidiary of the Alliance & Leicester Building Society. A London clearing bank, it offers a wide range of services, including full current account (cheque book) banking, with a cheque guarantee card available to qualifying customers. Girobank customers carry out much of their banking by direct mail and

288

telephone to the bank or at post offices around the country. All transactions are processed, and accounts ledgered, at the bank's Operations Centre in Bootle, Merseyside.

Banking

A bank offers the following services to its customers:

- It provides facilities to deposit and save money at interest.
- It lends money to approved borrowers (bank loans and bank overdrafts).
- By the cheque system, it provides an easy and safe means of payment (current account).
- It accepts standing orders, ie makes regular payment of bills.
- Direct debiting.
- It transfers credit by means of credit transfers and the BACS system (bankers' automated clearing service).
- Credit card/charge card.
- It provides facilities for withdrawing cash from autobanks (cash cards and switch services).
- Personal budget accounts.
- It discounts bills of exchange.
- It provides drafts (inland and foreign) and other methods for payment abroad, eg mail transfer, telegraphic transfer and a computer message switching system.
- It issues foreign currency and traveller's cheques.
- It takes charge of customers' securities, eg stock and share certificates, jewellery and other valuables.
- It provides night safe facilities.
- It acts as executor and/or trustee.
- It obtains information for customers concerning investments and makes investments on their behalf, as well as operating an investment management service.
- Insurance advisory service.
- Business advisory service which is available to small companies to improve their efficiency.
- Assistance to companies with their development, documentation and finance of exports and imports.

- Personal pension plans.
- Travel and financial services for business executives with an internationally recognised charge card.

Many of these services are also offered by Building Societies.

Deposit/savings accounts

These accounts are used for the purpose of earning interest on savings and sums of money surplus to current requirements. Up to £500 can usually be withdrawn without notice at cash machines using a cash card or by cheque after transferring any amount required to a current account. Sums in excess of £500 must be withdrawn at a bank counter. The money invested earns full interest right up to the day it is withdrawn. Interest gained in all bank accounts by personal customers who are not liable for higher rates of income tax has basic rate tax deducted at source, ie before it is paid to the customer. A high-interest savings account may be used to invest sums in excess of £5000 in return for considerably higher rates of interest. Withdrawals require 90 days (minimum £500). Usually the customer will also open a current account for their present requirements in addition to a deposit/savings account.

Current accounts for personal customers

A current account is an account into which payments are made and on which cheques are drawn. Money is paid into a current account by the use of a paying-in book or slip or by credit transfers. Withdrawals are made by cheque, standing orders or direct debits. Most banks now pay a small amount of interest on current accounts with credit balances. Account holders are also issued with autocheque cards (explained later in this unit) and may also use the standing order and direct debit services.

If accounts are overdrawn, there will normally be a charge and interest levied on the amount of the overdraft. A new kind of account is offered by certain banks in which, on payment of a monthly fee, customers can receive interest-free overdrafts, usually up to overdrawn amounts of £250.

Linked current and savings accounts

A number of accounts and services may be packaged together, as in the case of Midland's Orchard. This provides a current account (with interest on sums which are in credit); a savings account (with higher rates of interest); and 'automatic sweep' from the current account to the savings account, giving automatic transfer when the current account funds reach a predetermined level.

Business current accounts

In addition to the usual current account facilities, business current accounts provide access to a high interest account for any surplus funds and a business cash card for:

- daily cash withdrawals from self-service machines of up to £1000
- daily access to account balances and printed statements
- transfers between current and high interest accounts
- 'switch' facilities for the payment of goods and services

Special arrangements may be made for overdraft facilities.

A business start-up service is available, providing free consultations with a bank manager, a year's free banking while the account is in credit and other forms of assistance for small businesses.

High interest cheque accounts (HICA)

A high interest cheque account may be used by those who have large sums of money to invest (£2000 minimum) and require easy access to their money.

Money can be withdrawn, without loss of interest, by the following methods:

- cheque   for paying amounts in excess of £100
  for withdrawing a minimum of £100 cash from the branch where the account is held, or between £100 and £200 in cash from another branch, using a cheque and an autocheque card

- HICA card   for withdrawing up to £500 a day from a self-
  with PIN   service cash machine

Different rates of interest are payable, according to the amounts invested, and these are credited to investors at half-yearly intervals.

Flexi-loan accounts

These accounts provide a flexible means of borrowing money from banks. The customer selects a borrowing limit, which can be for any amount from £500 to £5000, and by special cheque may draw out as much as is required within these limits. Any sum from one tenth to one twenty-fifth of the borrowing limit may be selected for repaying the loan on a monthly basis from the customer's current account. The amount chosen determines how long it will take to repay the loan. A lump sum payment may also be made to reduce the amount owing, or the loan may be repaid completely. As soon as the amount borrowed has been repaid in full, the monthly transfer from the current account stops, but the loan facility remains open to the customer whenever it is required. Interest based on the amount owing is charged to the account each month on the same day as the payment is made from the current account.

An insurance protection plan may be entered into to cover loan repayments in the case of sickness, accident or unemployment.

Budget accounts

For these accounts customers estimate the total of their annual commitments which cannot normally be covered by standing orders, eg holidays, Christmas gifts, clothing, etc. By making a regular monthly standing order payment for one-twelfth of this total to their budget account, they can make out cheques from this account as and when required, thus spreading their outlay. Interest is only charged while the account is overdrawn.

Teenagers'/students' accounts

The banks offer special bank accounts for 'tomorrow's adults' which provide them with interest on savings, cheque book facilities and easy access to their money with autocheque cards. A minimum of £10 is required to open an account.

Telephone banking

A telephone operated account can be offered with First Direct. The normal range of services is available including current accounts, overdrafts, loans and savings accounts. An advantage of this type of bank is that it is open for telephoned transactions every day of the year for 24 hours a day.

Opening a current account

When opening a current account with a bank, a customer will be asked to provide the following:

1 One satisfactory form of identification from each party to the account. Normally only a full British passport or full driving licence

is acceptable. A credit register and voters' roll search is then taken to establish the creditworthiness of the customer. If these conditions are not met, then references may be taken up, either from the customer's employer or from an established customer, although most banks have now dispensed with the use of references altogether.

2 A specimen signature in the way in which the cheques will be signed. This is necessary for reference where a signature on a presented cheque needs to be verified.

3 If a joint account is being opened, both parties must sign a mandate authorising the banker to honour cheques with both signatures or with individual signatures. If a change of style of signature is adopted, the bank must be informed.

The bank provides the new customer with:

- a cheque book
- a bank statement
- a paying-in book

Cheque book

A cheque is a written order to a bank to pay on demand a stated sum of money and bears the name of the person to whom it is to be paid.

Each cheque has a serial number which is recorded when the cheque book is issued. Counterfoils are attached to the cheques and the particulars on the actual cheque are repeated on these for record purposes.

Bank statement

The bank statement is an account, on which the bank enters a record of all the transactions between the customer and itself involving the receipt and payment of money.

The balance of the bank statement is the sum which the bank has in hand of the customer's money in the current account. It may not agree with what the customer thinks their credit balance should be because of the following reasons:

a cheques paid into the bank but not credited

b unpresented cheques

c bank charges

d standing order and direct debit payments

e credit transfers

A business would make out a reconciliation statement in order to show why the cash book and bank statement balances disagree.

A typical bank statement is given in Fig 8.5.

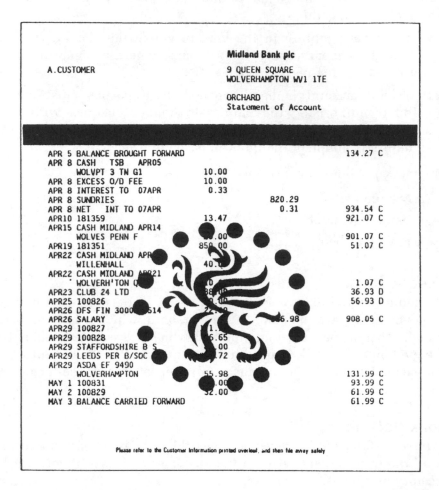

Midland Bank plc

A.CUSTOMER

9 QUEEN SQUARE
WOLVERHAMPTON WV1 1TE

ORCHARD
Statement of Account

APR 5 BALANCE BROUGHT FORWARD			134.27 C
APR 8 CASH TSB APR05			
WOLVPT 3 TN G1	10.00		
APR 8 EXCESS O/D FEE	10.00		
APR 8 INTEREST TO 07APR	0.33		
APR 8 SUNDRIES		820.29	
APR 8 NET INT TO 07APR		0.31	934.54 C
APR10 181359	13.47		921.07 C
APR15 CASH MIDLAND APR14			
WOLVES PENN F	.00		901.07 C
APR19 181351	850.00		51.07 C
APR22 CASH MIDLAND APR			
WILLENHALL	40.		
APR22 CASH MIDLAND APR21			
WOLVERH'TON Q			1.07 C
APR23 CLUB 24 LTD	88.		36.93 D
APR25 100826	.00		56.93 D
APR26 DFS FIN 3000 514	22.		
APR26 SALARY		6.98	908.05 C
APR29 100827	1.		
APR29 100828	6.65		
APR29 STAFFORDSHIRE B S	.00		
APR29 LEEDS PER B/SOC	.72		
APR29 ASDA EF 9490			
WOLVERHAMPTON	55.98		131.99 C
MAY 1 100831	.00		93.99 C
MAY 2 100829	52.00		61.99 C
MAY 3 BALANCE CARRIED FORWARD			61.99 C

Please refer to the Customer Information printed overleaf, and then file away safely

Fig 8.5   A bank statement

Paying-in book

A paying-in book is used for recording payments made into a current account. Each page is divided into two parts by perforated lines. One part is kept by the bank and the other part is left in the book and retained by the customer as an acknowledgement of the amount paid in. The bank clerk will initial and stamp the customer's copy. The

MIDLAND BANK plc

Date 2-08-19

Credit R. CARTER & SONS

£50 Notes		
£20 Notes	60	1
£10 Notes	70	1
£5 Notes	35	1
£1 Note/Coin	3	1
S. & I. Notes		
50p	1	50
20p		60
Silver		15
Bronze		25
Total Cash	170	50
Cheques, P.O.'s etc.	225	48
see over		
£	395	98

575-5   Counterfoil

COUNTER CREDIT

Date 2-08-19

Cashier's stamp and initials

Fee | Number of cheques 3

575-5

---

bank giro credit

Code No. 40-17-8

Bank   MIDLAND BANK plc

Branch   BRIGHTON

Customer's Name   R. CARTER & SONS

Account No.   21389642

Paid in by   J Carter

Address _____ Ref. No. _____

PLEASE DO NOT WRITE OR MARK BELOW THIS LINE

£50 Notes		
£20 Notes	60	1
£10 Notes	70	1
£5 Notes	35	1
£1 Note/Coin	3	1
S. & I. Notes		
50p	1	50
20p		60
Silver		15
Bronze		25
Total Cash	170	50
Cheques, P.O.'s etc.	225	48
see over		
£	395	98

70

Fig 8.6   Paying-in slip

precise details of the money paid in (cash, notes, cheques, etc) must be stated (see Fig 8.6).

Alternatively, the bank giro credit slips, inserted towards the end of cheque books, can be used for paying money into a current account.

A branch advice system enables a customer to pay money into their own account at any branch of the bank concerned. Moreover, a customer of one bank can pay in at a branch of any other bank. For example, a customer with an account at a bank in Brighton can pay in at a different bank in a small country town where there is no branch of their own bank. A small service charge may be made.

Standing orders

A customer may give a banker a standing order to pay a certain sum of money periodically from the current account to a person or business. The customer does not then have the trouble of remembering the dates of payment and writing and posting the cheques. The instructions, which must be given to the banker in writing, must contain the amount, dates and payee's name and bank. Standing orders are commonly used for paying customers' private financial commitments, such as monthly mortgage repayments, annual subscriptions and insurance premiums, etc.

Direct debiting

Direct debiting is another method of arranging for a bank to make periodic payments on behalf of its customer. When the standing order method is used, the drawer initiates the instruction to make payment, but in the case of direct debiting it is the payee who requests the bank to collect an amount from the drawer's account. This method can be used for fixed amounts at fixed dates or for varying amounts at irregular intervals.

The payee may send the drawer an invoice and, after an agreed interval, arrange for the bank automatically to transfer the appropriate amount of credit. By this process the drawer is given an opportunity to check the amount concerned.

The payee must in all cases have written authority from the drawer in order to arrange for direct debiting to take place.

Credit transfers (or Bank Giro)

A credit transfer enables the customer to pay creditors without having to prepare separate cheques for each account. A list, containing the names of the creditors and the amounts to be paid, is sent to the bank once a month together with a cheque for the total amount. The bank then arranges for credit slips to be sent out to the various creditors through their banks. Each creditor participating in this scheme must first be approached and must give written authority for payment to be made to them in this form.

A big saving can be made in stationery, postage and time and, if a computer is used, the bank lists, credit advices and the journal are compiled automatically.

The credit transfer system can be employed not only by a trader for the payment of creditors, but also by an individual for transferring money into a bank account of a person or business who is to be paid. The remitter takes the bill for payment into any bank, where it is necessary to complete a credit transfer slip, giving the remitter's own name and address, the name of the payee, the payee's bank and branch, the amount of money, and the date. The amount of the bill is paid over the counter of the bank with the credit transfer slip and a small charge. The bank clerk will initial and stamp the counterfoil and return it to the remitter as a form of receipt for the money. The credit transfer slips are then sent to the bankers' clearing house, which distributes them to the various banks, and the payee's account is credited with the amount of the bill. After the bank has recorded the payment, the slip is sent on to the payee for information.

By this system, payments are made directly into a bank account instead of cash, postal orders or cheques being handled by the payee. It is also possible for bank customers to have their salaries, commissions, etc, paid straight into their accounts by credit transfers.

The bankers' automated clearing service (BACS) is a fully computerised bank giro credit system in which the funds are paid into the payee's account the same day that the bank's account is debited, providing an even faster means of transferring credit from one account to another.

Credit cards

The credit card system enables a person to purchase goods on credit at shops or other establishments which have agreed to participate in the scheme. Card holders may also withdraw cash up to their credit limit without prior notice, from any branch of the bank group participating in the scheme.

Card holders are notified of their credit limit, which is the maximum amount that they can owe to the bank at any time. They also receive a plastic credit card which must be submitted to the supplier when ordering goods or services. The supplier makes out a sales voucher in duplicate which is signed by the purchaser and has an impression inserted on it from the credit card. The supplier retains the copy of the sales voucher and issues the customer with the second copy. The Credit Card Centre issues each card holder with a monthly statement of the amount owing and, provided the card holder makes a payment not later than twenty-five days after the date on the statement, no charge is incurred. The supplier deposits the sales vouchers at a branch of the bank and is credited with the amounts less discount.

The scheme has the effect of reducing the amount of cash carried by shoppers and handled by traders and also reduces the number of cheques in circulation, since card holders simply make out one cheque to the bank instead of separate cheques to each of their traders.

It is also possible to obtain extended credit by spreading the cost of paying for a purchase over a longer period of time by arrangement with the bank.

Charge cards

On payment of an annual membership subscription, a charge card such as American Express or Diners, may be used to borrow money for the payment of goods and services. With these cards there is usually no credit limit placed on the holder and no interest is charged. Accounts are paid monthly by cheque or direct debit.

Cheque cards

Banks issue to their current account holders a cheque card containing the holder's specimen signature and a code number which facilitates the acceptance of cheques by traders. A cheque up to the value of £50/£100 accompanied by a cheque card will normally be accepted by traders as they are assured that such a cheque will be honoured by the bank on which it is drawn. Cheque card holders are also entitled to cash cheques up to £50/£100 at any branch of the bank without prior arrangements or any additional charge being incurred.

This is not a credit card, but a card of authority which makes the cheque a more useful means of payment for the customer and relieves them of carrying substantial amounts of cash.

Some banks issue autocheque cards which are dual-purpose in providing a cheque guarantee card as well as a cash card for drawing cash from an autobank and obtaining a bank statement (see below).

Self-service cash dispensers

Autocheque cards may be issued to bank customers to enable them to withdraw cash from autobanks during the day and evening. When a customer applies for an autocheque card, the bank advises them of their personal number (PIN). This has to be remembered as it is not recorded on their card nor on any document, for security reasons. If the card is lost or stolen it cannot be used for withdrawing cash unless the personal number is known. To obtain cash the card has to be inserted in the autobank machine, the personal number keyed in and buttons pressed to select the service and amount required (Fig 8.7). The card is returned, followed by the cash and a receipt (if requested). Step-by-step directions are displayed on a screen to guide the user in operating the machine. The customer is allocated a weekly cash withdrawal limit by the bank which remains the same from week to week.

As well as obtaining cash, self-service cash dispensers can be used to check the customer's current account balance, order a bank statement to be sent by post to their address, and transfer funds between current and savings accounts.

Advice from the banks for autocheque card holders:

Fig 8.7   A self-service cash dispenser

- keep your cheque book and card separately
- never leave your card in public places or in your car
- keep your card away from any magnetic card used for opening security doors
- do not tell your PIN to anyone
- do not record your PIN in a way that allows another person to discover it
- do not keep a record of your PIN with your card
- never quote your PIN in correspondence or over the telephone
- if you think that someone has discovered your PIN, inform your bank immediately
- if your card is lost or stolen, inform your bank immediately

Crossed cheques

Two parallel lines across the face of a cheque constitute a crossing and prevent its being cashed across the counter of a bank. A crossed cheque cannot be paid to anyone except a banker, ie the payee must pay the cheque into their bank account and their banker must collect the amount from the drawee banker and place it to the credit of the payee. If a person requires cash for a crossed cheque made payable to them, they must make out their own cheque in the usual way. Crossing does not prevent theft, but it provides a means of tracing the cheque, since the thief must use a bank account to obtain the money.

The words 'A/C Payee' are normally printed between the lines of the crossing to ensure that the cheque can only be paid into the account of the person to whom it is made out. A cheque with this type of crossing is given in Fig. 8.8.

Cheques

There are three parties to a cheque:

1 The **drawer** — the person who draws, ie signs, a cheque and whose account will be debited.
2 The **drawee** — the bank on which the cheque is drawn, ie the drawer's bank.
3 The **payee** — the person to whom the cheque is made payable.

A cheque must always be written in pen and contain the points illustrated in Fig 8.8, the descriptions of which are as follows:

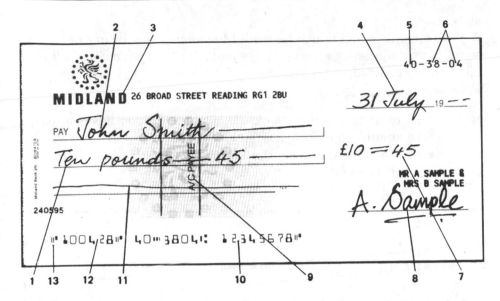

Fig 8.8 A specimen cheque with A/C Payee crossing

1 The amount of pounds in words.

2 The name of the payee.

3 The name and address of the drawee.

4 The date, written in the order of day, month and year.

5 The national number of the bank.

6 The branch number of the bank.

7 The amount in figures.

8 The signature of the drawer.

9 A crossing with 'A/C Payee'.

10 Drawer's account number.

11 Lines drawn to close up all blank spaces. The writing should be started well over to the left so that no spaces are left in which additional unauthorised words or figures could be inserted.

12 Serial number of the cheque.

13 Magnetic characters for sorting by computer.

Post-dated cheques

A post-dated cheque is one which is dated ahead of the current date. A bank does not credit the customer's account with the amount of a post-dated cheque until the due date.

Stale cheques

A stale cheque is one which is invalid because it has been drawn for some considerable time prior to presentation for payment. Validity normally expires after six months.

Alterations

If a mistake is made in writing a cheque and the drawer has to alter it, the drawer should sign their name or write their initials as near as possible to the alterations, as well as in the usual place, as in the example given in Fig 8.9.

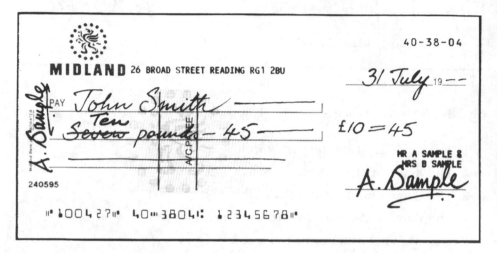

Fig 8.9   An altered cheque

Dishonoured cheques

Dishonoured cheques are those which a banker has refused to pay on presentation. Reasons for refusal may be attributed to one of the following causes:

1 Words and figures differ.

2 There are insufficient funds.

3 Irregular endorsement, ie the name on the reverse of a cheque does not correspond with the payee's name on the front.

4 Drawer's signature differs from that in the bank's records.

5 Notice of customer's death or act of bankruptcy, or that the customer has been certified as insane.

6 An alteration which requires signing.

7 A garnishee order (a notice sent to a person who owes money to judgement debtors) has been served on the banker.

8 The cheque is post-dated.

9 Payment has been stopped by drawer.

Usually the bank on which the cheque is drawn marks the cheque with an explanation before returning it to the payee through their bank. It should be noted that cheques issued under the protection of a cheque card cannot be dishonoured by the bank for reasons **2** and **9** above.

To stop payment
The payment of a cheque, after issue, can be stopped by the drawer. The drawer should contact their bank and give the following information:

- the date of the cheque
- the amount
- the name of the payee
- the serial number of the cheque, which can be obtained from the cheque counterfoil

Computerised banking services

Cheques are automatically sorted and recorded by computer using magnetic ink character recognition (MICR). You can see the magnetic ink numbers which are printed at the bottom of the cheque in Fig 8.9. The amount is also printed or encoded in magnetic ink characters at the foot of the cheque by the bank receiving it, using a machine called an encoder.

Computer terminals now allow bank customers to carry out more of their transactions in their own offices, homes or even while they are shopping. For example, in the Switch system the sales assistant passes your autocheque card through an electronic device that 'reads' the card and produces a voucher for you to sign. In this case, no cheque is used, but the process is similar, as the amount payable is debited to your account and included on your statement within 2 or 3 days. As well as using the card to pay for goods, cash up to £50 can be obtained at the same time from the sales assistant, and this is added to the sales voucher. This process, which uses electronic funds transfer (EFT), eliminates the need for a cheque or for paperwork.

The Home and Office Banking Service (HOBS) is operated by the Bank of Scotland throughout the UK. It links the customer via the telephone network direct to the Bank of Scotland's own computer, using a specially-designed screenphone for personal users or a compact integral keyboard and screen which is available to business users. Alternatively, HOBS can be linked to a PC.

By operating the keyboard in their own home or office, the customer can access accounts and carry out banking transactions at any time between 0600 and 0100 (next morning) from Monday to Friday and all day Saturday and Sunday until midnight. It is possible to view up to 600 separate transactions over the last three months without waiting for printed statements. Payments can be made by electronic transfer without writing cheques. Funds can also be transferred between accounts held with the Bank of Scotland. Instructions for transferring money from one account to another which have been keyed in before 1700 on any business working day are effected on that day.

Only the customer, or someone directly authorised by them, can key into the system. The customer is allocated their own exclusive codes for access to the HOBS system. Each set of codes includes a password, which the customer chooses and which they can change at any time. Using the code and password in the designated order ensures that access is gained to the customer's account.

HOBS customers are able to carry out most of their daily banking transactions without leaving their home or office and are not tied to traditional banking hours.

Questions

1 State the services provided by a banks, b the Post Office, for the payment of money and give examples of the types of transactions in which each is specially useful.

2 Name three ways of sending money by post. Say in what circumstances you would choose each of them and explain the procedures necessary. (RSA OP1)

3 Explain four of the following methods of payment and give one relevant example of the circumstances when each would be used.

a) Direct debit
b) Credit card

    c) EFT (electronic funds transfer)
    d) Credit transfer
    e) Standing order
    f) Banker's draft (*PEI OP2*)

4 a) What is a bank credit card?
    b) How would the card be used by a the customer, b the seller?

5 a) The Chief Accountant of your company is considering the possibility of using credit transfers instead of cheques for the monthly payment of creditors. He asks you to assist him by investigating the matter and giving him a report on the advantages and disadvantages of credit transfers, together with details of the changes which would be necessary in the system for making payments. Prepare the necessary report.
    b) List other methods of payment which could be used.

6 If you were going for a holiday abroad, how would you provide yourself with the necessary spending money? Where would you obtain it?

7 a) Why are cheques often used in payment of accounts?
    b) What effect has a crossing on a cheque?
    c) Is it customary to send a receipt if an account is paid by cheque? If not, why not?
    d) What action would you take if a creditor told you he had not received the cheque you sent him a week before?

8 State one advantage and one disadvantage to employees in being paid by each of the following methods:

    a) credit transfer
    b) cash

9 How would you turn the following into cash:

    a) your salary which had been paid by credit transfer
    b) a crossed cheque?

10 Describe the action you would take in the following cases:

    a) A cheque paid in to the company's bankers is returned 'RD'.
    b) You have just been informed that a cheque sent to a creditor more than a week ago has not been received.
    c) The cashier is absent unexpectedly at 1500 and your manager brings you cash and cheques collected from the cashier's workstation.
        You are asked to make it up for collection by a security company's armoured cash transit service at 1545. (*LCCI PSC*)

11 You are working in the General Office of a small firm called Easiglide Ltd.

a) This morning you opened the mail and among the correspondence were the following payments:

   i cheque for £75.32 sent by Dickenson & Brown

   ii crossed postal order for £6.50 from Miss L Waters

   iii registered packet from Joe Twining containing:

> 1 × £10 note
> 3 × £5 notes
> 2 × £1 coins

Enter these in a remittances book.

b) During the lunch hour you were looking after the Reception Desk and Mrs L M Oldenbourg from Central Cleaners called with a £16 cash refund (3 × £5 notes, 2 × 50p coins) on a cleaning bill for office curtains. Make out a receipt for Mrs Oldenbourg.

c) You are asked to take the payments received in the morning mail to the bank, together with the amount from Central Cleaners. Complete the paying-in book to cover the total. Your company's account number is 50347479.

d) Explain why Joe Twining sent his payment in a registered packet.

e) Give the reason why Miss Walters crossed the £6.50 postal order.

f) Explain in detail why a written record is kept of cash receipts and payments

In-tray exercise

12 You are employed at New Tech Office Services Bureau (Case Study 1) and are required to prepare cheques for signature by Mr Wood to pay the following bills:

a) Postage stamps to the value of £12.50

b) Catering, for a working lunch held on the premises, £48.12

c) Accountancy services for the year £540.00

Meetings

9.1   Servicing and recording meetings

The agenda

An agenda is a programme of the items of business to be discussed at a meeting in the order in which they are to be taken.

The agenda is sent to all members of the committee or organisation to give them adequate notice, and to enable them, prior to the meeting, to ponder over the items of business to be discussed. The period of notice to be given is laid down by the constitution of the organisation and is normally seven to fourteen days. It is customary at committee meetings to arrange at one meeting the date of the next. The agenda usually includes the notice convening the meeting, which contains the day, date, time and place of meeting.

The agenda is prepared by the secretary in consultation with the chairperson, and the items of business dealt with at the previous meeting are taken into consideration. The secretary should make a note of any matters requiring the attention of the committee, so that these may be included in the agenda for the next meeting.

Agenda items may be supplied from the following sources:

- the previous agenda (recurring items)
- the previous minutes (continuing items)
- the constitution (constitutional items)
- the chairperson and members who may request items to be included

Fig 9.1 is an example of an agenda for a committee meeting. The customary order of the business should be observed: if, for example, a chairperson were to be elected, that would be the first business of the meeting, and would be carried out under the supervision of a temporary chairperson.

THE XYZ WORKS SPORTS CLUB COMMITTEE

A meeting of the committee of the XYZ Works Sports Club will
be held at the Works Canteen on Friday 14 February 19__ at
1530 hrs.

A G E N D A
 1 Apologies for absence
 2 Minutes of the last meeting
 3 Matters arising
 4 Correspondence
 5 Treasurer's financial statement
 6 Fifth Annual Dinner arrangements
 7 Purchase of cricket bats and balls
 8 To consider suggestions for future sporting activities
 9 Any other business
10 Date of next meeting

J HANSON

Hon Secretary

Fig 9.1   An agenda for a committee meeting

The agenda for an annual general meeting differs slightly from the agenda for a committee meeting in two ways: copies are sent to all members of the organisation and not just to the elected committee; also, there is some variation in the type of business to be discussed. The items given in the example of an agenda for an annual general meeting in Fig 9.2 should be noted.

Chairperson's agenda

The chairperson's agenda contains more information than the ordinary agenda, and spaces are provided on the right-hand side of the paper for the chairperson to make notes. The additional information gives the chairperson all the relevant details which may be needed during the course of the meeting.

```
THE XYZ WORKS SPORTS CLUB


The Annual General Meeting of the XYZ Works Sports Club will
be held at the Works Canteen on Friday 21 February 19-- at
1900 hrs.


A G E N D A

  1  Apologies for absence

  2  Minutes of the last meeting

  3  Matters arising

  4  Correspondence

  5  Secretary's Annual Report

  6  Treasurer's Annual Report and Balance Sheet

  7  Election of: a  Officers

                  b  Committee

                  c  Honorary Auditor

  8  To consider the following proposed addition to

     the Club's Constitution:

     '15  All retired staff shall be installed as

          honorary members of the Sports Club.'

  9  To consider the formation of a Sub-Committee to

     arrange a programme of social evenings throughout

     the year

 10  Any other business


 J HANSON

 Hon Secretary
```

Fig 9.2   An agenda for an annual general meeting

Staff meeting notice and agenda

Staff meetings are generally quite informal. A sales manager, calling a meeting of his sales representatives, would send out a notice in the form given in Fig 9.3.

Business meeting terms

As a secretary, you will frequently meet, in the course of your duties,

```
THE LMN MANUFACTURING PLC

NOTICE OF MEETING

1 June 19__

To:  Sales Representatives

A meeting of sales representatives will be held in the Sales
Manager's Office at Head Office on Friday 10 June 19__,
commencing at 1430 hrs, when you are specially requested to
attend.
The agenda is set out below.



D PETTIFER
Sales Manager


AGENDA


1    To receive apologies for absence

2    To discuss the new selling lines which will be on the
     market in the spring

3    To report revised prices of established products

4    To consider suggestions for a simplified manner of
     submitting monthly returns

5    Any other business
```

Fig 9.3   An agenda for a staff meeting

many technical terms connected with business meetings. The most commonly used terms are given on the following pages.

Ad hoc This means 'arranged for this purpose'. An *ad hoc* subcommittee is appointed for the purpose of carrying out one particular piece of work, such as the arrangements for the visit of a very important person (VIP). These committees are sometimes called special or special-purpose committees.

Addendum An amendment which adds words to a motion.

Addressing the chair All remarks must be addressed to the chairperson, and members must not discuss matters between themselves at a meeting.

Adjournment Subject to the articles, rules or constitution of an organisation, the chairperson, with the consent of the members of the meeting, may adjourn it in order to postpone further discussion, or because of the shortage of time. Adequate notice of an adjourned meeting must be given.

Amendment A proposal to alter a motion by adding or deleting words. It must be proposed, seconded and put to the meeting in the customary way.

Attendance sheet A record of people present at a meeting, usually provided by an attendance sheet which is passed round for signature by members.

Casting vote A vote usually allowed to the chairperson, except in the case of a company meeting. A casting vote is used only when there is an equal number of votes 'for' and 'against' a motion.

Closure A motion submitted with the object of ending the discussion on a matter before the meeting.

Dropped motion A motion that has to be dropped either because there is no seconder or because the meeting wishes it to be abandoned.

En bloc The voting of, say, a committee en bloc, that is, electing or re-electing all members of a committee by the passing of one resolution.

In camera A meeting which is not open to the public.

Intra vires Within the power of the person or body concerned.

Lie on the table A letter or document is said to 'lie on the table' when it is decided at a meeting to take no action upon the business contained in it.

Majority The articles and rules of the organisation will define the majority of votes required to carry a motion.

Memorandum and articles of association These are regulations drawn up by a company setting out the objects for which the company is formed and defining the manner in which its business shall be conducted.

Motion A motion must normally be written and handed to the chairperson or secretary before the meeting. The mover of the motion speaks on it and has the right of reply at the close of the discussion. The seconder may then speak to the motion only once. If there is no seconder, a motion is dropped and cannot be introduced again. When put to a meeting, the motion becomes 'the question', and when it is passed, it is called 'the resolution'. A motion on a matter which has not been included on the agenda can be moved only if 'leave of urgency' has been agreed by the meeting or it has been included under the customary item 'any other business'.

Nem con (nemine contradicente) This means 'no one contradicting', ie there are no votes against the motion, but some members have not voted at all.

Next business A motion 'that the meeting proceed with next business' is a method of delaying the decision on any matter brought before the meeting.

Point of order This is a question regarding the procedure at a meeting or a query relating to the standing orders or constitution raised by a member during the meeting, eg absence of quorum.

Poll Poll is the term given for the method of voting at an election, and in a meeting this usually takes the form of a secret vote by ballot paper. The way in which a poll is to be conducted is generally laid down in the standing orders or constitution of the organisation.

Postponement The action taken to defer a meeting to a later date.

Putting the question To conclude the discussion on a motion it is customary for the chairperson to 'put the question' by announcing 'The question before the meeting is ...'

Question be now put When members feel that sufficient discussion has taken place on a motion, it may be moved 'that the question be now put'. If this is carried, only the proposer of the motion being discussed may speak and a vote is taken. If the motion 'question be now put' is defeated, discussion may be continued.

Quorum This is the minimum number of persons who must be in attendance to constitute a meeting. The quorum is laid down in the constitution or rules of the organisation.

Reference back This is an amendment referring a report or other item of business back for further consideration to the body or person submitting it. If the motion 'reference back' is defeated, the discussion is continued.

Resolution A formal decision carried at a meeting. It must be proposed, seconded and put to the meeting in the customary way. A resolution cannot be rescinded at the meeting at which it is adopted.

Rider A rider is an additional clause or sentence added to a resolution after it has been passed and it differs from an amendment in that it adds to a resolution instead of altering it. A rider has to be proposed, seconded and put to the meeting in the same way as a motion.

Right of reply The proposer of a resolution has the right of reply when the resolution has been fully discussed. He is allowed to reply only once, and afterwards the motion is put to the meeting.

Sine die Without an appointed day, or indefinitely.

Standing orders These are rules compiled by the organisation regulating the manner in which its business is to be conducted. They may also have the title 'Constitution'.

Status quo Used to refer to a matter in which there is to be no change.

Sub-committee A sub-committee may be appointed by a committee to deal with some specific branch of its work. The sub-committee must carry out such functions as are delegated to it by the committee and must report to the committee periodically.

Ultra vires Beyond the legal power or authority of a company or organisation.

Unanimous When all members of a meeting have voted in favour of a resolution it is said to be carried 'unanimously'.

Minutes

Minutes are a record of the proceedings of a meeting and are kept to preserve a brief, accurate and clear record of the business transacted.

The secretary is responsible for attending the meeting and taking down, in note form, details of the decisions reached. In resolution minutes it is necessary to record the exact wording of every resolution passed and the names of the proposers and seconders. A verbatim record is not necessary but all the arguments for and against the major decisions should be noted.

It is useful to keep minutes in a loose-leaf book as this enables them to be typed. If this method is used, very great care must be taken in ensuring their safety as papers can easily be lost or misplaced.

Secretarial duties for meetings

Before the meeting	*On the day of the meeting*	*After the meeting*
1 Prepare the agenda in consultation with the chairperson and distribute it to members.	1 Attend early, taking the items referred to in **5** of the previous column.	1 Ensure that all documents are returned to the office.
2 Prepare a chairperson's agenda.	2 Arrange for direction signs to the committee room to be displayed.	2 Prepare draft minutes for approval by the chairperson.
3 Book a suitable room.	3 Ensure that the seating arrangements are in order.	3 When approved, type the minutes in final form for distribution to members.
4 Obtain any necessary statements or documents from members who cannot be present but who are known to have strong views on items to be discussed.	4 See that each member has a supply of writing paper.	4 Type any correspondence resulting from the meeting and monitor its progress.
5 Collect together the following items required for the meeting:	5 Check that members sign the attendance register.	5 File any papers used at the meeting, as well as copies of correspondence typed in **4**.
a Stationery, including writing paper and shorthand notebook.	6 Read the minutes of the last meeting; letters of apology and any other correspondence.	6 If the chairperson is also your chief (the executive for whom you work), see that the date of the next meeting is entered in their diary and yours.
b Spare copies of the agenda.	7 Assist the chairperson in supplying information from files as required during the meeting.	
c Minutes of the previous meeting.	8 Record the details of the decisions reached, noting who proposed and who seconded motions as well as the results of the voting.	
d All relevant papers and files of the correspondence, including letters of apology received from members unable to attend.		
e Attendance register or sheet.		
f Any books of reference, standing orders, etc.		

The safe custody of the minutes is important as they provide a permanent record of the proceedings at a meeting and they can be referred to at a later date when the business discussed is being reviewed. They can also be consulted to discover why certain decisions were taken.

Action minutes are an alternative method of presentation which includes a column specifying who is responsible for taking action on the decisions made. This provides an effective reminder of follow-up action necessary and a clear delegation of duties.

Minutes should be written up as soon as possible after the meeting as it is much easier to be absolutely accurate when the discussions are fresh in the mind. They should be written wholly in the third person and in the past tense.

It is essential that minutes should be:

- **accurate** so that they present a true record of the proceedings
- **brief** so as to provide a summary of the important matters discussed and decisions reached for reading and confirmation at the next meeting and for future reference
- **clear** so those absent from a meeting can be fully informed of the proceedings, and so that there is no possible doubt about previous deliberations

When a set of minutes is typed, care should be taken to allow an adequate left-hand margin for the sub-headings. Minutes should be recorded in the following order:

1 A description of the meeting, which should include the type of meeting, time, date and place.

2 Names of those present, with the chairperson's name first and the names of the officers last.

3 Apologies for absence.

4 Reading of the minutes of the last meeting.

5 Matters arising from the minutes.

6 Correspondence.

7 General business — resolutions must contain the exact wording given at the meeting.

8 Any other business — this is recorded in the order in which it is taken at the meeting.

9 The date of the next meeting.

10 The signature block for the chairperson and the date of the meeting when the minutes will be signed.

A draft is generally submitted to the chairperson for approval before the final copy is typed.

At the meeting the chairperson will call upon the secretary to read the minutes of the last meeting. If the minutes have previously been circulated, they may be taken as read if this is agreed by all members. If a member points out a mistake in the minutes, the chairperson or secretary, subject to the approval of the meeting, may correct the error in the minutes, before they are signed as correct. Once the minutes have been signed, they should not be altered in any way.

Students of secretarial duties should note that minutes are a brief record of the proceedings of a meeting, and should not confuse them with a verbatim report or a summary/precis. The former is of a meeting, debate or discussion recorded and reported word for word; the latter is a summary of a literary passage, a speech, a report or of correspondence, expressing clearly and concisely all the important facts of the original.

Committee meeting minutes
Fig 9.4 is an extract from a set of minutes of a committee meeting embodying a formal resolution.

Informal meeting minutes
Fig 9.5 is an extract from a set of minutes of an informal meeting of an association. In this instance, formal resolutions were not required. The arguments for and against the decisions reached and the final conclusions are all that are required in narrative minutes of informal meetings.

Telecommunication services for meetings and conferences
See page 127.

Personnel involved in meetings

Chairman The title 'chairperson' or 'chair' may also be used. The chairman is appointed by a meeting to:

- manage the proceedings of a meeting and keep order
- approve the items to be discussed on the agenda

SPORTS COMMITTEE MINUTES

A Meeting of the Sports Committee of The Benning Welfare Association was held in the Sports Pavilion on Monday 30 June 19-- at 1930 hrs.

Present

Mr J H Thomas (in the chair)
Miss D Ashton
Mrs I Gardner
Mr A Evans
Mr J Ripley
Mr H Spence
Mr R T Bird (Secretary)

Minutes	The minutes of the last meeting were read, adopted and signed by the Chairman.
Matters Arising	Mr Evans reported that a reunion of the members of the Football Club proved very successful.
Financial Statement	A statement of the current financial position of the Committee was read and adopted. In addition, the statement for presentation to the Annual Meeting to be held on 14 July 19-- was approved.
Tennis	Miss Ashton pointed out that there was a lack of facilities for members wishing to play tennis. She stated that the one grass court belonging to the Committee was proving inadequate owing to the constant demand caused by the Club members' enthusiasm, and asked whether the Committee could see its way to secure a second court. Mr Ripley mentioned that members of the tennis section had contributed a large proportion of the funds at present in hand, and that he considered Miss Ashton's recommendation justifiable. The Chairman pointed out that the application would have to be submitted in the first place to the Board of Directors for their approval.
RESOLVED: R41	That the Secretary be instructed to make application to the Board of Directors for the provision of a second grass court adjoining the existing grass court.
Date of Next Meeting	It was decided to hold the next meeting of the Committee on Tuesday 23 July 19--.

Chairman
23 July 19--

Fig 9.4   Extract from the minutes of a committee meeting

```
MINUTES OF MEETING        A meeting of the Conference Organisation Committee of the National
                          Trad Association was held at Association Headquarters on Friday,
                          31 May 199- at 1430 hrs.


                          Present:


                          Mr J M Strang (in the Chair)
                          Miss J T Branson
                          Mr V E Carter
                          Mr B W White (General Secretary)
Apologies                 The Secretary reported that Mr Thomas had been admitted to
                          hospital. He was asked to communicate to Mr Thomas the Committee's
                          sincere wishes for a speedy recovery.


Minutes                   The minutes of the last meeting, which had been circulated, were
                          taken as read and approved and were signed by the Chairman.

Matters arising           There were no matters arising out of the minutes.

Conference                Miss Branson and Mr Carter had visited the conference town and
arrangements  venue       looked over the two proposed venues, the Royal Pavilion and the
                          Palace Ballroom. They stated that the acoustics were good in the
                          Pavilion but there were no refreshment facilities. The Ballroom
                          had good refreshment facilities, but the acoustics were poor. The
                          Secretary recommended that the pavilion would be more practical
                          from the point of view of effective speaking.


                          The Secretary's recommendation that the Pavilion should be used
                          was agreed, provided that the conference would adjourn for mid-
                          morning and mid-afternoon breaks. It was agreed that the Secretary
                          should make the arrangements for the booking.

Any other business

1  Future conferences     Miss Branson raised the matter of future conferences and asked
                          whether the conference was held at the right time of the year. She
                          though that March would be a much more appropriate time than June.
                          The Chairman said that it was rather late to open a discussion on
                          this matter and suggested that it should be discussed at the next
                          meeting of the Executive Committee, to which Miss Branson agreed.


2  Report to Council      The Secretary confirmed that he would make an appropriate report
                          for submission to the Council.



.............................
Chairman
14 July 199-
```

Fig 9.5 Extracts from the minutes of an informal meeting of an association

- conduct the business according to the agenda and constitution/ standing orders; keep the discussion within prescribed limits and allow all points of view to be expressed

- deal with points of order

- guide the discussion and assist the meeting to make decisions by passing resolutions, amendments, etc

- take a vote or poll and declare the result
- sign the minutes and ensure that action is taken, as approved
- close, adjourn or postpone meetings, as directed by the meeting

Convenor   A person authorised to call a meeting.

Co-opted member   A person who serves on a committee as a result of the committee's powers of co-option, ie the committee approves of the appointment of a co-opted member by a majority vote in order to engage the services of a person qualified to assist them in their work.

Ex-officio member   A person who is a member of a committee by virtue of office, eg the Restaurant Manager may be an ex-officio member of the Staff Welfare Committee.

In attendance   Those who attend a meeting to provide a service such as secretarial, legal, financial, etc but do not have voting powers.

Proxy   A person appointed to attend a meeting and vote on behalf of a member who is unable to attend.

Secretary   Responsible for the meeting arrangements as given on page 312.

Teller   A person who counts the votes at a meeting ballot.

Treasurer   A treasurer is involved when a meeting is responsible for the receipt and payment of money. Duties include:

- preparation and presentation of financial reports
- advice to the meeting on financial matters
- submission of audited accounts, when required.

Questions

1 You have been asked to check the maximum number of people who can be elected to the committee of your firm's sports club. How would you do this? Describe any means by which this number could be increased, either permanently or temporarily.

2 How are the matters for inclusion in the agenda of a meeting decided? Why is it necessary to include 'any other business' as a separate item?

3 A new satellite linking London and Malaysia is to be launched on 5 October. You have been requested to arrange a celebratory buffet luncheon at the London Headquarters. It is suggested that an *Ad Hoc* Committee be set up to assist you and a representative from each section will attend the first meeting.

a) Explain the purpose of an *Ad Hoc* Committee. List the preparations you will make for the first meeting and draft an agenda.

b) Draft a suitable formal invitation to the celebratory luncheon and list THREE reference books you might use to assist you in preparing the invitation list. Give details of why you would choose each book.

c) List the records which should be kept when organising such a function.

d) Describe the preparations you will make to arrange a video conference linking up offices in this country, and why would this method of a meeting be preferable to holding a meeting at Head Office?

e) As you will be absent for the video conference, prepare a checklist for your assistant on how to take and write the minutes. (*LCCI PSD*)

4 Your work involves the arrangement of a large number of committee meetings in regard to the various aspects and areas of operation of a large organisation. Some meetings — sometimes several on the same evening — are held after office hours and are attended by members who do not necessarily work in the building. Describe an efficient system to ensure that:

a) Sufficient notice is given of every meeting

b) It is immediately apparent, to the recipient of the notice, which activity of the organisation is involved

c) There is immediate evidence of notice and agenda having been sent out

d) Documents, minute books, etc, required for meetings are available for and collected after each meeting

e) It is clear to the caretaker which rooms are to be prepared and at which meetings refreshment is to be served

f) It is clear to the hall porter to which rooms people are to be routed (*LCCI PSD*)

5 One of the functions of the secretary of a meeting is to assist the chairman. What would you expect the secretary to prepare for the chairman beforehand and how might she help during the meeting?

6 a) What is the difference between the matters which would be dealt with at a general meeting of a club and at a meeting of one of its committees?

b) What is the reason for appointing committees?

c) Who may attend a general meeting of a club and who may attend committee meetings?

7 The MD's secretary in Case Study 4 is away on holiday and you have been asked to arrange a Board Meeting at short notice to be held in the company's Board Room. The meeting will probably last all day.

a) Make a checklist for yourself so you do not forget anything. Use the headings: Before, During, After Meeting.

b) Some members of the meeting will be travelling from different parts of the country. Not all these people will be directors but will have been asked to attend this meeting for various reasons. What special arrangements will you make for these people? (*PEI OP2*)

8 You are handing over the job of taking minutes for the firm's branch of the Trade Union to another employee who has asked for some guidance. Draft some notes on:

a) The purpose of minutes, indicating two alternative types of minute which might be taken.
b) The chief points to remember when taking minutes.
c) The procedure to be followed after the meeting regarding the minutes.
d) Briefly explain the following terminology:
   i quorum
   ii motion.

9 a) Prepare a draft notice and agenda for the monthly meeting of the Hotels Division Committee to be held at 1400 on 10 December 199- in the Committee Room. The major items are:

- Consideration of tenders for the kitchen fittings for the Olympia in Athens.
- Mr Lord will report on the current situation with regard to the opening of the Classic in Rome.
- List of people to be invited to the opening of the Classic in Rome.

b) Ms Davies will chair this meeting. What are her duties? (*LCCI PSC*)

10 You are Chairman of the Sports and Social Club.

a) From the following information draft *your* agenda for the next meeting:
- Angela Brown is to give details on a planned theatre visit.
- A note is on your desk from Louise Healey requesting that security be discussed following a break-in.
- Telephone message to say Jim Cook cannot attend the meeting, as he broke his leg playing football.
- Circular letter from Empire Theatre.

b) What is the importance of the agenda to you? (*LCCI PSC*)

11 Write the following in the form of a minute for inclusion in the Minutes of the Board:

'I suggest that we should allocate an appropriate sum for the purchase of desktop publishing equipment which would enable us to carry out our internal printing. In the long run this would be an economy.'

This suggestion, made by Mr Henderson, was agreed by the Board.

12 a) As secretary to your firm's Sports and Social Club, prepare the notice and agenda for their Annual General Meeting on 29 September.

    b) To whom will you send copies and when? (*LCCI PSC*)

13 a) What do you understand by an amendment to a motion?

    b) For what reason might a member of an organisation be co-opted on to a committee?

    c) Give one reason why a meeting might be adjourned for a few days.

    d) What is an *ex officio* member of a committee?

    e) What is the purpose of a quorum?

14 In a business meeting what is the correct way for a member:

    a) to address the chair

    b) to present a motion to the meeting

    c) to move an amendment to a motion?

In-tray exercise

15 You are employed at Office Products Ltd (Case Study 2).

    In your capacity as Secretary to the Social Club Committee, prepare the minutes of the last meeting from the following agenda and notes taken at the meeting (see page 323).

    NB Formal resolutions are not used in the minutes.

OFFICE PRODUCTS LTD
SOCIAL CLUB COMMITTEE

Notes:

A meeting of the Social Club

Committee will be held in the

Club House on Monday 4 October 19__

at 1930

AGENDA

Present: Mrs P Henderson
(Chairman)
Mr J A Watson
Miss B Light
Mr R A Partridge
Mrs L O Taylor
Miss T Macdonald
Mr G Walker
Me!

1 Apologies for absence —————— Mrs B O'Neill + Mr M Knight

2 Minutes of the last meeting
held on 20 September 19__

Approved

3 Matters arising

JW — Tennis club's annual
tournament v. successful 24 members
competed. G Harvey won cup

4 Newsletter ——————

LT — Costs of production
exceeding budget - agreed to
issue monthly instead of
fortnightly

5 Fireworks Display ——————

to be held on 4 Nov in
Sports Field. £200 allocated
from company for fireworks
GW agreed to organise

6 Fund-raising Event in aid of ——————
Oxfam

TM suggested a disco in
December at Club House —
£50 to be donated from Club
Funds. Further discussion at
next meeting

7 Any other business ——————

AGM on 20 October —
agreed to propose increase in
membership subs from 75p to
£1 per week

8 Date of Next Meeting ——————

Nov. 2 same time/place

UNIT 10 Travel and accommodation

10.1 Arranging travel and accommodation

If it is necessary for executives to make frequent business trips, it is essential that their private secretaries should be fully conversant with the preparation necessary. The three principal methods of travel — road, rail and air — are dealt with, giving (**a**) the reference books and other sources of information which should be available in the office and (**b**) the final preparation which must be made in each case. A fuller list of reference books for travel information is given on page 26.

Road

Reference books and sources of information

- *AA* or *RAC Handbook*
- Telephone numbers of the executive's garage, mechanic and nearest AA or RAC office
- Road maps

Final preparations

1 Arrange for the appropriate road maps and route plans to be available.
2 Verify weather conditions in the area in which the executive is travelling.
3 Confirm the booking of hotels.

4 Prepare the itinerary, and include telephone numbers of hotels, appointments, meetings, etc, and have a clear understanding of the times and places where the executive may be contacted.

5 Collect and hand to the executive all the documents required.

6 Prepare a supply of office stationery to enable the executive to write letters, reports, etc, during the visit.

7 Discuss outstanding matters.

Rail

Reference books and sources of information

- Railway *Guides*, plus a regular supply of the supplementary issues concerning train times
- Telephone number of the local British Rail Travel Advisory Centre

Final preparations

1 Confirm the departure time, station, and the time of arrival at destination.

2 Obtain the ticket for the journey plus one for a reserved seat if required.

3 Make arrangements for the executive to be met at the destination.

4 See points 3 to 7 listed under the heading of Final preparations for road.

Air

Reference books and sources of information

- *ABC World Airways Guide*
  World Atlas
  Airline timetables
  Car hire leaflets
  Royal Mail International Travel Guide
  Airport guides including car parking arrangements
- Current visa, passport, export licence, health and insurance regulations
- Telephone numbers for:
  a the local travel agent, including their 'out of hours' number

 b the executive's or organisation's bank for arranging currency, travellers cheques, etc

 c local taxi/car hire firm

Checklist for arranging travel abroad

First tasks

1 Agree dates for visit and enter them in the diary.

2 Book airline tickets.

3 Arrange insurance cover.

4 Book hotels.

5 Arrange medical preparations if necessary, such as vaccinations, first aid kit, etc.

6 Apply for visa, if required.

7 Check that the passport remains current.

8 Arrange meetings/appointments abroad.

9 Arrange for business visiting cards to be printed with information on reverse in the language of the country visited.

10 Send for information about country visited, eg *Hints to Exporters.*

11 Arrange for the executive to be met at the foreign airport or for a car to be hired.

12 Check if international driving permit is valid, if required.

One week before visit

1 Check receipt of:

• airline tickets

• insurance certificate

• visa, if required

• international driving permit, if required

2 Check confirmation of hotel booking.

3 Order travellers cheques and currency from bank.

4 Prepare itinerary.

5 Book transport to airport in this country.

1/2 days before departure

1 Collect traveller's cheques and currency from bank.

2 Assemble the following items and hand them to the executive:
- airline tickets
- insurance certificate
- vaccination certificate
- visa
- passport
- *Hints to Exporters* booklet
- travellers cheques and foreign currency
- itinerary
- hotel brochure, confirmation of booking and hotel voucher
- international driving permit
- confirmation of transport arrangements
- files/documents for meetings and appointments
- supply of stationery for use abroad
- business visiting cards

3 Discuss any outstanding matters.

On return

1 Follow up on the quality of:
- hotel
- flight
- entertainment/venues.

2 Follow up action points from meetings.

3 Make sure that reports are written, and that people are contacted.

4 File useful points of cultural interest for future reference.

5 Check exchange rate and preparation of expenses.

6 File trip information and itinerary for reference.

7 Discuss any changes for future trips.

Preparation of an itinerary

An example of an itinerary is given in Fig 10.1.

Notes on the construction of an itinerary
- Use appropriately-sized paper or card to fit inside a ticket wallet.
- Make a note of any special reservations, such as a sleeping berth,

```
ITINERARY FOR MR P JONES
14-17 October 199-

Tuesday, 14 October

Check-in:  London Heathrow Terminal 2   1000
Depart:    Heathrow (Flight AF811)       1135
Arrive:    Paris Charles de Gaulle       1340

Hotel:     Penta Hotel
           10 rue Baudin, Pl Charras,
           F-92400 Courbevoie, Paris
           Tel:   4788 5051
           Telex: 610 470  Fax: 4768 8332

Appointment with Mr M Petrescou
at hotel                                 1600

Wednesday, 15 October

Marketing Conference                     0930-
at Chambre de Commerce et D'Industrie    1700
2 Rue de Viarmes, 75001 Paris
Tel: 4508 3685  Fax: 4508 3580

Dinner at hotel with Mr E Delbaere       1930

Thursday, 16 October

Check-in:  Charles de Gaulle Airport     0915
Depart:    Paris (Flight LH 1745)        1045
Arrive:    Frankfurt                     1205

Hotel:     Sheraton
           Flughafen, Frankfurt
           Tel:   069 6977-0
           Telex: 841 418924
           Fax:   069 69772209

International Book Fair                   1400-
Reineckstrasse 3, Frankfurt              1800

Friday, 17 October

Check-in:  Frankfurt Airport             0950
Depart:    Frankfurt (Flight BA903)      1120
Arrive:    Heathrow (Terminal 1)         1200
```

Fig 10.1 Itinerary

seat numbers, smoking/non-smoking section, which have been made for the journey.

- Allow for transfer time between airports, hotels, railway stations.
- Sunday trains and sometimes Saturday trains are shown separately in some timetables. Care must be taken, therefore, to ensure that you are looking at the correct section for the day on which the executive is travelling.
- Ensure that the information is being taken from the current edition of the timetable, as considerable changes are made between the summer and winter services. Also, be sure to allow for time differences between different countries.
- The local BR Travel Advisory Centre may be contacted for times of trains; also, when using directories, it is advisable to check the train times with the Centre as there may be changes or cancellations to the published timetable.
- An itinerary should give:
  a name(s) of travellers
  b total and individual dates
  c departure and arrival times of trains and aircraft (also include check-in times, terminals and flight numbers for air travel)
  d hotel names, addresses, telephone numbers, telex and fax numbers
  e business names, addresses, telephone numbers and names of contacts
  f all times in the 24-hour clock system, as this saves any confusion which may arise between am and pm
- Keep a copy of the itinerary for use in the office and for any others who require information about the traveller's movements.

Flight schedules

Fig 10.2 is an extract from an airline timetable used for planning journeys which involve air flights.

You should note the following:

- Days of the week are represented by the numbers 1 to 7, ie 1 = Monday, 7 = Sunday.
- Arrival times are always given in the 'local' time and use the 24-hour clock system. For example, a flight leaving London at 0830 and arriving at Brussels at 1030 is actually of one hour's duration because Brussels is one hour ahead of London.

LON

From	To	Days 1234567	Depart	Arrive	Flight number	Aircraft /Class	Stops	Transfer Information Airport Arrive Depart			Flight number	Aircraft /Class

FROM LONDON CONTINUED

▶ **BRUSSELS**   *HL HZ*
🚭 All flights are No Smoking.

		Days	Depart	Arrive	Flight number	Aircraft/Class	Stops
		12345--	0700①	0900	SN614	737/CM	0
		12345--	0715①	0920	BA388	320/CM	0
		1234567	0750Ⓝ	0950	BA2412	737/CM	0
		1234567	0830①	1030	BA392	320/CM	0
		1234567	0830①	1030	SN602	737/CM	0
		123456-	0930①	1130	SN598	737/CM	0
		1234567	1000①	1200	BA394	320/CM	0
		12345--	1030①	1230	SN604	737/CM	0
		1234567	1155①	1355	SN606	737/CM	0
		12345--	1415Ⓝ	1615	BA2414	737/CM	0
		1234567	1430①	1630	BA396	757§/CM	0
		12345-7	1525①	1725	SN608	737/CM	0
		1234567	1600Ⓝ	1800	BA2416	737/CM	0
		1234567	1600①	1800	BA398	767§/CM	0
		1234567	1730①	1930	SN600	737/CM	0
		12345-7	1740①	1945	BA402	757/CM	0
		12345-7	1830①	2030	SN610	737/CM	0
		12345-7	1900Ⓝ	2100	BA2420	737/CM	0
		1234567	1930①	2130	SN612	737/CM	0
		12345-7	1930①	2130	BA404	737/CM	0

▶ **BUCHAREST**

		Days	Depart	Arrive	Flight number	Aircraft/Class	Stops	Airport	Arrive	Depart	Flight number	Aircraft/Class
		-2-4--7	0745①	1550	BA710	757/CM	1	ZRH	1025	1220	SR462	100§/CM
		1-3-56-	1000Ⓝ	1520	BA2894	737/CM	0					

▶ **BUDAPEST**   *HL MC HZ*

		Days	Depart	Arrive	Flight number	Aircraft/Class	Stops	Airport	Arrive	Depart	Flight number	Aircraft/Class
		1234567	0955①	1320	BA868	757/CM	0					
		1234-67	1245②	1605	MA611	73S/CM	0					
		----5--	1255②	1615	MA611	73S/CM	0					
		12345--	1435①	1940	BA704	320/CM	1	VIE	1745	1840	OS807	F50/CY
		12--567	1655①	2020	BA870	737/CM	0					
		12345--	1810①	2305	BA706	757/CM	1	VIE	2120	2210	OS809	F50/CY
		------7	1840②	2150	MA615	TU5/CM	0					
		-----6-	1840②	2200	MA615	737/CM	0					
		--3----	1945②	2305	MA615	737/CM	0					

▶ **BUENOS AIRES**   *MC HZ*

		Days	Depart	Arrive	Flight number	Aircraft/Class	Stops
		--3----	2055④	0725†	BA247	744/FJM	0
		-----6-	2055④	0725†	BA267	744/FJM	0
		1------	2125④	1015†	BA245	744/FJM	1

▶ **BUFFALO**   *MC HZ*

		Days	Depart	Arrive	Flight number	Aircraft/Class	Stops	Airport	Arrive	Depart	Flight number	Aircraft/Class
		1234567	1215④	1948	BA219	747/FJM	1	PHL	1535	1845	BA7443♦	737/FY

▶ **BULAWAYO**

		Days	Depart	Arrive	Flight number	Aircraft/Class	Stops	Airport	Arrive	Depart	Flight number	Aircraft/Class
		1------	2125④	1750†	BA053	747/FJM	1	HRE	0920†	1700†	UM341	73S/Y
		--3-5--	2125④	1850†	BA053	747/FJM	1	HRE	0920†	1800†	UM339	73S/Y

▶ **BURLINGTON, Vermont**   *HZ*

		Days	Depart	Arrive	Flight number	Aircraft/Class	Stops	Airport	Arrive	Depart	Flight number	Aircraft/Class
		1234567	1215④	2013	BA219	747/FJM	1	PHL	1535	1900	BA7461♦	DC9/FY

▶ **CAIRO**   *HL MC HZ*

		Days	Depart	Arrive	Flight number	Aircraft/Class	Stops
		1234567	1615④	2315	BA155	767/FJM	0

Fig 10.2 Extract from British Airways worldwide timetable

From	To	Days 1234567	Depart	Arrive	Flight number	Aircraft /Class	Stops	Transfer Information Airport Arrive Depart			Flight number	Aircraft /Class

FROM LONDON CONTINUED ✈

▶ **CALCUTTA** *T.I*

| | | -2---6- | 2145④ | 1525† | BA143 | 747/FJM | 1 | | | | | |

▶ **CAPE TOWN** *SU HZ*

| | | ----5 7 | 2005④ | 0940† | BA059 | 744/FJM | 0 | | | | | |

▶ **CARACAS** *HL HZ*

| | | ----5-7 | 1015④ | 1555 | BA249 | 744/FJM | 0 | | | | | |

▶ **CASABLANCA** *HZ*

| | | ------7 | 1010① | 1420 | GT120 | 73S/CM | 1 | | | | | |
| | | 1234--- | 1645① | 2100 | GT118 | 73S/CM | 1 | | | | | |

▶ **CHARLESTON, South Carolina** *MC HZ*

| 30 Oct-12 Nov | | 1234567 | 1055Ⓝ | 1730 | BA197 | 767/JM | 1 | CLT | 1525 | 1640 | BA7357♦ | 737/FY |
| 13 Nov-25 Mar | | 1234567 | 1055Ⓝ | 1741 | BA197 | 767/JM | 1 | CLT | 1525 | 1650 | BA7229♦ | 737/FY |

▶ **CHARLOTTE**

| | | 1234567 | 1055Ⓝ | 1525 | BA197 | 767/JM | 0 | | | | | |
| | | 1234567 | 1340④ | 2049 | BA177 | 747/FJM | 1 | JFK | 1645 | 1840 | BA7301♦ | DC9§/FY |

▶ **CHARLOTTESVILLE** *HZ*

| | | 1234567 | 1055Ⓝ | 1915 | BA197 | 767/JM | 1 | CLT | 1525 | 1805 | BA7185♦ | DH8/Y |

▶ **CHICAGO** *SU HL MC HZ*

| | | 1234567 | 1400④ | 1655 | BA297 | 747/FJM | 0 | | | | | |

▶ **CINCINNATI** *MC HZ*

| | | 1234567 | 1145Ⓝ | 1832 | BA199 | 767/JM | 1 | PIT | 1540 | 1730 | BA7489♦ | DC9/FY |

▶ **CLEVELAND** *MC RZ HZ*

| | | 1234567 | 1215④ | 1840 | BA219 | 747/FJM | 1 | PHL | 1535 | 1715 | BA7499♦ | 737/FY |

▶ **COLOGNE/BONN** *HZ*
⊘ All flights are No Smoking.

		12345--	0725①	0940	BA926	757/CM	0					
		-----67	0845①	1100	BA926	757/CM	0					
		12345-7	1530①	1745	BA928	757§/CM	0					

▶ **COLUMBIA**

| | | 1234567 | 1055Ⓝ | 1723 | BA197 | 767/JM | 1 | CLT | 1525 | 1645 | BA7325♦ | 737/FY |

▶ **COLUMBUS, Ohio** *MC HZ*

| | | 1234567 | 1145Ⓝ | 1757 | BA199 | 767/JM | 1 | PIT | 1540 | 1715 | BA7491♦ | M80§/FY |

▶ **COPENHAGEN** *HZ*

		1234567	0800Ⓝ	1050	BA2800	737/CM	0					
		1234567	0830①	1120	BA804	757/CM	0					
		12345--	1005Ⓝ	1250	DM112	737/CM	0					
		-----6-	1020Ⓝ	1305	DM114	737/CM	0					
		--3-5-7	1200①	1450	BA810	737/CM	0					
		12----	1215①	1505	BA810	737/CM	0					

CONTINUED NEXT PAGE

Fig 10.2 (continued)

- The schedule provides:
  a flight numbers, eg BA 388
  b type/class of aircraft, eg 747/FJM = Boeing 747 with first class, executive (club/business) class, and economy class
  c number of stops made (passengers do not change planes)
  d departure terminal in circle, eg terminal ④

- Other information given in the timetable includes:
  a aircraft seating plans
  b minimum connection times
  c minimum check-in times in UK
  d airport information
  e flight enquiries (telephone numbers)
  f reservations (telephone numbers)
  g baggage allowances

Travel agency checklist

Checklist of information to be supplied when using the services of a travel agent

- journey dates
- countries/places to be visited
- airline preference
- class of travel, ie first class, executive class (business/club) or economy class (tourist)
- smoking or non-smoking seats
- car hire
- if travelling by car, registration number, type of car and length of car
- hotel reservations
- insurance
- visa
- transport to airport

Hotel accommodation

It is an important responsibility of the secretary to select and book suitable hotel accommodation for their executives. The hotel selected should meet the following criteria:

- complies with the company's procedures and policy for travel and accommodation
- suitably located to allow the executives to make optimum use of their time
- cost effective and within the price range for the needs of the executive (hotel guides, such as the *AA Handbook*, grade hotels with stars according to a price range)
- terms for payment are acceptable and in accordance with organisational procedures
- caters for the individual needs of the executive, eg dietary needs, secretarial services, facilities for meeting clients, etc
- the personal wishes of the executive having regard to previous experience of using a particular hotel.

Hotel reservations made by telephone should be confirmed in writing by letter or fax and should supply the following details:

- name(s) of executives requiring the accommodation
- dates – specifying clearly the nights for which the room is required and approximate times of arrival and departure
- type of room required, ie single, double, twin
- facilities required (as referred to above)
- any special dietary needs
- arrangements for payment and confirmation of the rates quoted.

Claims for expenditure

Claims for expenditure relating to invoices for costs of travel and accommodation and expenses claims have to be checked carefully and verified against planned costs before they are approved for payment. This entails:

- verifying claims for expenditure to ensure that they comply with the company's code of practice and are within approved budgets
- checking accuracy of calculations
- checking that all the necessary information has been supplied
- investigating discrepancies and any problems which may arise from the above and taking appropriate action to rectify them
- ensuring that only correct invoices and claims for expenditure are authorised for payment.

Planning business visits abroad

Information

Useful information for the preparation of a business trip abroad can be obtained from the Department of Trade and Industry, Export Publications, PO Box 55, Stratford-on-Avon, CV37 9GE. The DTI publishes a series of booklets for different countries entitled *Hints to Exporters* containing general information about the country such as area, population, principal cities and towns, climate, clothing, hours of business; travel information relating to passport, visa and health regulations, currency, customs, travel routes, etc; hotels and restaurants; postal, telephone and telegraphic facilities; economic factors; import and exchange control regulations; government and commercial organisations; and methods of doing business.

Another useful publication is the *ABC Guide to International Travel* which gives details for each country of passports, visas, health regulations, currency, customs allowances, airport taxes, climate, clothing, bank holidays, business hours, driving licences, and business and social hints. Information can also be obtained from the local chamber of commerce and a chamber of commerce in the country visited, and from High Commissions and Tourist Boards.

Passport

A current passport must be obtained, as it is essential for visitors entering a foreign country. British passports are issued for a ten-year period.

An application form for a new passport or an extension of an existing one can be obtained from main post offices and travel agents. On completion, this should be sent to the regional passport office named on the form. Application must be made at least 28 days before the date of departure. The form has to be countersigned and the photographs certified by a British subject of standing, such as a bank manager, Justice of the Peace or headteacher who has known the applicant personally for at least two years.

Visa

A visa is also required for entry to many overseas countries. A travel agent can give advice on visas and can make arrangements for them to be obtained, or application can be made direct to the consulate of the country to be visited. It is also advisable to have a letter of invitation from the host firm or chamber of commerce of the country being visited. In certain cases it may be advisable for this letter to be sent to the embassy in this country, to arrive before application is made.

Money

A bank should be approached concerning the provision of money for a foreign visit (foreign currency, travellers cheques or Eurocheques and cards). The bank will usually require several days' notice to obtain foreign currency and to arrange for cheques.

Travellers cheques are supplied in different denominations and currencies. Before they can be issued, they have to be signed at the bank by the person who is travelling.

Eurocheques accompanied by Eurocheque cards having the symbol shown in Fig 10.3 are accepted in 40 countries at banks, shops, hotels, restaurants and petrol stations. The cheques are made out in the local currency and accounted for on the user's current account bank statement showing the amount both in foreign currency and sterling, including the bank's charges. Eurocheques can also be used in the UK and they are guaranteed by the Eurocheque card for up to £100 and, if necessary, more than one cheque can be used for a transaction. The Eurocheque card also serves as a cash card for operating autobanks. This is a convenient alternative as you are not dependent on the bank opening hours, but issuing banks do charge fees for the service and there is an additional fee for each transaction. It is, however, advisable to check in advance whether Eurocheques are acceptable in the country being visited.

If travellers cheques are lost or stolen, provided they are reported at the time of the loss to the hotel and police, it should be possible for them to be replaced locally through the representative bank. It is important, however, to keep travellers cheque receipts separately from the cheques for security reasons.

Fig 10.3 Eurocheque symbol

Rates of exchange for foreign currency may vary from day to day and the current exchange rates are given in newspapers, on television (viewdata), and in banks, airports and ports.

To convert sterling into the equivalent of a foreign currency, multiply the exchange rate for £1 by the number of pounds to be exchanged, eg to convert £25 into the equivalent of French francs, assuming an exchange rate of 9.80 francs per £:

£1 = 9.80
£25 = 25 × 9.80 = 245 francs

If it is required to convert foreign currency into sterling, divide the exchange rate for £1 into the amount of foreign currency to be exchanged, eg to convert 50 deutschmarks into sterling, assuming an exchange rate of 2.915 Dm per £:

2.915 Dm   = £1
50 ÷ 2.915 = £17.15

Driving licence

A traveller intending to drive a car abroad must be in possession of a full driving licence. An international driving licence is also required for some countries and in the UK this can be obtained from the AA or RAC motoring organisations. Also, if a car is to be taken to the continent and the car insurance policy does not include comprehensive cover for foreign travel, a green card should be obtained from the insurance company which insures the car. The car user should check with their insurance company concerning the use of a green card, as there may be an additional fee to be paid.

Health regulations

It is necessary to establish, well in advance of the visit, the inoculations and vaccinations required for entering the country and to obtain the relevant certificates. The local office of the Department of Health, or a travel agent, will supply a leaflet giving details concerning health protection when travelling abroad.

Insurance

Insurance cover for such contingencies as personal accident, medical treatment and loss of baggage can be arranged directly with an insurance company or by a travel agent. In certain countries such as USA it is desirable to take out maximum medical cover. Also ensure that, if a car is being driven abroad, a collision damage waiver is either paid for in this country or arranged by the local car-hire company. It is normal for medical insurance to cover repatriation 24 hours-a-day in case of dire need and the emergency telephone number to be used for this purpose should be stated on the insurance policy.

Tickets

The airline tickets should be obtained from a travel agent or direct from an airline booking office. Scheduled flights are the most expensive but can be obtained with very little delay and trouble. Cheaper fares are obtainable from such schemes as the advance passenger excursions (APEX and PEX), Euro budget, charter fares, group fares and standby. You can obtain further details of these schemes from a travel agent or airline. All of these cheaper fares have cancellation penalties and dates and times of travel may be unchangeable for certain fares, with no refunds applicable.

It should be noted that return or onward journeys must be reconfirmed at an airline or private charter office at least 72 hours before the flight.

Translation services

Translation and interpreting services are offered by the British Telecom Translation Bureau for:

- translation of documents, letters and contracts
- face-to-face interpreting
- on-line interpreting

These services may be booked by telephone.

International data for countries

Country	Capital	National telephone code	GMT* time difference (– earlier + later)	Currency
Afghanistan	Kabul	010 93	$+ 4\frac{1}{2}$	Afghani (AF)
Albania	Tirana	010 355	+ 1	Lek (L)
Algeria	Algiers	010 213	+ 1	Dinar (AD)
Argentina	Buenos Aires	010 54	– 3	Austral (Arg$)
Australia	Canberra	010 61	+ 10	Dollar (A$)

* Adjustments have to be made to the time differences to allow for British Summer Time which is one hour later than Greenwich Mean Time.

Country	Capital	National telephone code	GMT* time difference (– earlier + later)	Currency
Austria	Vienna	010 43	+ 1	Schilling (Sch)
Bahamas	Nassau	010 1 809	– 5	Dollar (BA$)
Bahrain	Manama	010 973	+ 3	Dinar (BD)
Bangladesh	Dhaka	010 880	+ 6	Taka (Tk)
Barbados	Bridgetown	010 1 809	– 4	Dollar (Bds$)
Belgium	Brussels	010 32	+ 1	Franc (BFr)
Bermuda	Hamilton	010 1 809	– 4	Dollar (Ba$)
Bolivia	Sucre	010 591	– 4	Peso (B$)
Bosnia-Hercegovina	Sarajevo	010 387	+ 1	Dinar (BD)
Botswana	Gaborone	010 267	+ 2	Pula (Pu)
Brazil	Brasilia	010 55	– 3	Cruzeiro (Cr)
Bulgaria	Sofia	010 359	+ 2	Lev (Lv)
Cameroon	Yaoundé	010 237	+ 1	Franc (CFAFr)
Canada	Ottawa	010 1	– 5	Dollar (C$)
Chile	Santiago	010 56	– 4	Peso (Ch$)
China	Peking/Beijing	010 86	+ 8	Yuan (Y)
Colombia	Bogota	010 57	– 5	Peso (Col$)
Costa Rica	San Jose	010 506	– 6	Colon (₡)
Croatia	Zagreb	010 385	+ 1	Kuna (CK)
Cuba	Havana	010 53	– 5	Peso (CubS)
Cyprus	Nicosia	010 357	+ 2	Pound (C£)
Czech Republic	Prague	010 42	+ 1	Koruna (Kcs)
Denmark	Copenhagen	010 45	+ 1	Krone (DKr)
Ecuador	Quito	010 593	– 5	Sucre (Su)
Egypt	Cairo	010 20	+ 2	Pound (E£)
El Salvador	San Salvador	010 503	– 6	Colon (₡)
Estonia	Tallinn	010 372	+ 3	Kroon (EK)
Ethiopia	Addis Ababa	010 251	+ 3	Birr (Br)
Fiji	Suva	010 679	+ 12	Dollar (F$)
Finland	Helsinki	010 358	+ 2	Markka (FMk)
France	Paris	010 33	+ 1	Franc (Fr)
Gambia	Banjul	010 220	Same as GMT	Dalasi (Di)
Georgia	Tbilisi	010 7	+ 4	Coupon (GC)
Germany	Berlin (Bonn until 2000)	010 49	+ 1	Deutschmark (DM)
Ghana	Accra	010 233	Same as GMT	Cedi (₡)
Gibraltar	Gibraltar	010 350	+ 1	Pound (Gib£)
Greece	Athens	010 30	+ 2	Drachma (Dr)
Guyana	Georgetown	010 592	– 3	Dollar (G$)
Haiti	Port-au-Prince	010 509	– 5	Gourde (Gde)
Hong Kong	Victoria	010 852	+ 8	Dollar (HK$)

Country	Capital	National telephone code	GMT* time difference (− earlier + later)	Currency
Hungary	Budapest	010 36	+ 1	Forint (Ft)
Iceland	Reykjavik	010 354	Same as GMT	Krona (IKr)
India	New Delhi	010 91	$+5\frac{1}{2}$	Rupee (Re)
Indonesia	Jakarta	010 62	+ 7	Rupiah (Rp)
Iran	Tehran	010 98	$+ 3\frac{1}{2}$	Rial (RI)
Iraq	Baghdad	010 964	+ 3	Dinar (ID)
Irish Republic	Dublin	010 353	Same as GMT	Punt (IR£)
Israel	Jerusalem	010 972	+ 2	Shekel (IS)
Italy	Rome	010 39	+ 1	Lira (L)
Ivory Coast (Cote d'Ivoire)	Abidjan	010 225	Same as GMT	Franc (CFA Fr)
Jamaica	Kingston	010 1 809	− 5	Dollar (J$)
Japan	Tokyo	010 81	+ 9	Yen (Y)
Jordan	Amman	010 962	+ 2	Dinar (JD)
Kenya	Nairobi	010 254	+ 3	Schilling (KSh)
Korea (North)	Pyongyang	010 850	+ 9	Won (NK W)
Korea (South)	Seoul	010 82	+ 9	Won (W)
Kuwait	Kuwait City	010 965	+ 3	Dinar (KD)
Latvia	Riga	010 371	+ 3	Lat (RL)
Lebanon	Beirut	010 961	+ 2	Pound (Leb.£)
Lesotho	Maseru	010 266	+ 2	Maloti (LSM)
Libya	Tripoli	010 218	+ 1	Dinar (LD)
Lithuania	Vilnius	010 370	+ 3	Lita (LL)
Luxembourg	Luxembourg City	010 352	+ 1	Franc (LFr)
Malaysia	Kuala Lumpur	010 60	+ 8	Dollar (M$)
Malta	Valletta	010 356	+ 1	Lira (LM)
Mauritius	Port Louis	010 230	+ 4	Rupee (MR)
Mexico	Mexico City	010 52	− 6	Peso (Mex$)
Monaco	Monaco	010 33	+ 1	Franc (Mon Fr)
Morocco	Rabat	010 212	Same as GMT	Dirham (DH)
Mozambique	Maputo	010 258	+ 2	Metzal (MzM)
Namibia	Windhoek	010 264	+ 2	Dollar (N$)
Nepal	Kathmandu	010 977	$+ 5\frac{3}{4}$	Rupee (NRp)
Netherlands (Holland)	Amsterdam	010 31	+ 1	Guilder (Gld)
New Zealand	Wellington	010 64	+12	Dollar (NZ$)
Nicaragua	Managua	010 505	− 6	Cordoba (C$)
Nigeria	Lagos	010 234	+ 1	Naira (N)
Norway	Oslo	010 47	+ 1	Krone (NKr)
Pakistan	Islamabad	010 92	+ 5	Rupee (Rp)

Country	Capital	National telephone code	GMT* time difference (– earlier + later)	Currency
Panama	Panama City	010 507	– 5	Balbao (Ba)
Paraguay	Asuncion	010 595	– 4	Guarani (G)
Peru	Lima	010 51	– 5	Sol (S)
Philippines	Manila	010 63	+ 8	Peso (PP)
Poland	Warsaw	010 48	+ 1	Zloty (Zl)
Portugal	Lisbon	010 351	Same as GMT	Escudo (Esc)
Puerto Rico	San Juan	010 1 809	– 4	Dollar (PR$)
Romania	Bucharest	010 40	+ 2	Leu (L)
Russian Federation	Moscow	010 7	+ 3	Rouble (Rub)
Saudi Arabia	Riyadh	010 966	+ 3	Rial (SAR)
Seychelles	Victoria	010 248	+ 4	Rupee (SR)
Sierra Leone	Freetown	010 232	Same as GMT	Leone (Le)
Singapore	Singapore	010 65	+ 8	Dollar (S$)
Slovakia	Bratislava	010 42	+ 1	Koruna (SK)
Slovenia	Ljubjana	010 386	+ 1	Tolar (ST)
South Africa	Pretoria	010 27	+ 2	Rand (R)
Spain	Madrid	010 34	+ 1	Peseta (Pe)
Sri Lanka	Colombo	010 94	+ $5\frac{1}{2}$	Rupee (SLR)
Sudan	Khartoum	010 249	+ 2	Pound (S£)
Swaziland	Mbabane	010 268	+ 2	Emalangeni(E)
Sweden	Stockholm	010 46	+ 1	Krona (SKR)
Switzerland	Berne	010 41	+ 1	Franc (SFr)
Syria	Damascus	010 963	+ 2	Pound (Syr£)
Taiwan	Taipei	010 886	+ 8	Dollar (T$)
Tanzania	Dodoma	010 255	+ 3	Shilling (TSh)
Thailand	Bangkok	010 66	+ 7	Baht (Bt)
Togo	Lomé	010 228	Same as GMT	Franc (CFA Fr)
Trinidad and Tobago	Port of Spain	010 1 809	– 4	Dollar (TT$)
Tunisia	Tunis	010 216	+ 1	Dinar (TD)
Turkey	Ankara	010 90	+ 2	Lira (TL)
Uganda	Kampala	010 256	+ 3	Shilling (USh)
Ukraine	Kiev	010 7	+ 5	Karbovanets (Ka)
United Arab Emirates	Abu Dhabi	010 971	+ 4	Dirham (DH)
United Kingdom	London	44	GMT	Pound (£)
Uruguay	Montevideo	010 598	– 3	Peso (Urug$)
USA	Washington DC	010 1	– 5	Dollar ($)
Venezuela	Caracas	010 58	– 4	Bolivar (B)
Vietnam	Hanoi	010 84	+ 7	Dong (D)

Country	Capital	National telephone code	GMT* time difference (− earlier + later)	Currency
Yugoslavia	Belgrade	010 38	+ 1	Dinar (Din)
Zambia	Lusaka	010 260	+ 2	Kwacha (K)
Zimbabwe	Harare	010 263	+ 2	Dollar (Z$)

Questions

1 It is necessary for your employer to make frequent business trips in the United Kingdom, often at short notice, sometimes using his car, sometimes travelling by rail or by air.

a) What reference books and information do you keep available?

b) What points would you check with him before he leaves? (*LCCI PSD*)

2 Your employer will shortly be travelling abroad. Where will you obtain

a) Passport

b) Visa

c) Foreign currency?

What other arrangements might you be expected to make in order to ensure a trouble-free journey for your employer? (*LCCI PSC*)

3 Your employer is travelling from London by plane to Aberdeen where he will stay for two nights, returning to London by train via Edinburgh where he will spend one night. He wishes you to:

a) book his tickets

b) make reservations for travel and hotels

c) arrange for him to be taken to and from the airports and the railway stations. How will you make these arrangements?

4 In the past, all travel arrangements for members of your company have been made by a travel agency. The amount of travel in Great Britain and abroad has now increased to such an extent that it has been decided to open a new department to deal with it.

a) Write a report to the Office Manager suggesting what reference books should be purchased.

b) The executive for whom you work wishes to travel by train to a neighbouring town in order to visit a factory which is situated three miles outside the town. He will return the same day. Write a memorandum to the travel department giving detailed instructions.

5 Your employer has to fly to New York (Kennedy Airport) on Tuesday 25 July 19–. He is to visit The Chuck Lucas Organisation, 500 5th Avenue, New York, telephone 721 6543621 on Wednesday and Muter, Levi & Gould Inc, 28th Floor, 1100 42nd Street, telephone 750 2296118 on the Thursday and Friday. He will return on the Saturday. He requires transport while in New York and he does not like to use travel agents.

a) List the arrangements you would make on his behalf.

b) Prepare an itinerary, using appropriate times.

6 Your employer, Mr Donald Jamieson, is shortly going on a business trip to Belgium, France, Germany, the Netherlands and Denmark. The various rates of exchange keep fluctuating and he would like you to check on today's rates against the £ sterling for each of these countries. In addition to foreign money he will need to take a number of travellers cheques. He finds the £20 units which he has used up to now on his business trips are too small for his use and asks you to ascertain what higher units of travellers cheques are obtainable. Type all the information requested, in memo form, to Mr Jamieson.

7 You are employed as secretary to Mr James Baker, Export Sales Director .

a) Mr Baker told you yesterday that he will be visiting West Africa on 3 September, returning on 10 September, to open a new cycle assembly plant for the subsidiary company there. He will be making a speech at the ceremony on 4 September.

    i List the things to be done in preparation for this visit (apart from last-minute arrangements before he leaves the office).

    ii Write a memo from yourself to John Eke, Managing Director of the Nigerian Company (Walter Cycles Nigeria Ltd), asking him to reserve a hotel room with private bathroom. Mr Baker also wants him to hire a car for Mr Baker during his visit. You will send flight details later.

b) In connection with his West African visit, Mr Baker has asked you to find out the following information:

    i   The telex answerback codes of the London office of Nigerian organisations.

    ii   The population of Nigeria, its currency and brief information on its trade.

    iii The current regulations on immunisation of a visitor to Nigeria.

    iv Biographical details of the British High Commissioner in Nigeria.

    v   Details of a speech recently made in the House of Lords concerning trade with Nigeria.

    vi The cost of telephone calls to Nigeria.

    vii The time difference between Great Britain and Nigeria.

viii How many British cycles were exported to Nigeria during the last five years.

Where would you find this information?

8 Ms Tricia Wright (Personnel Director) is to accompany Mr David Brackley (Managing Director) of Comlon International plc on a five-day trip to the Middle East, with the object of recruiting overseas agents. Neither Director has previously visited the Middle East. To ensure the success of the trip, what assistance might you obtain from the following organisations:

a) embassies
b) government agencies
c) banks
d) the company insurance broker
e) chambers of commerce
f) travel agents? (*LCCI PSC*)

9 Prepare Mr Wood's expenses claim figures so that he can complete his form for November.

a) On 7 November a meeting held in Manchester continued into the evening and it was necessary for Mr Wood to stay overnight. He arrived at the hotel car park at 1930 and left the following morning at 0845. The car park fee was 30p per hour or part thereof. The accommodation cost £58 plus VAT. Make the calculation.

b) Mr Wood's trip to Spain and France was unexpectedly extended for three days beyond the original 14—17 November arranged. He wishes to claim his expenses over and above the original company allowance for the trip. Calculate:

   i The total sum due on conversion to sterling of 50 000 pesetas and 2250 francs. (The rates of exchange were 197.50 pesetas and 10.87 francs respectively to the £.)

   ii The total cost in sterling of additional meals for which Mr Wood has receipted bills for 2300 pesetas, 1870 pesetas, 2140 pesetas, 295 francs, 230 francs and 300 francs. (*LCCI PSC*)

10 Prepare an itinerary for the visit of Ms Davies to the offical opening of the Comlon Classic in Rome. She is travelling on the Monday afternoon as she wishes to be in Rome one clear day beforehand to check arrangements. She will return on the Thursday to London. (*LCCI PSC*)

In-tray exercises

11 You are employed by Mr Brian Dobson, the manager of 'The Secretults (Case Study 3).

Take the necessary action requested below in connection with the first concert tour planned in In-tray exercise 11, page 245.

ACTION SLIP

To *Jane* URGENT ☑

Please:
- [ ] Draft a reply for my signature
- [ ] Give comments required
- [ ] Circulate and return to me
- [ ] Note and return to me
- [☑] Take appropriate action
- [ ] Note for your information

REMARKS *Please have the itinerary for the Group's first concert tour ready for tonight when they will be calling in to the office*

From: *BD*   Date: *10 Jan.*

12 You are employed at New Tech Office Services Bureau (Case Study 1). Use Fig 10.2 to supply Mr Wood with the information requested in the action slip on page 345.

ACTION SLIP

TO Martin

☐	1. URGENT ACTION REQUIRED
☐	2. Your comments please.
☐	3. Please see me.
☐	4. Answer, sending me a copy of your reply.
☐	5. Prepare reply for my signature.
☐	6. Attach previous correspondence and return.
☑	7. Take appropriate action.
☐	8. Your signature required.
☐	9. Note and return to me.
☐	10. Note and file.
☐	11. For your information.
☐	12. Note and destroy.

REMARKS I am flying from Heathrow to Brussels next Tuesday Flight SN 602. Please let me know: ① Terminal No. ② Name of air line ③ Time of arrival in Brussels.

FROM G. Wood

DATE 1 June 19 _

Index